Primitive Christianity
In Its Contemporary Setting

PRIMITIVE
CHRISTIANITY

In Its Contemporary Setting

by RUDOLF BULTMANN

Translated by Reginald H. Fuller

Fortress Press   Philadelphia

Nineteenth Printing and First Fortress Press Edition 1980

———————

Library of Congress Cataloging in Publication Data

Bultmann, Rudolf Karl, 1884–1976.
    Primitive Christianity in its contemporary setting.
    Translation of Das Urchristentum im Rahmen der antiken Religionen.
    Reprint of the ed. published by Collins, Cleveland, in series: A Fount book.
    Bibliography: p.
    Includes index.
    1. Christianity and other religions. I. Title.
[BR128.A2B83 1980]   270.1   80–8043
ISBN 0–8006–1408–9

———————

Printed in the United States of America   1-1408

95   94   93   92   91   4   5   6   7   8   9   10

TO MY FRIENDS

ERICH FRANK   PAUL FRIEDLÄNDER

FRIEDRICH SELL

ACKNOWLEDGMENTS

The publishers thank the following for giving permission to quote from the works mentioned:

Allen & Unwin Ltd.: *Aeschylus*, trans. Gilbert Murray; G. Bell & Sons Ltd.: *Aristophanes*, trans. B. B. Rogers; A. & C. Black Ltd.: *Early Greek Philosophy*, John Burnet; Basil Blackwell: *Companion to the Pre-Socratic Philosophers*, Kathleen Freeman; Rev. R. P. Casey: *Clement of Alexandria* (published by Christophers Ltd.); The Clarendon Press: *Apocrypha and Pseudepigrapha*, trans. R. H. Charles, and *Plato, The Republic*, trans. Professor Cornford; J. M. Dent & Sons Ltd.: *Thucydides*, trans. R. Crawley; W. Heinemann Ltd. and the Loeb Classical Library: *Euripides, Trojan Women*, trans. A. S. Way, *Homeric Hymn* and *Hesiod, Works and Days*, trans. H. G. Evelyn-White, *Plato, Phaedrus*, trans. H. N. Fowler, *Symposium* and *Georgias*, trans. W. R. M. Lamb, *Laws*, trans. R. R. Bury, *Epictetus, Dissertations*, trans. W. A. Oldfather, *Pliny the Elder, Natural History*, trans. H. Rackham, *Seneca, Moral Essays*, trans. J. W. Basore, *Epistles*, trans. R. M. Gummere, and *Apuleius, Metamorphoses* (or *Golden Ass*), trans. S. Gaselee; Macmillan & Co. Ltd.: *Homer, The Iliad*, trans. Lang, Leaf and Myers; John Murray Ltd.: *Herodotus*, trans. G. Rawlinson, editor A. J. Grant; Singer's Prayer-book Publication Committee: *Singer's Prayer Book*; S.P.C.K.: *Sayings of the Jewish Fathers*, trans. W. O. E. Osterley; University Press, Cambridge: *Sophocles, Antigone, Ajax* and *Niobe*, trans. R. C. Jebb, and University of California Press: *Solon the Athenian*, I. M. Linforth.

The text of the Authorized Version of the Bible is Crown copyright and the extracts from this version are reproduced by permission.

Contents

TRANSLATOR'S PREFACE

IN ACCORDANCE WITH THE DESIRE of the publishers, the biblical quotations (frequently given by Dr. Bultmann in modern translations) are taken from the Authorized Version. I have however deemed it necessary to make slight modifications in a few places, where the point which Dr. Bultmann is illustrating demands it.

I wish to express my thanks to my colleague, F. R. Newte, Esq., Lecturer in Classics at St. David's College, for the help he has given me with regard to the quotations from classical authors, and in connexion with the English bibliographies to Chapters III and IV.

REGINALD H. FULLER

ST. DAVID'S COLLEGE,
LAMPETER.
May 1955.

INTRODUCTION

THE CRADLE OF PRIMITIVE CHRISTIANITY as an historical phenomenon was furnished by late Judaism, which in turn was a development from Hebrew religion as evidenced in the Old Testament and its writings. Yet, despite the predominance of the Old Testament and Jewish heritage, primitive Christianity remained a complex phenomenon. At a very early stage in its development it came into contact with Hellenistic paganism, a contact which was to exercise a profound influence on Christianity itself. This paganism was itself equally complex. Not only did it preserve the heritage of Greek culture; it was also enlivened and enriched by the influx of religions from the Near East.

Such then, in brief, were the historical antecedents of primitive Christianity. It was no more an inevitable product of historical causes than was any other great movement of the past, yet its uniqueness is thrown into sharper relief by setting it against the background of its environment. From this it assimilated many traditions, while to other traditions it adopted a critical attitude. It also took up the same questions as were being asked in these other religions, and by attempting to answer them it found itself *ipso facto* in competition with the other missionary religions and philosophies of its time. Only by paying attention to what Christianity has in common with these other movements shall we be able to discern its difference from them.

We have no apologetic axe to grind. We do not seek to prove that Christianity is true, nor even that it is the climax of the religious evolution of antiquity, as an Hegelian philosophy of history might argue. Nor do we intend to explain the reasons why Christianity finally triumphed over its competitors, thus assuming its superiority over them. Such motives are alien to the historian. The truth of Christianity, like that of any other religion or philosophy, is always a matter of personal decision, and the historian has no right to deprive any man of that responsibility. Nor, as is often asserted, is it his business to end up by assessing the value of what he has been describing. He can certainly clarify the issues involved in the decision. For it is his task to interpret the movements of history as possible ways of understanding human existence, thus demonstrating their relevance to-day. By bringing the past to life again, he should drive home the fact that here *tua res agitur*: this is your business.

Such then will be the aim of this book. It is not an original piece of historical research. It does not claim to offer any new material for the study of comparative religion or fresh combinations of facts already known. It takes such research for granted. Its purpose is rather that of *interpretation*. We shall ask what understanding of human existence is enshrined in primitive Christianity, what new philosophy of life. Or, to put it more cautiously, is there such an understanding, and if so, how far does it go?

THE OLD TESTAMENT HERITAGE

THE OLD TESTAMENT HERITAGE

I

GOD AND THE WORLD

The Doctrine of Creation

UNLIKE GREEK PHILOSOPHY, the Old Testament never indulges in any speculation about the *arché* ($\dot{\alpha}\rho\chi\acute{\eta}$), the origin of the world which is inherent in it so long as it endures, and which makes the continuance of the world and the events staged within it rationally intelligible as a unity. Certainly, God is the Creator, the source of all life from of old and for all time. But he is the *Creator* of the world. The doctrine of creation is not a speculative cosmogony, but a confession of faith, of faith in God as Lord. The world belongs to him, and he upholds it by his power. He sustains human life, and man owes him obedience.

It is symptomatic that Hebrew monotheism did not originate in theoretical reflection. It was implicit in the Israelite belief in God from the outset, and it was only gradually clarified in the course of historical experience.[1] Jahweh, the God of Israel, started as a tribal god, like the other Semitic deities. The existence of these other deities was never questioned, though they were no concern of Israel's. Hebrew thought, in its initial stages, was not monotheistic; it stood rather for henotheism or monolatry. It was only when Israel became a national state, somewhere about 1000 B.C., that Jahweh became the God of the nation. And then, when Israel was forced to enter into formal relation with other states, polytheism became a serious problem. Through the teaching of the prophets it came to be realized that Jahweh was a 'jealous God', who tolerated no other gods but himself. To believe in Jahweh meant to acknowledge him exclusively as Lord. He was the one true God. As Lord, Jahweh had dealings with other nations besides Israel. He 'hissed' for

the people from the north, summoning them to wreak judgement upon Israel (Isa. 5.26). Asshur was the 'rod' of his anger
and the 'staff' of his indignation, whose function was to chastise
Israel (Isa. 10.5). Pharoah was the 'great dragon' who couched
in the Nile: 'I will put hooks in thy jaws . . . and I will bring
thee out of the midst of thy rivers' (Ezek. 29.4). And Deutero-
Isaiah was quite explicit about it:

> Thus saith the Lord the King of Israel
> and his redeemer the Lord of hosts;
> I am the first, and I am the last;
> and beside me there is no God.

To this Lord, moreover, the creation of the world was
attributed.[2] Israel, like other nations, had its creation myths.
God was depicted as the master workman, forming the earth
and all that is therein out of pre-existent matter. Such myths
lie behind the creation stories in Genesis 1 and 2. According to
Genesis 2.7 God 'forms' man out of the dust like a potter.
The later creation story in Genesis 1 is based on the notion that
God creates the world out of primeval matter, 'chaos', by
separating off the mingled elements and rearranging them to
suit his purpose. But there is little attempt to describe the
actual process of creation for its own sake. God speaks the
word and it is done (Gen. 1.3, 11, 14):

> God said, Let there be light: and there was light.
> God said, Let the earth bring forth grass . . .
>   and it was so.
> God said, Let the earth bring forth the living creature after his
> kind . . .
>   and it was so.

The myth has faded into the background before the conception
of God as the omnipotent Ruler, who calls into existence that
which is not by a mere fiat.

Hence Israel never developed its mythology along the lines
of the Greek *arché*. The world was never conceived after the
analogy of a work ($\check{\epsilon}\rho\gamma o\nu$) or a product of craftsmanship ($\tau\acute{\epsilon}\chi\nu\eta$).

The problem of the relation between form and matter, which so much exercised the Greek mind, is conspicuously absent from the Old Testament. There is no conception of the 'cosmos' (κόσμος = harmonious structure), of 'nature' (φύσις), of the law of nature (νόμος φύσεως). The world is never objectified as a natural order whose eternal laws are open to intellectual apprehension. There is no natural science or physics. The Greek saw the divine power in the cosmic law whose existence he had apprehended by reason. In this way he brought the deity into relation with the universe. The Bible on the other hand regards God as transcending the world.[3] He 'hath prepared his throne in the heavens; and his kingdom ruleth over all' (Ps. 103.19). The transcendence of God receives its classical expression in the doctrine of the *creatio ex nihilo*, a notion utterly inconceivable to the Greek mind, though a logical development from the premisses of Biblical thought (Jubil. 12.4; 2 Macc. 7.28, etc.).

God's wisdom and skill in creation certainly evoked awe and wonder. He established the world like a disc upon the waters, so that it could never be moved (Ps. 24.2). But it was a matter for awe and wonder, not rational comprehension. It is true, God created the world for a purpose, as Psalm 104, for instance, teaches. But this was conceived in a naïve fashion: God put the plants and springs there so that the wild beasts might satisfy their hunger and quench their thirst, corn and wine to make men prosperous, and the sun and moon to mark the seasons and order the movements of the wild beasts and the labours of men. But the Old Testament never speculates about the purpose (τέλος) of creation, or inquires into the rational intelligibility of the universe. It never thinks of each separate entity as articulated into a whole, each part having its own purpose, and the whole its purpose in an organic unity. And with the absence of the idea of the law of nature there is also no conception of providence (πρόνοια). Nor is the problem of theodicy raised in connexion with the universe at large. God's revelation in nature is not seen in the ordered course of natural history, but in unusual and terrifying occurrences like storm and earthquake. The very fact that the world is not susceptible to rational understanding makes it an object of awe as the handiwork of God.[4]

> Who hath measured the waters in the hollow of his hand,
> and meted out heaven with the span,
> and comprehended the dust of the earth in a measure,
> and weighed the mountains in scales,
> and the hills in a balance?
> Who hath directed the Spirit of the Lord,
> or being his counseller hath taught him? (Isa. 40.12).

The contemplation of nature may evoke the wonder of the psalmist (Ps. 147), though it can just as easily silence any attempt to reason with God (Job 42.2-6).

In the last analysis, the Old Testament doctrine of creation expresses a sense of the present situation of man. He is hedged in by the incomprehensible power of Almighty God. The real purpose of the creation story is to inculcate what God is doing all the time. As he once created man, so he is continually forming him wonderfully in his mother's womb (Ps. 139.13). As he once gave him the breath of life, so he imparts it again and again (Job 33.4). If he withdraws that breath, man returns to the dust from which he sprung. And when God restores that breath, he rises again and God renews the face of the earth (Ps. 104.29f.).

> O Lord, thou art our father;
> we are the clay, and thou our potter;
> and we are all the work of thy hand (Isa. 64.8).

Thus the doctrine of creation expresses man's sense of utter dependence on God:

> Woe unto him that striveth with his Maker!
> Let the potsherd strive with the potsherds of the earth.
> Shall the clay say to him that fashioneth it, What makest thou?
> or thy work, He hath no hands?
> Woe unto him that saith unto his father, What begettest thou?
> or to the woman, What hast thou brought forth?

> Thus saith the Lord, the Holy One of Israel, and his Maker,
> Will ye ask me concerning things to come,
> and will ye command me concerning the work of my hands?
> I have made the earth, and created man upon it:
> I, even my hands, have stretched out the heavens,
> and all their host have I commanded (Isa. 45.9-12).

And the devout man can say:

> Thy hands have made me and fashioned me:
> give me understanding that I may learn thy commandments
> (Ps. 119.73).

Man is therefore nothing in the sight of God,[5] and the prophet hears a voice saying to him:

> Cry: All flesh is grass,
> and all the goodliness thereof is as the flower of the field:
> The grass withereth, the flower fadeth:
> because the Spirit of the Lord bloweth upon it: . . .
> The grass withereth, the flower fadeth:
> but the word of our God shall stand forever (Isa. 40.6-8).

But this faith in creation can also give rise to confidence and gratitude:

> When I consider thy heavens, the works of thy fingers,
> the moon and the stars which thou hast ordained;
> What is man that thou art mindful of him?
> and the son of man, that thou hast visited him?
> For thou hast made him a little lower than a God,
> and hast crowned him with glory and honour.
> Thou madest him to have dominion over the works of thy
> hands;
> thou hast put all things under his feet (Ps. 8.3-6a).

> Like as a father pitieth his children,
> so the Lord pitieth them that fear him.
> For he knoweth whereof we are made;
> he remembereth that we are dust (Ps. 103.13-14).

This sense of God as our Creator implies an awareness of our own status as creatures. But this is no abject grovelling or self-annihilation. Of course, man is as nothing before God; but God has given him a certain dignity in the world. Genesis 1.26f. says that man was made in the image of God. This was originally meant to imply that man had a physical likeness to God. But in the text as it stands it means man's sovereignty over all the other creatures, as in Psalm 8.6ff. (see above).

Man then is a creature. But this does not mean that he is just a part of nature or its processes. He is not a part of the objective world, but stands over against it. This aspect of human nature is never a problem in the Old Testament as it is with the Cynics, the Stoics and the Epicureans. For the Old Testament the world is the field of man's experience, the stage on which his work and destiny are played out. Man is not interpreted in the light of the world, but the world in the light of man.[6] The world is not only man's home, a place he knows how to cope with; at the same time it is a dangerous place. For it is not just a dead place, but alive, confronting man also in the shape of fate. It is the place where God rules. Yet once we become aware of our dependence upon him we know we can trust him.

All this is admirably expressed in Psalm 100, which was composed as an introit hymn for the thank-offering:

> Make a joyful noise unto the Lord, all ye lands.
> Serve the Lord with gladness:
> come before his presence with singing.
> Know ye that the Lord he is God:
> it is he that hath made us, and we are his,
> we are his people and the sheep of his pasture.
> Enter into his gates with thanksgiving,
> and into his courts with praise:
> be thankful unto him and bless his name.
> For the Lord is good; his mercy is everlasting;
> and his truth endureth to all generations.

If the world as nature is the sphere of God's sovereignty and the stage for man's labours and the working out of his destiny, that means that in the last resort it is regarded as history, rather than nature. The real sphere where God rules is history. He makes his works known in the history of Israel.[7] In its early stages Hebrew thought did not think of Jahweh as the God of the world. But he came to be conceived as such in the teaching of the prophets. He was essentially righteous will, demanding righteousness from men. He could not therefore be confined to the limits of a single nation. By acting as Judge in the history of Israel, he became Lord over other nations as well as over natural events, which were now made into a part of the historical process.[8] The creation story in Genesis I is not just a piece of speculation, but the first chapter. in history.[9] Beginning with creation, the course of history moved forward through the age of the patriarchs to Israel's development into a nation under Moses and the giving of the Law on Mount Sinai. In this history, in which men knew they were involved, they saw the exercise of God's judgement extending over all nations.

History is the major theme of the Old Testament literature. It is never content with brief annals or chronicles, but describes a continuous historical course from one generation to another. But it has no sense of historical laws working throughout the universe.[10] History is not, as in Greek literature, the scientific study of the past as a means of finding out the eternal laws which govern all events. Rather, it looks towards the future, to a divinely appointed goal.[11] The prophets call attention to God's favour and punishment in the past. They show how he is ever carrying out his purpose in the teeth of the rebellion of his people. They pass judgement on the present, and drive home to the people their responsibilities in face of the future, whether of weal or woe.

Apart from chronicles, there is no history in the real sense among the nations of the East. The same was originally true of the Romans. "Historiography in the proper sense of the word, not just its early beginnings, is to be found only in Greek and Hebrew literature. Quite independently of one another, these two nations produced original and creative characters who left the stamp of their personalities on the raw materials of history."[12] In both cases the writing of history was the direct outcome of historical experience—with the Greeks, their wars of liberation against the Persians, in Israel, the victorious struggle against the Philistines and the conquest of the cities of Canaan.[13] In their earliest stages, both exhibited a predominant interest in myth and genealogy, in the short story and folklore; but as they developed they began to diverge. Among the Hebrews interest in 'periegesis' (detailed description of landscape and people), so typical of Greek literature, as the product of a nation of seafarers and merchants, soon faded into the background.

But the most important point about Hebrew historiography is that the centre of interest is not politics, as with the Greeks. It is the purpose of God and his moral demands. Thus there is no concern with history as a science, no interest in the forces immanently at work in it. Its real interest is in relating the course of history to its end. Hence the division of history into epochs and the reflection on their significance for the whole historical process. Hence, finally, a preoccupation with eschatology as the clue to its meaning. Historiography is sustained by a sense of responsibility on the part of the present toward the past and its heritage in weal or woe, and towards the future whether it brings salvation or disaster. History is not, as for Thucydides, material for educating the statesman, but homiletics for the people, driving home to all and sundry their responsibility.

The Knowledge of God

God cannot be seen.[14] The Greeks also believed that. God was not perceptible to the physical senses. But the Greeks did not believe that God could not be known. Though it needed tremendous effort on man's part,[15] he could apprehend him by reason, and even adduce rational proofs of his existence. The Old Testament never reflects in this way. God is not invisible to the senses as a matter of principle. Indeed, Hebrew has no word for 'invisible'.[16] God is invisible because he wills to be so.

To see God would be to die. 'We shall surely die, because we have seen God' (Judges 13.22; cf. 6.22f.); 'Woe is me! for I am undone; because I am a man of unclean lips, and I dwell in the midst of a people of unclean lips: for mine eyes have seen the King, the Lord of hosts' (Isa. 6.5). Such cries of terror are wrung from men to whom God has shown himself. God's invisibility is his holiness, his unapproachableness, his being beyond man's control. To be able to see God would mean to be able to stand upright in his presence. God is not therefore invisible, as he is for the Greeks, because he is a metaphysical being and as such beyond the apprehension of our physical senses. Man cannot get God into his possession or control; he knows about God only because God speaks to him.

Hearing is the means by which God is apprehended. In the last resort this is no more acoustic apprehension than seeing is optical apprehension. Just as seeing (whether physical, or spiritual) means perceiving at a distance an apparently stationary object, thus ascertaining its shape and measurements—so hearing is a sense of being encountered, of the distance being bridged, the acknowledgment of a speaker's claim on us. The Greek tends to think of the world as an objective closed system, susceptible of mathematical measurement. Thus for him sight tends to be the most important of the senses. For the Old Testament, however, hearing is the most important.[17]

> It has been *said* to thee, O man, what is good,
> and what the Lord doth require of thee . . . (Mic. 6.8).

Priests and prophets proclaim the *Word* of God, that is to say, his will. The father teaches Jahweh's commandments to his family. The prophet is not a man with a deeper knowledge or experience of God than his fellow Israelites. Knowledge of God has nothing to do with God's metaphysical nature. It means to know his *will*. To know his will is to acknowledge him. Thus the prophet reminds the king: 'Did not thy father . . . do judgement and justice? . . . He judged the cause of the poor and needy . . . was not this to know me, saith the Lord?'

(Jer. 22.15-16). God reveals through his prophets the reason why he has sent his people into exile: 'I will give them an heart to know me, that I am the Lord: and they shall be my people, and I will be their God; for they shall return to me with their whole heart' (Jer. 24.7). And then there is the promise:

> I will put my law in their inward parts,
> and will write it in their hearts;
> and will be their God,
> and they shall be my people.
> And they shall teach no more every man his neighbour
> and every man his brother saying: Know the Lord:
> for they shall all know me, from the least of them unto the
> greatest of them (Jer. 31.33f.).

Compare also the synonymous parallelism of the psalmist's prayer:

> O continue forth the loving kindness unto them that know thee;
> and thy righteousness unto the upright in heart (Ps. 36.10).

Truth, in the Old Testament, means primarily not propositional knowledge, but that which is valid and demands recognition, that which can be trusted.[18] Wisdom, for Israel, is not abstract science, but practical morality, knowledge about the way the world works, what happens to the righteous and the wicked, the truthful man and the liar; above all it is knowledge of what God demands. The wisdom of Israel is enshrined in proverbs. Its basic principle is the fear of God.

> The fear of the Lord is the beginning of wisdom:
> but fools despise wisdom and instruction (Prov. 1.7).
> The fear of the Lord is the instruction of wisdom;
> and before honour is humility (Prov. 15.33).

The prophet similarly admonishes men to fear God:

> Sanctify the Lord of hosts himself;
> and let him be your fear, and let him be your dread (Isa. 8.13)

There is a similar admonition in the Law:

Ye shall walk after the Lord your God, and fear him,
and keep his commandments, and obey his voice,
and ye shall serve him, and cleave unto him (Deut. 13.4).

Then there is the promise God makes through the prophet:

I will give them one heart and one way,
that they may fear me for ever . . .
I will put my fear in their hearts,
that they shall not depart from me (Jer. 32.39f.).

This fear of God is no craven terror—that is just what he
delivers us from by granting us security. It is rather a sense of
awe, of submission to the will of God encountering us in his
demand as it does in fate. Terror is precisely what we are
supposed *not* to feel.

Fear not; for I have redeemed thee,
I have called thee by the name; thou art mine (Isa. 43.1).

Fear of God rules out all fear of men: 'What this people
feareth, ye should not fear' is the prophet's admonition, while
the psalmist says:

I will not be afraid of ten thousands of the people,
that have set themselves against me round about (Ps. 3.6).

'Therefore will we not fear, though the earth be removed'
(Ps. 46.3). Thus the fear and love of God go hand in hand.
To love Jahweh and keep his commandments, to serve him
and walk in his ways—all this is the same thing (Deut. 6.4f.,
13, 10.12).

God's Care for the World

It goes without saying that God cares for the world he has
made. That care is depicted by the psalmists with awe and
gratitude:

Who covereth the heaven with clouds,
who prepareth rain for the earth,
who maketh grass to grow upon the mountains.

> He giveth to the beast his food,
> and to the young ravens which cry (Ps. 147.8f.).[19]

This trust in God's providential care is no light-hearted optimism. The psalmists never shut their eyes to the fact of suffering, nor do they ever imagine that man can be free of it. God satisfies all things in their season, but:

> Thou hidest thy face, they are troubled:
> thou takest away their breath, they die (Ps. 104.29).

As they contemplate God's rule and care in nature they never forget that nature is beyond man's control, and that man is nothing in the sight of God. To this extent suffering and death present no problem, and sickness or natural disasters never evoke questions which might lead to the working out of a theodicy or throw doubt on the existence of God. The denial of God's existence on intellectual grounds is outside the purview of Old Testament thought.[20] The only kind of atheism it knows is a practical one:

> The fool hath said in his heart, there is no God.
> They are corrupt, they have done abominable works,
> there is none that doeth good (Ps. 14.1).

The wicked ignore God by oppressing the widows and orphans and maltreating the lowly. They say:

> The Lord shall not see,
> neither shall the God of Jacob regard it (Ps. 94.7).

> How doth God know?
> and is there knowledge in the Most High? (Ps. 73.11).

Belief in God's care is therefore poles apart from the Stoic doctrine of providence, for which, as we have seen, there is no actual word in Hebrew. It is not based on a conviction of the harmonious unity of the cosmos, in which all separate things have their organic place and serve their purpose. Thus there is no attempt to find out the purpose and meaning behind misfortune and suffering, no suggestion that they are merely apparent. There is no idea that everything is necessary when seen in the context of the whole, and is therefore good. The devout men of Israel know that suffering is always suffering. Every sufferer must bear his own burden. There is no getting rid of it by seeing oneself in the wider context of the whole. The Bible never says, 'Look at things as a whole', as did Marcus Aurelius.[21] Doubt and anxiety are not to be banished by rational argument of this sort. Man is not encouraged to think of himself as just the particular instance of the universal. Instead, he is told to look to the future. If we cannot find God in the present we shall find him then.

No, the problem is not suffering in general, but the suffering of the righteous. Suffering can be explained as God's punishment for sin. But why then should the righteous suffer? And why do so many of the wicked prosper? The common answer to this problem is that in the end it will be the wicked who will suffer and the righteous who prosper.

> Fret not thyself because of evil men,
> neither be thou envious at the wicked;
> For there shall be no reward to the evil man;
> the candle of the wicked shall be put out (Prov. 24.19f.).

> For evil doers shall be cut off:
> But those that wait upon the Lord, they shall inherit the earth
> For yet a little while, and the wicked shall not be
> yea, thou shalt diligently consider his place, and it shall not be.
> But the meek shall inherit the earth;
> and shall delight themselves in the abundance of peace
> (Ps. 37.9-11).

This answer does not satisfy everybody, for it is all too often refuted by experience. Consequently we occasionally hear expressions of resignation. Life is like that: some prosper, others suffer misfortune. There is nothing we can do about it, nor is it possible to lay down any rule on the subject.

> The poor and the deceitful man meet together:
> the Lord lighteneth both their eyes (Prov. 29.13).

This mood of resignation finds classical expression in Ecclesi-astes:[22]

> Vanity of vanities, saith the Preacher,
> vanity of vanities; all is vanity.
> What profit hath a man of all his labour
> which he taketh under the sun?
> One generation passeth away, and another generation cometh:
> but the earth abideth for ever . . .
> The thing that hath been, it is that which shall be;
> and that which is done is that which shall be done:
> and there is no new thing under the sun (1.2-9).

> The work that is wrought under the sun is grevious unto me:
> for all is vanity and vexation of spirit (2.17).

> So I returned and considered all the oppressions
> that are done under the sun:
> and behold the tears of such as were oppressed,
> and they had no comforter;
> and on the side of their oppressors there was power;
> but they had no comforter.
> Wherefore I praised the dead which are already dead
> more than the living which are yet alive.
> Yea, better is he than both they,
> who hath not seen the evil work that is done under the sun
>   (4.1-3).

> There is a vanity which is done upon the earth;
> that there be just men unto whom it happeneth according to the
>   work of the wicked;
> again there be wicked men, to whom it happeneth according to
>   the work of the righteous:
> I said that this also is vanity (8.14).

What are we left with?

> There is nothing better for a man,
> than that he should eat and drink,
> and that he should make his soul enjoy good in his labour (2.24).

Eat thy bread with joy,
and drink thy wine with a merry heart . . .
Let thy garments be always white;
and let thy head lack no ointment.
Live joyfully with the wife whom thou lovest
all the days of the life of thy vanity,
which he hath given thee under the sun (9.7-10).

If such resignation comes pretty near to the practical atheism we spoke of above, we get the opposite extreme in the book of Job. This work wrestles with the problem of suffering, and comes to the conclusion that the only way out is to submit uncomplainingly to the will of God. His wisdom surpasses all human understanding. When his friends insist that Job's sufferings must be the punishment of some sin he has committed, he protests his innocence, and as he contemplates he realizes that God is oppressing him like a tyrant.

Whom, though I were righteous, yet would I not answer,
but I would make my supplication to my judge.
If I had called, and he had answered me;
yet would I not believe that he had hearkened unto my voice.
For he breaketh me with a tempest,
and multiplieth my wounds without cause.
He will not suffer me to take my breath,
but filleth me with bitterness.
If I speak of strength, lo, he is strong:
and if of judgement, who shall set me a time to plead?
If I justify myself, mine own mouth shall condemn me:
if I say, I am perfect, it shall also prove me perverse (9.15-20).

But that does not quieten his heart. He must insist on getting justice from God. It is not a reward he wants, but recognition.

Surely I would speak to the Almighty,
and I desire to reason with God (13.3).

God refuses such advocates, so anxious to prove him in the right by proving Job in the wrong!

Will ye speak wickedly for God,
and talk deceitfully for him?
Will ye accept his person?
Will ye contend for God? (13.7f.).

Your remembrances are like unto ashes,
your bodies to bodies of clay.
Hold your peace, let me alone, that I may speak,
and let come on me what will.
Wherefore do I take my flesh in my teeth,
and put my life in my hand?
Though he slay me, yet will I trust in him:
but I will maintain my own ways before him (13.12-15).

Oh that I knew where I might find him!
that I might come even to his seat!
I would order my cause before him,
and fill my mouth with arguments.
I would know the words which he would answer me,
and understand what he would say unto me.
Will he plead against me with his great power?
No, but he would give heed unto me.
There the righteous might dispute with him;
so should I be delivered for ever from my judge (23.3-7).

He begs God to let him have his accusation in black and white,
so that he can refute it.

Surely I would take it upon my shoulder,
and bind it as a crown to me.
I would declare unto him the number of my steps;
as a prince would I go near unto him (31.36f.).

God takes up the challenge, appears to Job and gives him his
answer, which takes the form of a counter-question:

Where wast thou when I laid the foundations of the earth?
declare, if thou hast understanding.
Who hath laid the measures thereof, if thou knowest?
or who hath stretched the line upon it? (38.4f.).

Wilt thou disannul my judgement?
wilt thou condemn me, that thou mayest be righteous?
Hast thou an arm like God? or canst thou thunder with a voice
  like him?
Deck thyself now with majesty and excellency;
and array thyself with glory and beauty . . .
Then will I confess unto thee
that thine own right hand can save thee (38.8, 10, 14).

Job is reduced to silence:

Behold, I am vile; what shall I answer thee?
I will lay my hand upon my mouth.
Once have I spoken; but I will not answer:
yea twice, but I will proceed no further (40.4f.).

I know that thou canst do every thing,
and that no thought can be withholden from thee . . .
therefore have I uttered that I understood not;
things too wonderful for me, which I knew not . . .
I have heard thee by the hearing of the ear:
but now mine eye seeth thee.
Wherefore I abhor myself,
and repent in dust and ashes (42.2f., 5f.).

Confronted by God's omnipotence and unfathomable wisdom, man's only recourse is to hold his peace. The problem of his suffering has no answer. It is not for man to reason why, but to make his submission to God. The author of Job illustrates this point by inserting his poem in the framework of the traditional story of Job as a religious man who, when all was taken from him, says meekly: 'Naked came I out of my mother's womb, and naked shall I return thither: the Lord gave, and the Lord hath taken away; blessed be the name of the Lord' (1.21). And when his wife pours scorn on him: 'What? shall we receive good at the hand of the Lord, and shall we not receive evil?' (2.10).

The book of Job is an exception in the Old Testament, for here the conventional picture of God's righteousness as evidenced in the fortunes of men breaks down. The author had discovered that even the righteous must suffer. Yet he keeps within the limits of Old Testament thought. He does not doubt God, and although his conception of God provides no clue to the problem of suffering, he does not abandon it on that account. Indeed, he accentuates it. The omnipotence of God is infinite, and the wisdom in his apparent caprice surpasses all comprehension. All man can do is to hold his peace.[23]

This is an extreme development of an element found everywhere in the Old Testament faith in God: submission to his unfathomable purpose. Such acquiescence may go together with a confidence that God will redress the situation in the future, particularly if man is content to renounce his self-will and wait quietly upon him. Thus there grows up a unique conception of faith. To believe in God is not simply to believe in his existence, but meekly to submit to his will and wait upon him in quietness and confidence. That is what the psalmist means when he says:

> Nevertheless I am continually with thee:
> thou hast holden me by my right hand.
> Thou shalt guide me with thy counsel,
> and afterward receive me to glory.
> Whom have I in heaven but thee?
> and there is none upon earth that I desire beside thee.
> My flesh and my heart faileth:
> but God is the strength of my heart, and my portion for ever.
> For lo, they that are far from thee shall perish;
> thou hast destroyed all that go a-whoring from thee.
> But it is good for me to draw near to God:
> I have put my trust in the Lord God (Ps. 73.23-8).

And when Jeremiah complains:

> Woe is me, my mother, that thou hast borne me
> a man of strife and a man of contention to the whole earth!
> I have neither lent on usury, nor men have lent to me on usury;
> yet every one of them doth curse me.

God answers:

> Verily it shall be well with thy remnant
> verily I will cause the enemy to entreat thee well

in the time of evil and in the time of affliction.
Shall iron break the northern iron and the steel? (Jer. 15.10-12).

The religious man can still fly to God in prayer and find refuge
and consolation. He lifts up his eyes unto the hills from whence
cometh his help (Ps. 121).

Unto thee, O Lord, do I lift up my soul.
O my God, I trust in thee:
let me not be ashamed, let not mine enemies triumph over me
   (Ps. 25.1f.).

My soul, wait thou only upon God;
for my expectation is from him.
He only is my rock and my salvation:
he is my defence; I shall not be moved.
In God is my strength and my glory:
the rock of my strength, and my refuge, is in God (Ps. 62.5-7).

But the problem of suffering receives another peculiar twist.
This is because pious Israelites know that their destiny as individuals is bound up with that of the nation. Sometimes this
feature fades into the background, as is the case with Ecclesi-
astes, Job, and many of the psalms. Elsewhere however it receives great prominence. On the one hand part of the sufferings
which fall to the lot of the individual are inextricably bound
up with the sufferings of the nation, while on the other hand
the very fate of the nation as such raises the whole question of
the righteousness of God. One answer is that found in the
denunciations of the prophets. The sufferings are meant to
punish and correct a recalcitrant people, and must therefore be
willingly borne. The nation must 'turn' so that God can turn to
it again. But besides these admonitions and threats there are
also passages which promise a good time coming, when God
will create his people anew.

The sufferings of the nation must be faced in the same way
as those of the individual—by meekly submitting to the will of
God, by waiting and trusting in him.

For thus saith the Lord, the holy One of Israel;
In returning and rest shall ye be saved;

in quietness and in confidence shall be your strength:
and ye would not.

But ye said, No; for we will flee upon horses;
therefore shall ye flee:
and, We will ride upon the swift;
therefore shall they that pursue you be swift (Isa. 30.15f.).
If ye will not believe, surely ye shall not be established (Isa. 7.9b).

He that believeth shall not make haste (Isa. 28.16b).

In both cases—individual and national—there is no idea of order and purpose in the universe. Instead there is a future to be inaugurated by God. That is the Old Testament answer to the problem of theodicy, in so far as there is any answer at all. God confronts man with his blessing and demand, judging him in each successive moment. Every such moment however points towards the future. God is always a God who comes. He always transcends the here and now. But this transcendence (there is no actual word for it in the Old Testament) is not a metaphysical transcendence of spirit over matter or the transcendence of the world of ideas over the world of growth and decay. For the religion of the Old Testament everything turns on how seriously a man is prepared to take this idea of a God who comes. Is he prepared to wait for God's coming in every future moment, and in the future as a whole? Or does he expect the future simply to produce a happy ending, whether for himself, or for the nation at large? Does he in other words look for a state of permanent bliss in this world? Such a state of bliss would bring all activity to a standstill. God's transcendence in the sense that he is always the God who comes would be reduced to a transcendence within this world. And that would mean the end of faith. The only way out of this dilemma is to bring in a life after death to redress the balance. But such a notion was foreign to ancient Israel, and only grew up gradually in post-exilic Judaism, leaving its sole traces in a few quite late passages in the Old Testament.[24] The main problem in Old Testament religion is its development of thought about the relation between God and his people.

II

GOD AND THE NATION

The Divine Covenant

OLD TESTAMENT RELIGION was a national religion. The life of the community and its religion formed a unity. God and the nation belonged together. Jahweh was Israel's God, though other nations might have theirs. This association between Jahweh and Israel was the outcome of a particular history. Moses in the wilderness had welded a number of nomadic tribes into a nation. The bond of unity was the worship of Jahweh. He was the God of the nation. Israel's wars were his wars, Israel's glory his glory. The land belonged to him, the land which Israel conquered, though he gave it to the nation for their heritage. In time of peace he was the Lord of the whole life of the community, the patron of justice. By his name men used to swear, and in his name they made treaties.[25] This relationship with God was conceived in terms of a covenant. In this covenant God was the major party. But by offering it to the people God had entered into mutual obligations with them. He dealt with the people as a corporate entity, not with its individual members—or more precisely, he dealt with the male members of the community. The nation bound itself to worship only Jahweh, and Jahweh bound himself to succour and protect the nation. This covenant was inaugurated by a sacrifice and was perpetuated through the cultus. It was irrevocable so long as the cultus was duly performed. Quite soon however the prophets raised their protest against the popular conception of the covenant.

As a consequence of the occupation of Canaan and the influence of Canaanite religion there was a very real danger of Israel coming to believe that God was tied to the land. This would have destroyed the distinctive feature of Hebrew religion and have made it just like any of the other Semitic religions. In these religions the deity was tied to the land, with its mountains and fields, its vegetation. Their gods were worshipped as the power of fertility, the force at work in nature. It was just this idea that the prophets set out to combat. According to them God was not tied to the land, but to the nation. This is the distinctive feature of Hebrew religion, giving it a certain affinity with the Greek religion of the city state. But Israel never regarded herself as a *polis* or city state in the Greek sense. The city state was constituted by the total will of a community of free citizens, that will providing the norm of community life. The deity was conceived as the guardian of this norm, and therefore, in the last analysis as the personification of the will of the community. Hence the problem which constantly beset the city state: Would this idea of the community continue to command respect? Would the community continue to maintain its priority over the individual? Or would the community come to be thought of as derivative from the individual, as the product of the subjective will of its individual members? This is the problem of democracy.

Such a problem, however, never arose in Israel, because there the nation was never conceived as the result of the individual will of its members, developing its own life as a city state. The nation was the product of history. There the problem was one of loyalty to history. Since the contemporary scene was always the product of a past it had not itself created, the past was not the story of man's exploits and achievements, but a *gift*— the sign of God's grace. 'And say thou not in thine heart, My power and the might of my hand hath gotten me this wealth. But thou shalt remember the Lord thy God: for it is he that giveth thee power to get wealth . . .' (Deut. 8.17f.).

The emergence of the nation might therefore be described as an act of creation. The deliverance from Egypt was depicted as the destruction of the dragon in primaeval times (Isa. 51.9f.). Similarly national calamity was depicted as the return of chaos.

According to the Old Testament, the nation is not constituted by the forces and purposes inherent in it at any given time, but through the mighty acts of God in the past. It was he who brought the nation out of Egypt and made his covenant with it on Mount Sinai. It was he who led it through the wilderness and gave it the land—the land which is now their heritage, the land of their fathers. These fathers are not dim figures of a distant past, but the abiding witnesses of the nation's history.

This sense of history was reflected in the principal feasts. Originally the festivals of a pastoral and agricultural people, they were transformed into historical commemorations.[26] The passover was originally the new year feast, when the first-born of the herd was presented to the deity. In Palestine this was combined with the *Mazzoth*, the feast of the first-fruits, when the sickle was put to the corn. Later however, it was transformed into the commemoration of the Exodus, when the Hebrew tribes became a nation and national history began. The feast of weeks began as the thanksgiving for the corn harvest. Later it became the commemoration of the giving of the Law on Mount Sinai. The feast of the tabernacles, originally another new year's festival and the feast of the ingathering (the thanksgiving at the end of the harvest as a whole) was later transformed into the commemoration of the time when Israel dwelt in tents in the wilderness.

Unlike the cult legends of classical Greece and Hellenistic times, the legends associated with the feasts do not tell of the fate of the deity, but the history of the nation. The cult itself lost much of its former magical associations as a means of securing the prosperity of the nation and its land. There are indeed traces of such notions in the rites of purification and atonement. But the chief thing about the feasts is that they became themselves moments in the redemptive history. In the feasts, that history becomes a present reality in which the participators share.

This belief in the historical origins of the covenant finds its theological expression in the doctrine of election—the election of Israel. Here the underlying idea is that the nation owes all it has and is, not to itself, but to God who rules its history.[27] Israel's election does not rest on her own merits:

> Speak not thou in thine heart, after that the Lord thy God hath cast out the nations before thee, saying, For my righteousness the Lord hath brought me in to possess this land. . . . Not for thy righteousness, or for the uprightness of thine heart, dost thou go to possess this land. . . . (Deut. 9.4-5).

The divine election is unmotivated and free, so that Israel is perpetually dependent on the grace of God, while her election is beyond her control. God's mighty acts in the past never become an assured possession: they must be appropriated ever anew. For Israel, to observe the terms of her covenant means to be loyal to her history. This sense of calling and election is, in its original form, a conscious determination to remain loyal to history, with the blessings and obligations that entails.

Israel can rely on the faithfulness of God, but only on condition that she remains faithful herself. Her faithfulness is demonstrated first and foremost in the cultus. It is here that she acknowledges her God and her history.

> A Syrian ready to perish was my father, and he went down into Egypt, and sojourned there with a few, and became there a nation, great, mighty, and populous: And the Egyptians evil entreated us and afflicted us, and laid upon us hard bondage: And when we cried unto the Lord God of our Fathers, the Lord heard our voice, and looked on our affliction, and our labour, and our oppression: And the Lord brought us forth out of Egypt with a mighty hand, and with an outstretched arm, and with great terribleness, and with signs, and with wonders: And he hath brought us into this land, even a land flowing with milk and honey. And now behold, I have brought the first fruits of the land, which thou, O Lord, hast given me (Deut. 26.5-10a).

It is to loyalty to history that the prophets exhort:

> Yet destroyed I the Amorite before them. . . .
> Also I brought you up from the land of Egypt,
> and led you forty years through the wilderness,
> to possess the land of the Amorite.

And I raised up of your sons for prophets,
and of your young men for Nazarites.
Is it not even thus, O ye children of Israel? saith the Lord.
But ye . . . (Amos 2.9-11).

Israel's disloyalty is denounced as adultery by the prophets.
The covenant is compared to a marriage, the election of Israel
to an espousal (Hosea, Jeremiah).

Loyalty consists in the due performance of the cultus and in
offering it exclusively to Jahweh. But it also—and with the
prophets particularly so, if not exclusively—consists in obedience to the Law of Jahweh, which embraces the whole life of
the nation, requiring above all righteousness and justice. The
prophets combat the security of national pride. If God chose
Israel he can also reject her!

Woe to them that are at ease in Zion,
and trust in the mountain of Samaria.
Gather yourselves, ye firstlings of the nations,
and come, thou house of Israel.
Pass ye to Calneh, and see;
and from thence go to Hamath the great:
then go down to Gath of the Philistines:
be they better than these kingdoms? or their border greater than
    your border? (Amos 6.1f.).

Hear this word that the Lord hath spoken against you,
O children of Israel, against the whole family
which I brought up from the land of Egypt, saying,
You only have I known of all the families of the earth;
therefore I will punish you for all your iniquities! (Amos 3.1f.).

Are ye not as children of the Ethiopians unto me,
O children of Israel? saith the Lord.
Have I not brought up Israel out of the land of Egypt?
and the Philistines from Caphtor, and the Syrians from Kir?
    (Amos 9.7).

Yet I am the Lord thy God from the land of Egypt,
and thou shalt know no God but me:
for there is no saviour beside me.

I did know thee in the wilderness, in the land of great drought.
When they came to the pasture, they were filled;
they were filled, and their heart was exalted;
therefore have they forgotten me.
Therefore I will be unto them as a lion:
as a leopard by the way will I observe them (Hos. 13.4-7).

God will exact terrible vengeance on disloyalty. He will destroy his faithless people. Maybe a remnant will be left and will 'turn'. But judgement will come upon the nation as a whole. It will be wrought out in history. It is God who has called Assyria as the chastening rod to smite Ephraim and Judah. It is God who raises the King of Babylon to destroy Jerusalem. As for King Manasseh's idolatry (698-643):

> Therefore thus saith the Lord God of Israel, Behold I am bringing such evil upon Jerusalem and Judah, that whosoever heareth of it, both his ears shall tingle. And I will stretch over Jerusalem the line of Samaria, and the plummet of the house of Ahab: and I will wipe Jerusalem as a man wipeth a dish, wiping it, and turning it upside down. And I will forsake the remnant of mine inheritance, and deliver them into the hand of their enemies; and they shall become a prey and a spoil to all their enemies; Because they have done that which was evil in my sight, and have provoked me to anger, since the day that their fathers came forth out of Egypt, even unto this day (II Kings 21.12-15).

God, according to the traditional view, exercises his power on behalf of Israel: for the prophets he can also exercise his power *against* Israel, and owing to the people's wickedness will actually do so. Logically, this means the end of national religion.[28] The more the prophets emphasize ethical obedience as opposed to the performance of the cultus as the *sine qua non* for the maintenance of the covenant, the more they abandon the old naïve sense of the latter. If the covenant depends primarily on loyalty to history, its maintenance is bound to be always in doubt. Thus, in the last resort, the past poses a question to the nation: the covenant can never be fully realized until the future. It can never have been concluded definitively in the past, nor can its permanence be secured by the performance of the cultus. If, as the naïve view supposed, the security of the individual rests on his membership of the elect nation, then conversely, according to the prophetic view, the election of the people depends on the individual's obedience to the demands of God. And the less that is the case in the empirical course of history, the more the covenant develops into an eschatological concept. In other words, the covenant is not capable of realization in actual history: its realization is only conceivable in some mythical future of redemption.

> Behold, the days come, saith the Lord,
> that I will make a new covenant with the house of Israel,
> and with the house of Judah:
> Not according to the covenant I made with their fathers
> in the day that I took them by the hand
> to bring them out of the land of Egypt;
> which my covenant they brake,
> and I rejected them.
> But this is the covenant
> that I will make with the houses of Israel;
> After those days, saith the Lord,
> I will put my law in their inward parts,
> and write it in their hearts;
> and will be their God,
> and they shall be my people.
> And they shall teach no more every man his neighbour,
> and every man his brother, saying,
> Know the Lord:
> for they shall all know me,
> from the least of them unto the greatest of them,
> saith the Lord:
> for I will forgive their iniquity,
> and I will remember their sin no more (Jer. 31.31-3).

> Moreover I will make a covenant of peace with them;
> it shall be an everlasting covenant with them:
> and I will multiply them,
> and will set my sanctuary in the midst of them for evermore.

My tabernacle shall also be with them:
yea, I will be their God,
and they shall be my people.
And the heathen shall know
that I the Lord do sanctify Israel,
when my sanctuary shall be in the midst of them for evermore
(Ezek. 37.26-8).

The Holy People

The actual course of Israel's history, the settlement of nomadic
pastoral tribes in Canaan, made Israel a nation of agricultural-
ists. This brought them into contact with urban cultures. It was
these influences which turned them eventually into a national
State, thus involving them in political relations with other
nations, both great and small, in the semicircle between Egypt
and Babylon. All this meant danger to the religion of Jahweh.
With the tilling of the soil, customs from the fertility cults
of foreign nations, and even those cults themselves, found their
way into Israel. Political change brought social upheaval in its
train, with a consequent lowering of moral standards. Social
differences began to emerge, and social sins to abound.

In protesting against this moral decline, the prophets also
raised their voice against the foreign cults and the customs which
came in from them. Unfortunately, however, the prophets
combined their preaching of social righteousness with a protest
against all political and economic progress as such. They called
for a return to a golden age of the past, to the simple life before
the State began. They depicted that age as a time when the holy
people were faithful to the covenant and lived at peace with
God—a Utopian requirement in view of the actual course of
history; Israel was so small that she was unable to pursue an
independent policy of her own, especially after the schism between the northern and southern kingdoms. And then came the
exile,[29] as a result of which the Utopian policy of the prophets
gained the upper hand, and an attempt was made to put the
idea of a holy people into practice.

Like other Semitic nations, Israel regarded God as her King. His will was law for his people. He was the judge and arbiter in all disputes, the patron of justice at home and the wager of Israel's wars abroad. At the new year's feast his accession to the throne was celebrated with the cry: 'Jahweh is King.' The hymns sung at the feast praised him as the God exalted above all other gods and as Lord of the world.[30] His kingship became a present reality through the performance of the cultus.

With Israel having thus become a State and with the institution of monarchy, a conflict arose between the kingship of Jahweh and that of the earthly monarch. The prophets resisted the introduction of monarchy. The story in I Samuel 8.1ff. records how the elders came to Saul at Ramah and demanded: 'Make us a king to judge us like other nations.' 'But the thing displeased Samuel.' And when he prayed to the Lord, the Lord answered him: 'Hearken unto the voice of the people in all that they say unto thee: for they have not rejected thee, but they have rejected me, that I should reign over them.' The prophets dated all Israel's sin from the day that Saul was crowned king at Gilgal (I Sam. 11.11f.):

> All their wickedness was done in Gilgal:
> for there I hated them (Hos. 9.15).

With the prosperity during David's reign, the monarchy became so popular that his reign was later regarded as a golden age. When the time of salvation came, there would be a new Davidic king. But at the outset the earthly monarchy was regarded as a threat to the kingship of God. The old tribal structure was replaced by a new organization in provinces. The native organization of the people was replaced by one which met the technical requirements of an organized state. A new aristocracy of bureaucrats and officers came into being. The army, which hitherto had been a popular muster, now consisted of professional soldiers. This made it necessary to raise taxes, as we hear in I Samuel 8.10-18. The kings of Israel were obliged to seek treaties with other nations. Jahweh became the

God of the state and a temple was built for him in accordance with Canaanite custom. National shrines were erected at Jerusalem, Bethel and Samaria. With the redistribution of wealth the old communal law of village life declined, and the administration of justice became uncertain. Among the ruling classes the old inhibitions disappeared with the old moral sanctions and there were ceaseless complaints about injustice and violence.

The prophets fulminated against the new institutions and their moral consequences. But they failed to perceive the necessities of state. If kings were willing to accept the responsibilities of government, they were simply not in a position to follow the ideals of the prophets. They were bound to be anxious about defence. They had to ensure that the State was strong, and to that end they had to enter into foreign alliances. The prophets for their part were equally incapable of presenting their ideals in such a way as to make them practical politics in the new situation. Their demand of righteousness and justice would in itself have been practicable in any proper kind of State, but when associated with a demand for a return to the old family, clan and tribal organization they were doomed to failure from the outset. And when they sought to uphold the sovereignty of God by denying the right of the State to administer justice, and insisting that judicial functions should be placed in the hands of the priestly caste, they were undermining the very foundations of the State.

When Israel lost her independence at the exile the Utopia of the prophets lived on and became the mainstay of the nation in its bondage to foreign rule. To begin with, the old aristocratic order of the patriarchs was re-established, though this was increasingly supplanted by the rule of the priestly caste. Israel was now organized on an hierarchical basis, with the high priest at its head. In this way the theocratic ideal of the sovereign rule of God was realized at last—but at a cost. Israel ceased to be a nation and became a Church. All the functions of government, except the administration of justice, which remained in the hands of the priests, were managed by the foreign power.

Cyrus, who restored the Jews from exile, was hailed by the devout as the Lord's anointed. Ezra (444 B.C.), under a direct commission from the Persian emperor, set up the Jewish Church State, which was peculiar in that Israel was at once a Church and a national community. As a national community, Jewish society derived its cohesion from the tradition of its past, preserving its national distinctiveness through its ritual. Hence the importance of circumcision and the sabbath. Israel looked for a return of the old days when she had been an independent State, for a restoration of the kingdom of David. But that could not be brought about by direct political action. It had to be left to supernatural intervention. In fact the new kingdom of David was not to be a real State on earth at all.

Thus the conception of a holy nation with God as its King was realized in the peculiar form of a Church-State. Any other alternative was out of the question, if the people of God were to be identified with any empirical community. This is shown by the way in which the full realization of the ideal of the holy people, together with that of the covenant, was projected into a mythical future. The genuine idea of God as a God who was to come was abandoned, and with it the conception of God as the Lord of history. In the eschatological hope, history was expected to come to an end. By its anticipation of the eschatological future Israel lost its historical moorings. This it did by moulding the ritual pattern of its whole life in such a way as to emphasize its distinctiveness from all other nations as the holy people of God.

III

God and Man

An Anthropology in Outline

IN THE PERSPECTIVE of the Old Testament man consists of body and soul, or more accurately, flesh and soul. The Old Testament knows nothing of the body in its proper sense of 'figure' or 'shape'. Flesh and soul are not opposed to one another in a dualistic sense. The soul does not belong intrinsically to a higher world, here imprisoned in a material body. Instead, the soul is the energy which gives life to the flesh. Its seat is generally in the blood, though it is sometimes equated with the divine breath. The ego or self of man is called indifferently 'soul' or 'flesh'. Life is not treated as a natural phenomenon or made the object of scientific observation. It is the vitality which makes itself known in hunger and thirst, in wish and desire, in love and hate, in zeal and hope, in fact in all man's conative impulses, in all his striving and purposefulness. Life like the flesh itself is mortal, and ceases to be upon death. The idea of the immortality of the soul is quite foreign to the Old Testament. It only entered later from the Greek world into Hellenistic Judaism. Palestinian Judaism, on the other hand, adopted the Iranian conception of the resurrection of the body, a belief which appears only in a few late passages in the Old Testament.[31] Otherwise, the Old Testament invariably confines human life to this earth. The departed live a shadowy existence in Sheol.

Death is not seen as a natural process any more than life. There is no suggestion that it should be faced with equanimity, or that man should adjust himself to the cosmic order by an act of resolution. Equally absent is that other typical Greek idea, that death is the supreme triumph of human life—man should die nobly ($\kappa\alpha\lambda\hat{\omega}\varsigma$ $\dot{\alpha}\pi o\theta\nu\dot{\eta}\sigma\kappa\epsilon\iota\nu$). Nor is there any attempt to white-wash suicide as an act of heroism. There is no remedy for death, except to wish for a long life, at the end of which a man may go down tired but contented to the grave. A long and happy life is the supreme blessing the individual can enjoy, and that is what God promises to those who keep his commandments. The sinner is punished with premature death. There is as yet no idea in the Old Testament of punishment after death. The punishment of Adam's transgression is not death, but his expulsion from Paradise and the curse of hard labour.

A long and happy life, then, is man's greatest boon. There is no idea that long life might not necessarily be genuine life. The devout Israelite does not distinguish between the natural and the spiritual life, nor does he ask, like the Greek philosopher, what the true life is. Life is never described as good or bad in a moral sense. To live does not mean to live in any particular way. For the Old Testament, life is ζωή never βίος. It is always a vital, and never a spiritual phenomenon.

Old Testament man never shows any disposition to reflect on the tension between the higher and lower elements of his being. Hence he never thinks about shaping his life in one way or another. There is no antithesis between body (flesh) and spirit, as though one were base and the other noble. Nor is any distinction drawn between the higher and lower elements in the soul itself. There is no contrast between sensuality and spirit, and therefore no scale of values to define the relation between spirit and sensuality in the light of the ideal of 'pleasure' (ἡδονή), to say nothing of the Platonic ideal of justice (δικαιοσύνη) or the Stoic 'fortitude' (καρτερία), or the Hellenistic idea of asceticism, achieved by the successive stages of harmonic, musical, scientific and philosophical education. Nor is there any idea of education or formative training as such. Man is not regarded as a work of art, to be moulded after an ideal pattern. There is a complete absence of the typical Greek concept of the 'gentleman' (καλὸς κἀγαθός, i.e. a man who combines the ideals of beauty and goodness), no idea of virtue (ἀρετή) or technical efficiency (ἔργον), of eros (ἔρως), the urge or striving for the ideal. There is no conception of life as a competitive race (ἀγών), that Homeric maxim of αἰὲν ἀριστεύειν καὶ ὑπείροχον ἔμμεναι ἄλλων. No use is made of the argumentative dialogue (διαλέγεσθαι) as a method of education. The Platonic image of the soul as a chariot, like Faust's 'two souls within the breast' is completely foreign to the Old Testament, as foreign as the belief that the body is the prison of the soul.

Since there is no ascetic way for the purification of the soul from the defilement of the physical senses, no system of sacramental purification, no mysticism or mystical ecstasy,[32] there are no *homines religiosi*, no 'divine men' (θεῖοι ἄνδρες). But the ideal of personality is equally absent. Just as there is no sculpture, no representation of the human form, so there is no biography as a branch of literature. There are, for instance, no biographies of Moses or the prophets, no attempt to portray human character. The characters and passions of men are never made a theme for poetry. There is no drama or comedy, or even romance. Lyric becomes more and more exclusively religious—the hymn, the lamentation, the prayer and the song of thanksgiving.[33] And where lyric is used to express an individual's personal troubles or his trust or gratitude to God, these are not revelations of the secrets of his heart. The single exception is furnished by the Lamentations of Jeremiah.[34]

Good and Evil

The judgements passed on man and his activity are not derived from an ideal conception of man or the Good. The ethical vocabulary of the Old Testament is not derived, as with the Greeks, from the plastic arts or craftsmanship. It comes partly from the law court and commerce,[35] partly from the cultus. Hence there are no such laudatory epithets as 'becoming', 'decent', 'harmonious', 'well-proportioned', 'graceful' and the like (εὐσχήμων, κόσμιος, εὐάρμοστος, ἔμμετρος, εὔρυθμος, etc.). Instead, we get such terms as 'true', 'faithful', or (from the cultus) 'whole', 'without blemish', 'unspotted'.[36]

This ethical vocabulary suggests no ideal conception of man. It simply tells him how to satisfy the claims of society by upright, reliable and irreproachable conduct. 'Righteousness' is the omnibus term to describe this character. It means the respect a man enjoys in the sight of his fellows and in the sight of God who is the supreme instance of justice. 'Righteousness' is also used in the further, more specific sense of judicial impartiality. But it is never used to denote the harmony between the various faculties in the soul, as in Plato. Similarly, evil is positive opposition of the will to the Good, not just an inadequacy or deficiency in ethical education, a stage which it is both possible and necessary to get over. It is an offence which must be either punished or forgiven.

Even if the ethical precepts are addressed to the community rather than the individual, there is no idea of the city state as a political Utopia. Social life can only thrive on sound principles. Hence any behaviour which promotes the general welfare is to be encouraged, such as respect for law and order. No distinction is drawn between social justice and personal morality. Men must treat their neighbours properly, for they are their fellow Israelites. Most of the explicit ordinances are negative in character, as in the Decalogue, for instance. They lay down what must *not* be done. If any list of specific precepts is provided, there is no attempt to be exhaustive, still less systematic. No general principles are furnished from which specific duties may be deduced. There is no conception of 'virtue' or 'duty', no need to offer rational motives for morality. Common sense is sufficient to indicate what is conducive to the welfare of society. Right from the earliest days the tradition included concrete injunctions.

These precepts of righteousness and morality are regarded as the commandments of God.[37] As King and patron of justice, God requires righteousness and justice. No distinction is drawn between the moral and ceremonial law, both being of equal importance. In fact, there is more scrupulousness in fulfilling the latter when the former is neglected. The prophets are concerned to protest against this view. For them—or at any rate for the earlier prophets—God demands only righteousness and justice, not the performance of the cultus.

I hate, I despise your feast days,
and I will not smell in your solemn assemblies.
Though ye offer me burnt offerings and your meat offerings,
I will not accept them:
neither will I regard the peace offerings of your fat beasts.
Take away from me the noise of your songs;
for I will not hear the melody of thy viols.
But let judgement roll down as waters,
and righteousness as a mighty stream (Amos 5.21-4).

For I desire mercy, and not sacrifice;
and the knowledge of God more than burnt offerings (Hos. 6.6).

To what purpose is the multitude of your sacrifices unto me?
  saith the Lord:
I am full of the burnt offerings of rams,
and the fat of fed beasts;
and I delight not in the blood of bullocks or of lambs or of he-
  goats . . .
Bring no more vain oblations;
incense is an abomination unto me;
the new moons and sabbaths and your appointed feasts my soul
  hateth:
they are a trouble unto me;
I am weary to bear them.
And when ye spread forth your hands,
I will hide mine eyes from you:
yea, when ye make many prayers, I will not hear:
your hands are full of blood.
Wash you, make you clean;
put away the evil of your doings from before mine eyes;
cease to do evil; learn to do well;
seek judgement, judge the fatherless, plead for the widow
  (Isa. 1.11-15).

True, the prophets did not succeed in abolishing the cultus.
The outcome of their work was its centralization at Jerusalem,
which brought to an end the Canaanite vegetation rites and the
corruption of the worship of Jahweh. And in addition to this
there was an attempt to discover a unity between the cultus

and the judicial and moral law. A partial solution was found in the reinterpretation of the ancient ceremonial observances. The sabbath, for instance, was given a moral motive. More important, however, was the transformation of worship into a demonstration of obedience towards God and an effective symbol of Israel's separation from the surrounding nations, with the temptations of their paganism. Thus the later prophets ceased to attack the cultus, and interpreted it as obedience to a divine institution. According to them, what God really wants is radical obedience—or the 'heart' of man. Hence the denunciation of the prophet:

> Forasmuch as this people draw near to me with their mouth,
> and with their lips do honour me,
> but have removed their heart far from me,
> and their fear toward me is taught by the precept of men:
> Therefore will I proceed to do a marvellous work among this
>   people (Isa. 29.13-14a).

and the psalmist's prayer:

> Create in me a clean heart, O God;
> and renew a right spirit within me (Ps. 51.10).

The old condition laid down for the sacrificial victim, viz., that it should be entire and without blemish, is reapplied to the worshipper himself.

Sin and Grace

Sin is disobedience against the demand of the here and now. And since such demands come from God himself, sin is in the last analysis disobedience against God. All particular transgressions are expressions of the same underlying spirit, man's rebellion against lawfully constituted authority, his desire to be his own master. This means that it is rebellion against God. Disobedience deprives God of the honour due to his name. But God is a jealous God; he will not suffer anyone else to have that honour. He hates pride and arrogance, and casts it down to the ground.

> For the day of the Lord of hosts
> shall be upon every one that is proud and lofty,
> and upon every one that is lifted up;
> and he shall be brought low
> And upon all the cedars of Lebanon,
> that are high and lifted up,
> and upon all the oaks of Bashan,
> and upon all the high mountains,
> and upon all the hills that are lifted up,
> And upon every high tower,
> and upon every fenced wall,
> And upon all the ships of Tarshish,
> and upon all costly barks.
> And the loftiness of man shall be bowed down,
> and the haughtiness of men shall be made low:
> and the Lord alone shall be exalted in that day (Isa. 2.12-17).

In his hour of triumph the Assyrian imagines: 'By the strength of my hand have I done it, and by my wisdom.' But:

> Shall the axe boast himself against him that heweth therewith?
> Or shall the saw magnify himself against him that shaketh it?
>   (Isa. 10.13-15).

When the morning star sought to rise up to heaven, God cast it down to the depths of the underworld:

> How thou art fallen from heaven,
> O Lucifer, son of the morning!
> How thou art cut down to the ground,
> which didst lay low the nations!
> For thou hast said in thine heart,
> I will exalt my throne above the stars of God:
> I will sit upon the mount of the congregation high in the north:
> I will ascend above the heights of the clouds;
> I will be like the most High.
> Yet shalt thou be brought down to Sheol, to the sides of the pit.
> They that see thee shall reflect upon thee and consider thee, saying,

Is not this the man that made the earth to tremble,
that did shake kingdoms;
that made the world as a wilderness, and destroyed the cities
 thereof;
that opened not the house of his prisoners?
All the kings of the nations, even all of them lie in glory. . . .
But thou art cast out of thy grave
like an abominable branch (Isa. 14.12-19*a*).

Come down, and sit in the dust,
O thou virgin daughter of Babylon . . .
Thou saidst, I shall be a lady for ever. . . .
Therefore hear now this, thou that art given to pleasures,
that dwellest carelessly, that sayest in thine heart,
I am, and none else beside me . . .
Therefore shall evil come upon thee;
thou shalt not know from whence it ariseth (Isa. 47.1-11).

Let not the wise man glory in his wisdom,
neither let the mighty man glory in his might,
let not the rich man glory in his riches;
But let him that glorieth glory in this,
that he understandeth and knoweth me,
that I am the Lord,
which exercise loving kindness, judgement, and righteousness,
 in the earth (Jer. 9.23f.).

Even if God exalts Israel by destroying her enemies, she has no
ground for pride, for:

For my sake, even for mine own sake, will I do it:
for how should my name be polluted?
and I will not give my glory to another (Isa. 48.11).

I do not this for your sakes, O house of Israel,
but for my holy name's sake,
which ye have profaned among the heathen . . .
The heathen shall know that I am the Lord . . .
when I shall be sanctified in you before their eyes (Ezek. 36.22f.).

We are reminded of the jealousy of the Greek gods, and of the
judgements that befall man's *hybris*. But the Old Testament

conception of God's jealousy is different. It is not excess of good fortune as such which provokes God's jealousy—the Old Testament contains nothing analagous to the 'Ring' of Poly-crates—but pride and self-confidence. The Greeks of course believed that those things were wicked too. But in the Old Testament God's aim goes further. Sin is not only ostenta-tion, but self-will. Self-will and arrogance are sins because they are born of ingratitude to God, ingratitude for his creation and preservation of his people. The Greek saw no reason why he should be grateful for his existence. In the Old Testament ingratitude to God is ingratitude to history and disobedience to its claims. It is exactly for this reason that distrust is ingratitude and an insult to God. Both arrogance and pusillanimity are an insult to God. His jealousy is the jealousy of love.

Sin is therefore not only the specific transgression of a com-mandment, but also doubt in God's sovereignty and in the force of his demands. That was what lay behind the serpent's beguiling words in Paradise, 'Yea, hath God said?' It is also doubt in the truth of his promises. Sin is complaining about God's providence in the past and distrust of his guidance in the future. It is ingratitude, faithlessness and unbelief, the opposite of fear of God and of faith in the sense of trustful waiting upon God.[38]

Sin, then, is not a lower element in human nature, not a deficiency or imperfection to be got over by moral endeavour, but guilt in the sight of human society and in the sight of God. That is why man cannot get rid of sin by himself. That must be done by society and by God. Since it involves guilt, it requires atonement. This may take the form of punishment at the hands of the aggrieved party—and in the last resort that means God, the author of the law. But he can also administer punishment directly, by sending sickness, misfortune, or prema-ture death. But God has provided another way of atonement. That is the cultus, with its sacrifical system. Israel's thinking about the cultus is profoundly coloured by judicial notions. The more the ceremonial rites of atonement lose their original magical associations and are reinterpreted as symbols of man's obedience, and the more sin is interpreted in terms of moral guilt, the more do the ceremonies of atonement come to be regarded as an institution of the forgiving grace of God. Man knows he is thrown back upon God's forgiveness.

Two factors led to an increasing sense of sin. First, there were the experiences of misfortune and distress, in which the devout saw the punishment of God. Secondly, there was the teaching of the prophets, with their insistence on the inadequacy of the cultus, which led to a refined sense of conscience. Man was driven more and more to take refuge in the forgiving grace of God and to supplicate for pardon.

> Out of the depths have I cried unto thee, O Lord:
> Lord, hear my voice.
> Let thine ears be attentive to the voice of my supplication.
> If thou, Lord, shouldest mark iniquities,
> O Lord, who shall stand?
> But there is forgiveness with thee,
> that thou mayest be feared (Ps. 130.1-4).

> Create in me a clean heart, O God;
> and renew a right spirit within me.
> Cast me not away from thy presence;
> and take not thy holy Spirit from me.
> Restore unto me the joy of thy salvation;
> and uphold me with the face of thy spirit . . .
> For thou desirest not sacrifice; else would I give it thee:
> thou delightest not in burnt offering.
> The sacrifices of God are a troubled spirit:
> a broken and contrite heart, O God, thou wilt not despise
> (Ps. 51.10-12, 16f.).

It is in this sense that repentance is demanded of man. Repentance is not just a change of mind. That would only be a subjective process, leaving man's relation with God unaffected. Repentance means returning to God from the isolation of self-will. It means recognizing God as the Judge in whose sight man is guilty, and whose forgiveness alone can restore him to the community. Repentance thus involves an acceptance of God's judgement. It is more than remorse. It is an explicit act of self-surrender, an acknowledgment of a life forfeited. Of course, this turning to God does involve a change of disposition, a resolve to do good and obey God's will in time to come. But there is no suggestion that this resolve in itself is able to avert the wrath of God. All man can do is to ask God's forgiveness and hope to receive it. Compare the admonition of the prophet:

> O Israel, return unto the Lord thy God;
> for thou hast fallen by thine iniquity.
> Take with you words (of confession):
> say unto him, Take away all iniquity,
> and receive us graciously:
> so will we render the fruit of our lips (Hos. 14.1f.).

> Seek ye the Lord while he may be found,
> call ye upon him while he is near:
> Let the wicked forsake his way,
> and the unrighteous man his thoughts:
> and let him return unto the Lord,
> and he will have mercy;
> and to our God, for he will abundantly pardon (Isa. 55.6f.).

And God promises through his prophet:

> I dwell in the high and holy place,
> with him also that is of a contrite and humble spirit,
> to revive the spirit of the humble,
> and to revive the heart of the contrite ones (Isa. 57.15*b*).

Since for ancient Israel life was confined to this world, and the only future after death was the future of the people, God's forgiveness and grace were seen or expected in a change of worldly fortune. But since experience taught that sin was as permanent as personal misfortune and national suffering, the hope of his forgiveness and grace was transferred to an eschatological future: 'In those days and at that time, saith the Lord, the iniquity of Israel shall be sought for, and there shall be none; and the sins of Judah, and they shall not be found: for I will pardon them whom I reserve' (Jer. 50.20).

JUDAISM

JUDAISM

I

Synagogue and Law

Jewish Legalism

FROM THE TIME OF THE EXILE, Israel lost her independent existence as a state. Thenceforth, the nation lived under foreign rule; first of all, the Persians (until *ca.* 350 B.C.). Under them the Jewish Church enjoyed freedom of religion and worship. The Jews could organize themselves as the people of God and realize the ideal of theocracy. Further, during the Greek period, i.e. under the rule of the Ptolemies, this freedom went unchallenged. It was only after Judaea came under the yoke of Syria in the time of the Seleucids that the situation changed (*ca.* 200 B.C.). Antiochus IV (175-164 B.C.) adopted a policy of forcible Hellenization for the Jews, as a result of which the Maccabean revolt broke out. This party fought for national liberty, and under the Hasmonean kings Judah became once more an independent state until Pompey entered Jerusalem in 63 B.C. and set up Roman rule. As a puppet king under the Romans, Herod the Great reigned in Judaea from 37 to 4 B.C. After his death his kingdom was divided among his sons and grandsons, Judaea proper being ruled by Archelaus (4 B.C.-A.D. 6) until it came under the rule of Roman procurators; it was only later that the northern and eastern districts came under direct Roman administration. The revolts of A.D. 66-70 and A.D. 132 led to the final destruction of the Jewish nation in the form in which it had existed hitherto.

Until the fall of Jerusalem in A.D. 70 the city and the temple were the focal point of the nation's life. Devout Jews made pilgrimages to the Temple for the great feasts, even from the Diaspora. These feasts acted both as a demonstration of national solidarity and loyalty to law, and also as an anticipation of the eschatological joy. But the worship of the temple was no longer the focal point of Jewish piety. That status was gradually taken over by the synagogue. Here we have something unique in the ancient world, viz. a non-sacrificial form of worship. Its pattern was as follows. It began and ended with prayer, and its central feature was the reading of 'the scripture' (i.e. the Old Testament) and its exposition in the sermon.[1]

By its loyalty to the scriptures the community bound itself to its history. Its God was the God of the fathers,[2] the God of Abraham, Isaac and Jacob, the God who brought the people out of Egypt by the hand of Moses, made his covenant with them on Mount Sinai and gave them the Law. It was the God who from time to time had raised up prophets, who had punished his people by sending them into exile, and who was chastening them by making them subject to foreign rule. Yet some day this God would fulfil his promises to the fathers and grant his people a glorious future. This loyalty to its past gave the community a strong sense of history and election. It was this that distinguished Israel from all other nations.

But there is a curious inner contradiction here. By binding herself to her past history, Israel loosened her ties with the present, and her responsibility for it. Loyalty to the past became loyalty to a book which was all about the past. God was no longer really the God of history, and therefore always the God who was about to come. He was no longer a vital factor in the present: his revelations lay in the past. History was likewise brought to a standstill. The nation lived outside history. God no longer raised up prophets and kings as he had done in the past; he no longer poured forth his Spirit. He would not do so until the last times. The national leaders were not men of political or social action, but teachers who expounded the scriptures. There was no possibility there of science and art, nor could there be any cultural intercourse with other nations. Israel (apart from Hellenistic Judaism) cut herself off from the outside world and lived in extraordinary isolation. As a result she cut herself adrift from history. The redemption she hoped for in the future was not a real historical event, but a fantastic affair in which all history had been brought to an end for good and all.

Once the idea of God's transcendence was lost in the sense of constant futurity, another idea of transcendence came instead. God, like his people, was cut adrift from history. Just as the nation isolated itself in its religion, so God was no longer bound to his people. The reason for this was that God seemed no longer to reveal himself in history as he had done in former times. He now became the universal Lord of heaven and earth, and therefore of other nations besides Israel. He was the Judge of the world. The doctrine of his omnipotence and universal judgement were developed. It is symptomatic that his name could no longer be uttered aloud—except, perhaps, on very special occasions. His transcendence was now conceived in metaphysical terms. He was a superior cosmic power, spacially distant and ontologically distinct from all worldly phenomena. The apocalypses provide fantastic pictures of his cosmic rule, with his hosts of angels and the blinding glory of heaven. God's purpose was no longer confined to Israel, but embraced the whole universe.

He was the Judge before whose tribunal all must one day give account. Therefore everybody was given a chance to worship him. Judaism might have been an exclusive religion, but it was also a missionary religion. Jesus holds up to ridicule its methods of propaganda in his saying addressed to the Pharisees and scribes about their going over land and sea to make one proselyte (Matt. 23.15). Of course, it goes without saying that the true worship of God was confined to the Jews. Only they worshipped him in accordance with the commandments of scripture. Proselytes actually had to join the Jewish community.[3] Here is another instance of the way Israel was cutting herself adrift from history. The bond of unity seems no longer to have been a common history, but a common ritual.

This inner contradiction, which is the clue to our whole understanding of Israel, appears again in the treatment of the

Bible in synagogue worship. It was no longer primarily an historical record of God's dealings with his people, but a book of divine Law. The focal point of worship was no longer the cultus, but the preaching and hearing of the sermon, which was intended to regulate the whole of life. Thus daily life itself became an act of worship, ideally, at any rate. This had two different consequences. First, it meant that the whole of life was dominated by religion. Religion was not confined to a special sphere of its own, as distinct from daily life. On the other hand, however, life was alienated from history, which is the natural sphere to which it belongs. The Law inculcated not only morality, but ritualism. Ritual became the more important of the two, with the result that men lost sight of their social and cultural responsibilities. The 'chosen people' were not called to fulfil a special mission in history, but to be the 'holy nation', above all worldly interests and ideals.

The national leaders were neither the politicians (the Herodian dynasty were regarded as aliens no less than the Roman procurators) nor the priests, but the scribes, who combined the functions of lawyers and theologians. Both religion and morality were enjoined in the Law, and were not therefore separable from jurisprudence. Both civil and criminal law were considered to be divine in origin. The exposition of the Law controlled the administration of justice no less than day-to-day behaviour.

Fundamentally, the Law was incapable of undergoing any further development. Since it was God's Law, it was valid for all time in the exact form in which it was delivered from the time of Moses. To be sure, it contained many precepts which changing circumstances had rendered obsolete and meaningless. Yet they had still to be obeyed unquestioningly. Again, the Law failed to give guidance for the new circumstances which, despite the isolation of the people, inevitably arose through the influence of the outside world. It was therefore necessary for the scribes to apply the old laws to the new conditions. They had to be as true as possible to the original meaning, and yet derive practical regulations for contemporary situations. It was necessary for instance to state exactly what work was prohibited on the sabbath, and to draw a clear line of demarcation between prohibited and permissible forms of conduct. This led to a good deal of discussion among the scribes, and to the forming of various schools of thought which took the place of political parties. Broadly speaking, there were two such schools, the Sadducees and the Pharisees.[4] The Sadducees were the conservatives, the 'orthodox', accepting only those laws which were codified in the Pentateuch (that is, those laws which were incontrovertibly Mosaic), and rejecting the traditions which had grown up around the original deposit through generations of scribal activity. To accept the latter would have been to place them on a par with the scriptures themselves. The Sadducees also rejected certain new-fangled doctrines, such as the resurrection of the dead. The Pharisees were opposed to them on both points. They were the 'liberals', who sought to modify the harshness of the old punishments of the Law by interpretation and inference. For them the oral tradition was as authoritative as the written law itself. Yet at the same time the Pharisees were more strict in the way they tied daily life to the observance of the Law. By their exposition of it they extended it to cover the whole of daily life down to the smallest details.

These different schools of thought were by no means confined to the scribes, who represented a closed caste of jurists and theologians. The laity also ranged themselves on one side or the other. The Pharisees, with the zeal for the strict regulation of daily life, formed a kind of monastic order. The very name 'Pharisee' means 'separatist'. They called themselves 'associates' or 'people of the fellowship'. It is evident that Pharisaic tendencies were dominant in the religion of the ordinary people, while the Sadducees had their following mainly among the upper and wealthier classes.[4] After the fall of Jerusalem the Pharisees had a monopoly, and the traditions assembled in their exposition of the law became the standard of Jewish orthodoxy.

The scribes laid down a course of training leading to ordination to the rabbinate. As already suggested, this course of study was centred upon the exposition of the Old Testament. But it was not scientific knowledge in the Greek sense. There was no attempt to lay down certain fundamental principles from which all knowledge could be systematically developed, and applied to the study of the universe, no constant testing and revision of these principles. The scribes regarded the foundation as immutable, for it consisted in the holy scriptures themselves. Their method of exegesis was primitive, and, despite certain variations, stereotype. The progress of scientific knowledge was limited to painstaking exegesis. But there was no attempt to reach a deeper understanding of the context, to discover the ideas underlying the text itself, or the circumstances in which it took shape. The only kind of progress they recognized was the accumulation of possible interpretations. There was therefore no attempt to work out a particular thesis, or to abandon it in the light of further criticism. New interpretations were simply recorded side by side with the old, and no attempt was made to decide which was the true one. It was the function of learning to preserve as many existing interpretations as possible. In teaching there was no attempt to ask questions of the pupil and thus train him to think for himself. The Greek method of seeking the truth in the cut and thrust of argument was entirely unknown. The pupil asked the teacher for his opinion, and tried to memorize the views of all the different authorities. The opinions of previous scholars were faithfully preserved, indeed, verbatim, wherever possible, with the name of the rabbi who had first uttered it.[5]

Eventually the tradition, as was inevitable, was fixed in writing, though the scribes resisted this development as long as they could. The oldest codification is the 'Mishna', a re-edition of earlier collections undertaken towards the end of the second century A.D. We also have a parallel collection in the 'Tosephta'. The Talmud represents a continuation and commentary on the Mishna. It is extant in two versions, both defective, viz. the Jerusalem and the Babylonian, from the fourth and fifth centuries respectively. In addition to these collections, the rabbinic tradition is deposited in the 'Targums', translations of Old Testament books into Aramaic, and in the 'Midrashim', which comment on those books.

Life under the Law was still worship and service of God.[6] Not only was it based on the rhythm of the week, with the sabbath at the end of it with worship in the synagogue and a rigid abstention from work,[7] but also it contained certain liturgical observances which accompanied daily life. Every morning and evening the male Israelite had to recite the *Shemah*,[8] which served as the Jewish creed. It consists of sentences from the Old Testament (Deut. 6.4-9, 11.13-21; Num. 15.37-41). It begins: 'Hear, O Israel: The Lord our God is one Lord: And thou shalt love the Lord thy God with all thine heart, and with all thy soul, and with all thy might'; and it concludes: 'I am the Lord your God, which brought you out of the land of Egypt, to be your God: I am the Lord your God.' In the morning, at midday, and in the afternoon (the times of the sacrifice called the *Minha*) everyone, including women, children, and slaves, had to recite the *Shemoneh 'esre* or Eighteen Benedictions, while, of course, grace was said before and after meals.

Beyond this however, the whole of life was covered by ritual observances. The Pharisees, in their zeal, imposed upon the laity the laws of purity which had originally applied only to the priesthood, thus giving the whole of life the character of ritual holiness. No part of daily living was beyond the scope of these regulations. Hence the innumerable precepts about 'eating and drinking, the slaughter of animals and the preparation of meat, about cooking utensils and about keeping the body clean from all defilements, about washing, about impurities occasioned by infectious diseases, birth, death, adolescence and senile decay, and contact with other impurities'.[9] Naturally, all contact with the uncircumcised required careful regulation.

These regulations went into detail to the point of absurdity. Since all work was forbidden on the sabbath, you were not allowed to pluck ears of corn if you were hungry (Mark 2.23). There were minute regulations about what was and what was not permissible on the sabbath, such as sewing on a button, or taking one off! There were solemn discussions about the legality of wearing a false tooth on the sabbath (the carrying of burdens being forbidden!) or whether it was permissible to eat an egg laid on the sabbath. It was indeed permissible to incur a breach of the sabbath regulations for the purpose of saving life, though the limits one might go to were carefully defined. We should of course remember that such discussions were largely academic in character. It is doubtful whether they were seriously intended to be put into practice in such border-line cases as these.[10]

At the same time, however, it was just this ritualism which sanctified the life of the community. But that sanctity was an entirely negative affair, since most of the regulations are negative and prohibitive in character.[11] It was calculated during the third century A.D. that there were 613 regulations, 365 of which were negative and 248 positive. This also shows the vast number of the regulations, and their lack of unifying principle. To take them seriously meant making life an intolerable burden. It was almost impossible to *know* the rules, let alone put them into practice. All the same, we should not exaggerate this side of the matter. No one was obliged to observe *all* the Pharisaic precepts. Moreover, while there was still a regular communal life prior to the fall of Jerusalem the regulations had not yet been elaborated to the extent they later were in the Mishna and Talmud. And the sabbath and the basic laws of purity were taken so much as a matter of course by the ordinary Jew, who had been familiar with them from childhood, that he would not have felt them to be a burden at all. Such minute regulations were mainly a matter of academic discussion in learned circles. In practice there were always a number of alternatives, although it would be true to say that the precision of the scribal jurists was a typical expression of Jewish legalism.

Some attention was paid to a difference of importance between the regulations, and they were classed as of primary and of secondary importance. Hillel, who taught at the time of Herod the Great, at the end of the first century B.C., is said to have been the author of the 'golden rule' summary of the Torah: 'What is hateful to thee, do not do to anyone else: this is the whole Law and the rest is commentary.' The following teaching is attributed to the rabbis of Jabneh: 'It makes no difference whether one does little or much, so long as one's heart is fixed on heaven [i.e. God].' Johanan ben Zaccai, who flourished about the time of the fall of Jerusalem, is said to have asked his disciples about the 'good way', and gave the prize to the one who answered, 'A good heart.' Another saying runs: 'Whosoever in his dealings and behaviour with the creatures is guided by faithfulness is accounted as having fulfilled the whole Torah.' R. Akiba (ca. A.D. 110-15) summed up the whole Law in the saying: 'Love thy neighbour as thyself.' In the *Testament of the Twelve Patriarchs* the term 'simplicity' (ἁπλότης) is suggested as the fundamental principle for an ethic of disposition. 'All depends', it is said, 'on goodwill.' So long as men are of goodwill their sins are absorbed by their good deeds, while conversely the good done by a man of ill will is worthless.[12]

Finally, it should not be forgotten that while ritualism received so much prominence, the moral precepts of the Old Testament, and in particular the Decalogue, were still in force. Traditional wisdom, with its formulation of ethical rules in proverbs, was also still alive.[13] The old precepts of honesty, reliability and faithfulness were still observed, while in the realm of sexual purity and reverence for marriage Judaism was exemplary, and always sensitive of its difference from paganism in this respect. But life makes demands which lie beyond the purview of the devout Jew, and Jewish morality became over-scrupulous and pettifogging. Modesty and amiability, characteristic traits which often enough became kindness and compassion, also degenerated frequently into mere pliability. Instead of the Greek maxim, ὑπείροχον ἔμμεναι ἀλλῶν, we get: 'Give no offence.'

Most important of all, no distinction was drawn between the moral and ritual law in respect of their divine authority.[14] Jesus must have had good reasons for saying what he did about straining at the gnat and swallowing the camel (Matt. 23.24). The ritual commandments having lost their original meaning, man's relation to God was inevitably conceived in legalistic terms.

The motive of ethics was obedience. The commandments were obeyed because they *were* commandments. Johanan ben Zaccai answered a critic thus: 'Death does not make unclean, nor the water make clean. But the Holy One says: I have prescribed a statute for you, I have issued a decree to you. You have no right to transgress my decree, for it is written. This is the statute of my law.'[15] Belief in divine retribution was as strong as ever: God still punished the sinner and rewarded the righteous. Yet this was not to be the motive for obeying the Law. Antigonus of Soko, who flourished in pre-Christian times, is reported to have said: 'Be not like slaves who minister unto their Lord on condition of receiving a reward; but be like unto slaves who minister unto their lord without expecting to receive a reward.'[16] A similar saying is attributed to Johanan ben Zaccai: 'If thou hast practised much Torah, claim merit not for thyself, since for this purpose thou wast created.'[17] The underlying motive for the fulfilment of the Law was therefore obedience, or, as the Jews called it, the 'fear of God'. This fear was not misconstrued as slavish fear: the rabbis said that the love of God must actuate human behaviour, just as much as the fear of him.[18]

Radical obedience would have involved a personal assent to the divine command, whereas in Judaism so many of the precepts were trivial or unintelligible that the kind of obedience produced was formal rather than radical. The equality of importance attached to ritual and moral precepts was no less conducive to formalism. The Law failed to claim the allegiance of the *whole* man. Although in theory it provided for every possible contingency in daily life, there were inevitably an infinite number of possibilities for which there was no provision. In the absence of a specific ruling, a man was free to decide for himself what to do. Thus there was plenty of scope for egoistic impulses and passions, as well as for works of supererogation. Here we have a clear indication of the legalistic way in which the divine decrees were conceived. The Law could not possibly embrace every conceivable contingency, and, besides, it was essentially negative in character, with very few positive injunctions. This encouraged the notion that it is possible to do one's whole duty and leave nothing undone. What was required was specific actions, or specific abstentions from action. Once these had been got through, a man was free to do what he liked. There was thus scope for works of supererogation, 'good works' in the technical sense of the term. These provided a basis for merit in the proper sense of the word. The accumulation of merits might serve to atone for breaches of the Law. Among these works of supererogation were charitable deeds of every kind, including almsgiving and voluntary fasts.

With the unintelligibility of many of the precepts and the scope for works of supererogation, it was impossible to entertain a radical conception of obedience. Where the motive of obedience is simply that a certain course of action is prescribed, there is no personal assent to the requirements of the Law. Radical obedience is possible only where the Law is understood and answered by personal assent. So long as there are occasions in life which are directly or indirectly free from God's claim, there cannot be radical obedience. For in radical obedience a man knows himself to be claimed by God in his entirety and in every conceivable contingency.

The legalistic conception of obedience produced an equally legalistic conception of divine retribution.[19] If God's demand was conceived as a legal demand, its breach required a legally fixed punishment. Just as human criminal law was based on the principle of the *lex talionis*, so too God had to make the punishment fit the crime. 'Wherewithal a man sinneth, by the same also shall he be punished.'[20] One day, when he saw a skull floating on the water, Hillel remarked: 'Because they drowned thee thou art drowned, but they that drowned thee shall themselves be drowned at the last.'[21] Gad was visited by a liver complaint because his 'liver' was unmerciful towards Joseph (Test. Gad 5). The punishments applicable to particular sins could be calculated to the last detail.

Divine punishment was at first looked for during this life, as in the Old Testament. Whenever a man met with unusual misfortune or distress, the question inevitably arose as to the latent cause of his sufferings. But the calculation often went astray, as was the case with the friends of Job. Consequently, a belief in retribution after death was gradually developed, and with it a theology of suffering.[22] God allowed the wicked to prosper in this life in order to punish them in the next, whereas the righteous paid for their sins in this life in order to receive a full reward for their righteousness in the next.

A further consequence of the legalistic conception of obedience was that the prospect of salvation became highly uncertain. Who could be sure he had done enough in this life to be saved? Would his observance of the Law and his good works be sufficient? For in the day of judgement all his good works would be counted up and weighed, and woe to him if the scales fell on the side of his evil deeds! When his friends visited Johanan ben Zaccai on his sick-bed, they found him weeping because he was so uncertain of his prospects before the judgement seat of God;[23] The prospect of meeting God as their Judge awakened in the conscientious a scrupulous anxiety and morbid sense of guilt. Sin appeared to be an ineluctable power, spreading its tentacles over the whole world and affecting the heart of the individual in a way that could be felt.[24] It was the great enigma. Nobody wants to sin, and if he does sin he is bound to be terrified. It must have been the devil who brought sin into the world. Adam brought it on all his descendants when he fell. Those were the answers. There was also the further doctrine of the evil impulse dwelling in the heart of man side by side with the good impulse. True, man could repent: renew his will to do good;[25] but if he was powerless to do good, the only way out was by penitential prayer in which God's forgiveness was implored. 'We have sinned in thy sight' was a prayer constantly on the lips of the devout. Jewish literature is full of confessions of sin and penitential prayers.[26] Especially after the fall of Jerusalem, when the sacrificial cultus ceased, remorse or repentance took the place of sacrifice as the means of obtaining the forgiveness of God.[27]

It is a remarkable fact that side by side with this sense of sin and urge to repentance we find the 'righteous' proud and self-conscious. They look down on the publican and sinner and preen themselves on their own good works. 'I thank thee, that I am not as other men are, extortioners, unjust, adulterers, or even as this publican. I fast twice in the week, I give tithes of all that I possess' (Luke 18.11f.). And, strangely enough, this self-praise can be combined with a sense of sin. Thus, after a lengthy penitential prayer the seer in IV Ezra hears the angel saying to him:

> Thou, however, hast many times ranged thyself with the ungodly. This must not be!
> But even on this account thou shalt be honourable before the Most High;
> because thou hast humbled thyself, as it becomes thee,
> and hast not assigned thyself a place among the righteous;
> and so shalt thou receive the greater glory (IV Ezra. 8.47b-9).

Thus repentance itself became a good work which secured merit and grace in the sight of God. In the end the whole range of man's relation with God came to be thought of in terms of merit, including faith itself. Originally obedient loyalty and hope in God's providential guidance, it came to mean faith in retribution or merit. Thus although it was not reckoned explicitly among good works, but placed alongside of them, the concept of meritorious faith began to take shape.[28]

The Proclamation of Jesus

The proclamation of Jesus must be considered within the framework of Judaism.[29] Jesus was not a 'Christian,' but a Jew, and his preaching is couched in the thought forms and imagery of Judaism, even where it is critical of traditional Jewish piety. It is in fact a tremendous protest against contemporary Jewish legalism, thus renewing under changed conditions the protest of the ancient prophets against the official Hebrew religion. As the prophets contrasted God's demand of righteousness with the formalism of the cultus, so Jesus preaches radical obedience in place of ritualism and a legalistic conception of man's relation to God. Unlike the ancient prophets, however, he is not concerned with social righteousness. Such a concern would have been irrelevant now that Israel had lost her independence. It was in fact the teaching of the prophets which had been codified in the Law. But this no longer served primarily for the ordering of society, but as a means of regulating man's personal relation to God. It was just this legalism that Jesus protested against. God demands radical obedience: he claims the whole man.

The Sermon on the Mount (Matt. 5.21-48) contrasts the Law and the will of God: 'Ye have heard that it was said to them of old time. . . . But I say unto you . . .' God does not claim man only in so far as his behaviour is covered by formulated precepts, as though outside that area man were free. He forbids not only murder, adultery and perjury, but even anger and abuse, lust and untruthfulness. His demand embraces not only external behaviour (which the Law can take cognizance of), but inner motive. God is concerned not only with *what* man does, but with the spirit in which he does it. The Law's prohibitions of murder, adultery and perjury (Matt. 5.21f., 27f., 33-7) are made radical to a degree unknown before, as well as other laws which were concessionary in character and left a loophole for man to do as he pleased. These too, in the light of God's will, are null and void. Thus he abrogates divorce and the *jus talionis*, and the restriction of love to man's neighbour (Matt. 5.31f., 38-41, 43-8). God demands the complete surrender of man's will, and knows no concessions:

Do men gather grapes of thorns,
or figs of thistles?
Every tree is known by its fruits;
a good tree bringeth not forth corrupt fruit (Luke 6.43f. and
Matt. 7.16, 18).

The light of the body is the eye:
if therefore thine eye be light, thy whole body shall be full of
light;
But if thine eye be evil, thy whole body shall be full of darkness
(Matt. 6.22f.).

Man has no freedom over against God. God claims him as a
whole, and man must answer for his life as a whole, as the
parable of the Talents teaches (Matt. 25.14-30). Therefore he
cannot claim anything from God on the ground of personal
achievement. He is like a slave who can do no more than his
duty (Luke 17.7-10). God will certainly reward the performance
of duty.[30] But any attempt to reckon up merit and reward is to
be deprecated. The labourer who did his duty in the last hour
receives the same reward as those who had borne the heat and
burden of the day (Matt. 20.1-15). Those who suppose inordin-
ate misfortune to be a punishment for particularly heinous sin
are reminded that they themselves are no better than anyone
else (Luke 13.1-5). The proud are an abomination in the sight of
God (Luke 16.15), and the self-righteous Pharisee must yield
place to the sinful publican, who dares not so much as lift up his
eyes to heaven (Luke 18.9-14). Man must approach God like a
child, content to receive a gift, and innocent of any appeal to
privilege or merit (Mark 10.15).

Without contesting the authority of the Old Testament,
Jesus discriminates between its various precepts. Moses may
have permitted divorce, but what God really intends is that
marriage should be permanent (Mark 10.2-9). 'Woe unto you
scribes and Pharisees, hypocrites! for ye pay tithe of mint, anise
and cummin, and have omitted the weightier matters of the
law, judgement, mercy and faith. Ye blind guides, which
strain at a gnat, and swallow a camel' (Matt. 23.23f.).[31] Actually

God has revealed his will in the Old Testament, and those who
want to know his will are referred to the moral precepts of the
Old Testament like the rich man (Mark 10.17-19), and the scribe
who inquires which is the great commandment of the law
(Mark 12.28-34). The rich man, it is true, only thought he had
kept the Law, for he shrinks from giving up everything for
God's sake (Mark 10.20-2).

The upshot is that the Old Testament, in so far as it consists
of ceremonial and ritual ordinances, is abrogated.[32] Jesus directs
a polemic against the legalistic ritualism of the scribes, whose
correct external behaviour so often went hand in hand with an
impure will. Thus he quotes from the prophets:

> This people honoureth me with their lips,
> but their heart is far from me.
> In vain do they worship me,
> teaching for doctrines the commandments of men (Mark 7.6f.).

> Woe unto you, scribes and Pharisees, hypocrites!
> for ye make clean the outside of the cup and of the platter,
> but within ye are full of extortion and excess.
> Woe unto you, scribes and Pharisees, hypocrites!
> for ye are like unto whited sepulchres,
> which indeed appear beautiful outward,
> but are within full of dead men's bones, and of all uncleanness.
> Even so ye outwardly appear righteous unto men,
> but within ye are full of hypocrisy and iniquity (Matt. 23.25-8).

How easy it is to pray, fast and give alms in order to show off
before others! (Matt. 6.1-4, 5f., 16-18.) How easy it is to nullify
the fifth commandment by claiming priority for the ceremonial
law! (Mark 7.9-13.) The laws of purity are meaningless, for
'There is nothing from without a man, that entering into him
can defile him: but the things which come out of him, those are
they that defile the man'(Mark 7.15). 'The sabbath was made for
man, and not man for the sabbath' (Mark 2.27). Even the scribe
knows this,[33] but Jesus pushes it to its radical conclusion: 'Is it
lawful to do good on the sabbath day, or to do evil? to save life,

or to kill?' (Mark 3.4). In other words, there is no third alternative, no holy *dolce far niente*. To refrain from action when charity
demands that we should do something positive is to do evil.
Unless it be an expression of genuine sorrow, fasting is pointless (Mark 2.18f.). That is why Jesus consorted with publicans
and sinners and harlots (Mark 2.15-17; Matt. 21.28-32). He is
reproached as a 'glutton and winebibber' (Matt. 11.19), but no
matter. He can hold up a Samaritan as an example (Luke
10.30-6).

And what does God really require? Love. The second commandment, 'Thou shalt love thy neighbour as thyself' is
inseparable from the first, 'Thou shalt love the Lord thy God
with all thy heart, and with all thy soul, and with all thy mind,
and with all thy strength' (Mark 12.28-34). There is no need for
formulated definitions. The parable of the Good Samaritan
shows that there is no difficulty in seeing what we ought to do
when our neighbour needs our help. The phrase 'as thyself'
indicates both the unlimited measure and the direction of love
as a principle of conduct. We all know how we would like
others to treat us if we were in the same situation ourselves.

The commandment of love is neither a blueprint for society
nor a programme for Utopia. Although in practice it may have
far-reaching implications for national and social life in general,
it is addressed in the first place to the individual. It points him
to his encounter with his neighbour. In this way it takes the
future out of his hands. Thus Jesus' ethic is a transcendental
or eschatalogical ethic. This does not mean, however, that the
prospect of future judgement provides the motive for the
precept. It is significant that neither the imperatives of the Sermon
on the Mount nor the criticisms of the Law are motivated by a
reference to the judgement. There is nothing, for instance, like
the Old Testament 'Do this and ye shall be saved'. Nor is there
any suggestion of escapism or asceticism about it. Its transcendence is the future of God. His demand is always present anew in
each successive encounter with our neighbour.

Jesus also has a place in his teaching for the imminence of

judgement. He too can challenge men to repentance. Here he begins where John the Baptist left off. Clearly it was John who gave him the first impetus, just as he also submitted to baptism at his hands. The Baptist had been at work before he came on the scene as an ascetic preacher of repentance, crying out in the wilderness: 'Repent ye, for the Reign of God has drawn nigh.' He baptizes those who come to him confessing their sins. And through baptism they receive forgiveness (Mark 1.5). He rebukes the complacency of the 'children of Abraham', and tells them to bring forth fruits worthy of repentance (Matt. 3.8; Luke 3.8).

Though Jesus' teaching about the will of God is hardly influenced by his expectation of an imminent end of the world and the threat of judgement, yet, when he is confronted by the indifference and hostility of the authorities and the people, his preaching does assume the form of denunciation and a summons to repentance:

> Woe unto you, scribes and Pharisees! (Matt. 23.1ff.; Luke 11.37ff.).
>
> Woe unto you that are rich! for ye have received your consolation.
> Woe unto you that are full! for ye shall hunger.
> Woe unto you that laugh now! for ye shall mourn and weep (Luke 6.24-6).

'The time is fulfilled, and the kingdom of God is at hand'— thus does Mark 1.15 briefly summarize the preaching of Jesus. But 'this generation' is an 'adulterous and sinful generation'. Men say Yes to God's decrees and then forget all about them (Matt. 21.28-31). They are not ready for repentance (Matt. 12.41f.; Luke 11.31f.; cf. Matt. 11.21-4; Luke 10.13-15). Therefore judgement will come upon this generation (Luke 13.1-5), and all the old prophecies of judgement will be accomplished upon it (Matt. 23.34-6; Luke 11.49-51), especially on Jerusalem (Matt. 23.37-9; Luke 13.34f.) and its temple. No stone of it will remain unbroken (Mark 13.2). Only the outcast, the publicans, sinners and harlots are ready to repent. Jesus knows that it was to them he was sent (Mark 2.17). Those who first said No repent later (Matt. 21.28-31). God takes more pleasure in one sinner who repents than in ninety and nine just persons (Luke 15.1-10). It is the hungry and those who mourn, those who know they are poor, who receive the promise of salvation (Luke 6.20f.; Matt. 5.3-6).

For Jesus, as for the Old Testament and Judaism, God is the Creator who governs the world with his providential care. It is he who feeds the birds and gives their beauty to the flowers, without whose will not even a sparrow falls from the roof-top, and who has even numbered the hairs of our head (Matt. 6.25-34; 10.29f.; Luke 12.22-31). All this fear and anxiety, all the hurry to lay up goods in store as a means of security, are therefore pointless. For when all is said and done we are in God's hands. We cannot add a cubit to our stature or make our hair white or black (Matt. 6.27, 5.36; Luke 12.25). We may think wealth is the key to security, but we do not know whether we may not die this very night (Luke 12.16-20). God wants men to have a sense of dependence as well as trust.

Thus Jesus' teaching of God seems no different from that which he had been taught. But the terms used to express this sense of dependence and trust show that Jesus had brought God out of the false transcendence to which he had been relegated by Judaism and made him near at hand again. God is transcendent, but in the sense that he is always the coming God. He defines the present, embracing us all, delimiting us and making demands upon us. All this is clearly expressed in the opening words of the Lord's Prayer. Jewish prayers generally began by piling up sonorous predicates: 'God of Abraham, God of Isaac, God of Jacob. God most High, Creator of heaven and earth. Our shield and the shield of our fathers.'[34] But Jesus just gives the simple address: 'Father.' The Lord's prayer is not distinguished from Jewish prayers by any original matter, but by its brevity and simplicity. God is near, and hears the petitions we address to him as a father listens to the requests of his children (Matt. 7.7-11; Luke 11.9-13; cf. Luke 11.5-8, 18.1-5).

But Jesus also brings God near in another sense. While for him, as in Judaism, God is the God who *demands*, for him the will of God is not confined to the letter of the Law and its scribal interpretation. The limitations imposed by the written Law and tradition are swept aside. Man learns God's will directly from the situation of encounter with his neighbour. Thus belief in God as the Judge, in itself already familiar to Judaism, indeed an article of their faith, acquires a new urgency: 'Fear not them which kill the body, but are not able to kill the soul: but rather fear him which is able to destroy both soul and body in hell' (Matt. 10.28; Luke 12.4f.).

But the God who demands and judges is also the God who forgives, the God of grace. If only men 'turn' to him, they can be sure of this. The scribes shut men out of the kingdom of God (Matt. 23.13; Luke 11.52). But Jesus' summons to repentance *opens* the door. No need for long penitential prayers! It is the publican who is justified, the publican who smites on his breast and says: 'God be merciful to me a sinner' (Luke 18.13). And when the prodigal son comes to himself and decides to return home, all he can say is: 'Father, I have sinned against heaven and in thy sight, and am no more worthy to be called thy son'—but even then his father's love is already going out to him (Luke 15.21).

Clearly the repentance Jesus requires is not just a human achievement, thus creating a claim to the grace of God. It is rather self-recollection and self-knowledge, leading to a sincere confession of sin and a readiness to stand before God as a sinner and throw oneself wholly upon his grace (Luke 18.9-14). The commandment of love, the summons to repentance are clearly two facets of the same thing. As in turning away from self he prepares for encounter with his neighbour, so a man throws himself in penitence upon God and thus opens the way for his grace. Only those who themselves forgive can ask God for forgiveness (Matt. 6.12; Luke 11.4). Only those who become loving themselves as a result of forgiveness have really received it (Matt. 18.23-5; cf. Luke 7.47).

Jesus agrees with Judaism that God no longer reveals himself in the history of the nation. When he speaks of his judgement, he is not thinking of disasters in history—wars between nations and the like—as was the case with the ancient prophets, any more than he expects the Reign of God to take the form of a magnificent terrestrial empire for Israel. The judgement he speaks of is the judgement of the individual. Everyone must stand before God's tribunal and give an account of himself (Matt. 12.36f., 25.31-46). The coming salvation will bring bliss to the individual. Since judgement and salvation are thus detached from history, Jesus' conception of God is similarly non-historical, just as in Judaism, as also his conception of man. But there is an all-important difference between them at this point. For Judaism God has become remote. He governs the world by means of angels, while his relations with man are mediated by the book of the Law. In the same way the holy people are marked off from the outside world by an elaborate ritual. Through its legalism the Jewish community achieves an artificial kind of otherworldliness. For Jesus however, God's distinction from and transcendence over the world means that he is always the God who comes. He meets man not only in the future judgement, but already here and now in daily life, with its challenges and opportunities. In the same way man is distinct from the world in the sense that he has no security in it. He cannot trust in any tangible reality. His real life consists in his encounter with his neighbour and his response to the claims of God.

II

IN THE *Shemoneh 'esre* the devout Jew prays every day:

> Sound the great horn for our freedom;
> lift up the ensign to gather our exiles . . .
> Restore our judges as at the first,
> and our counsellors as at the beginning . . .
> And for the slanderers let there be no hope,
> and let all wickedness perish as in a moment . . .
> And to Jerusalem, thy city, return in mercy,
> and dwell therein as thou hast spoken;
> rebuild it soon in our days as an everlasting building,
> and speedily set up therein the throne of David.

In Judaism there was a lively hope that God would deliver the nation from its bondage and restore its former glory. This hope fed upon the predictions of salvation in the prophets, and lived on in prayers and hymns like the so-called Psalms of Solomon.[35] Its classical expression is to be found in the apocalyptic literature.[36] Men long for the end; and the greater the oppression, the more excited the expectations and the more certain the conviction that the end is at hand and the greater their eagerness for its dawning. 'May he establish his kingdom during your life and during your days, and during the life of all the house of Israel, even speedily and at a near time.' That is a petition in one of the prayers of the synagogue.[37] 'Blessed be they that shall be in those days', say the Psalms of Solomon (17.50, 18.7), while the seer of the Fourth Book of Ezra, who lived through the destruction of Jerusalem, asks anxiously: 'How long and when shall these things be coming to pass? For our years are few and evil' (4.33). True, he is told: 'Thy haste may not exceed that of the Most High' (v.34). Yet despite that he is allowed to hear that the end is nigh at hand (4.44-50).

Again and again these hopes were dashed to the ground.

First, hopes ran high after the exile, when Haggai and Zechariah hailed Zerubbabel, a descendant of David appointed as governor by the Persians, as their Messianic King. Later, when the Maccabees fought for liberty and independence from the Syrians, it seemed that the age of redemption had dawned at last. But again they were disappointed, as can be seen from Psalms of Solomon 17.6-9. At the time of Jesus the impatience and excitement had reached such a pitch, that, during the revolt over the census under the governor, Quirinius (6 or 7 B.C.), the party of the zealots was formed with the object of casting off the Roman yoke by force. And down to the great rebellion of A.D. 66 there was a series of prophets and pretenders to the throne who created disturbances and had to be bloodily suppressed by the Romans. Besides these political agitations there were other Messianic movements which were awakened by the preaching of John the Baptist and the appearance of Jesus.

In its traditional form the hope of Israel was nationalistic in character. It looked for a restoration of the Davidic kingdom under a Davidic King, the 'Messiah'.[38] To begin with, the Messiah was not a supernatural agent of redemption, but the restorer of the Davidic dynasty. He was a human figure, and he would set up his throne at Jerusalem. The twelve tribes of Israel would be brought back from the Dispersion, assembled in the holy land, and have the land divided out among them. The Messiah would also be a warrior hero, who would destroy his enemies and restore Israel's sovereignty over the world—though by this time the war was hardly thought of as a real one, but as decided by supernatural powers. The Messiah would destroy his enemies by the word of his mouth (Ps. Sol. 17.27, 39). His rule was no longer conceived in earthly terms.

> For he shall not put his trust in rider and bow,
>> Nor shall he multiply for himself gold and silver for war,
>> Nor shall he set his hope upon the multitude for the day of
>> battle.
>> The Lord himself is his King . . .
>> All nations shall be in fear before him (Ps. Sol. 17.37f.).

He would rule in wisdom and righteousness. In the counsels of the nation his word would have the force of the word of an angel. All injustice would be done away from the face of the land. All Israelites would be holy, the sons of God: 'a good generation living in the fear of God in the days of mercy' (Ps. Sol. 18.10).

In the last analysis, the Messiah would really be no more than a figurehead. The real king would be God himself. In fact it is expressly stated of the Messiah that 'the Lord himself is his King'. Thus Psalms of Solomon 17 begins and ends with a confession of God as King over Israel. This explains why in many of the prophecies, even in early times, there is no Messiah at all (e.g. the Book of Daniel), or if he appears, he plays only a subordinate role. The theocratic ideals of the priestly school and the legalism of the scribes really left no logical place for the Messianic king.

Yet this is not the only form the hope of Israel took. The most important development in this period was the growth of apocalyptic writings, where, under Babylonian and Persian influence, there was worked out a cosmic eschatology, which, although intrinsically different from the nationalist hope, was capable of entering into various combinations with it.[39] Under the impact of present disasters as well as through Babylonian and Persian mythology, the Jewish world view was modified along the lines of a pessimistic dualism, though without abandoning the doctrine of creation. This earth, the scene of so much distress and misery, sickness and death, sin and violence, is the habitat of evil spirits with Satan at their head, opposing the sovereignty of God.[40] The power of darkness makes war on the power of light. But the power of darkness is not eternal and static, so that the way to regain freedom from it would be by sacraments and asceticism, which enable the soul to rise to the realm of light, where it will ascend one day after death. As in Iranian religion the present state of affairs will come to an end, and God will vindicate his kingly rule.

Then shall his kingdom appear throughout all his creation,
And then Satan shall be no more,
And sorrow shall depart with him.[41]

The course of the world is divided into two ages, this age and the age to come. 'The Most High has not made one age, but two' (IV Ezra 7.50). It is the conviction of the apocalyptic writers that the turning point between the two ages is near at hand. 'Creation is already grown old, and is already past the strength of youth' (IV Ezra 5.55; cf. 4.26). The epochs of world history are predetermined, one succeeding another in such a way that the apocalyptists can calculate the point which history has reached at the present moment by looking back on the past. The course of history is depicted in poetical imagery or mythological allegory. Nebuchadnezzar dreams that he sees the world empires succeeding one another in the form of different metals (Dan. 2), while in the vision of the seer in Daniel 4 there appear fantastic, gruesome beasts, which are succeeded by the Reign of Israel as 'the saints of the most High' (Dan. 7).

It is supremely important to recognize the signs of the approaching end. It will be heralded by the 'Messianic woes', when Satanic evil reaches its climax in the coming of Antichrist. There is confusion among men and nations, friends and relations, fighting on opposite sides. The whole of nature is out of course: there are unnatural births, cosmic disturbances, the sun shining by night and the moon by day, fountains running blood, the stars running out of course, fire bursting forth from the bowels of the earth, trees dripping blood, stones crying out, and so forth (IV Ezra 5.4-12).

Finally, the end will be there, with the resurrection of the dead and the judgement. The resurrection of the dead, a doctrine still foreign to the Old Testament[42] was clearly taken over by Judaism from Iranian sources. By the time of Jesus it was widely accepted, though not by the Sadducees. There was no need to fear that only those who were alive at its coming would share in the age of redemption. 'I will liken my judgement to a ring;

just as there is no retardation of them that are last, even so there is no hastening of those that are first' (IV Ezra 5.42).[43]

> The earth shall restore those that are asleep in her,
>   and the dust those that are at rest therein,
> and the chambers shall restore those that were committed unto
>   them (IX Ezra 7.32).

The judgement is a great forensic act. The earliest description we have of it is to be found in Daniel 7. God comes forth to judgement in white hair as the Ancient of Days. He takes his seat on his throne, surrounded by his court of angels. The books are brought in, in which all the deeds of men are recorded. Then the judgement itself takes place (Dan. 7.9-12).

> The Most High shall be revealed upon the throne of judgements
>   and then cometh the end,
>   and compassion shall pass away,
>   and pity be far off,
>   and longsuffering withdrawn;
> But judgement alone shall remain,
>   truth shall stand,
>   and faithfulness triumph.
> And recompense shall follow,
>   and the reward be made manifest:
> Deeds of righteousness shall awake.
>   and deeds of iniquity shall not sleep.
> And then shall the pit of torment appear,
>   and over against it the place of refreshment;
> The furnace of Gehenna shall be made manifest,
>   and over against it the paradise of delight (IV Ezra 7.33-7).

Then the new age begins:

> Then shall the heart of the inhabitants of the world be changed,
> and be converted to a different spirit.
>   For evil shall be blotted out,
>   and deceit extinguished;
>   Faithfulness shall flourish,
>   and corruption be vanquished:
>   And truth . . . shall be made manifest (IV Ezra 6.26-8).

> Corruption is passed away,
>   weakness is abolished,
>   infidelity is cut off;
> while righteousness is grown,
>   and faithfulness is sprung up (V Ezra 7.113f.).

For the righteous the new age brings eternal life. When they rise they shall be changed into radiant glory (Syr. Bar. 49-51), and arrayed in celestial robes and crowns on their heads, like angels. 'In the age to come there is no eating or drinking, no begetting of children, or multiplying, but the righteous sit with crowns on their heads, and rejoice in the radiance of the Godhead'—so runs a Rabbinic saying [Bab. Berakoth 17a, Trans.]. It should, however, be added that there are other sayings which speak of women in the age to come giving birth daily. By and large, fantasy has free scope to elaborate the details of life in the age to come. A typical expectation is the return of Paradise and the heavenly Jerusalem coming down to earth. All the blessings of salvation have been predetermined by God from of old, indeed they are often regarded as being actually pre-existent in heaven.

> For you
>   is opened Paradise,
>   planted the tree of life:
>   the future age prepared,
>   plentiousness made ready;
>   a city builded,
>   a Rest appointed;
>   Good works established,
>   wisdom preconstituted;
> The evil root is sealed up from you,
>   infirmity from your path extinguished;
> And death is hidden.
>   Hades fled away;
> Corruption forgotten,
>   sorrows passed away;
> and in the end the treasures of immortality are made manifest
>   (IV Ezra 8.52-4).

> For everything that is corruptible shall pass away,
> And everything that dies shall depart,
> And all the present time shall be forgotten, . . .
> And the hour comes which abides forever.
> And the new world . . . (Syr. Bar. 44.9, 12).

But the fate of the ungodly is destruction or eternal torment in hell fire. The idea of hell as a place of torment was still foreign to the Old Testament, and was adopted only much later from Iranian sources. It is called 'Gehenna', after the Valley of Hinnom, where children were sacrificed to Moloch in olden times.

Nationalistic and cosmic hopes are in some places combined unsystematically by an interchange of imagery. The rabbis achieve this more systematically by making the Messianic age a prelude to the new age. Hence the doctrine of the intermediate kingdom, which is expected to last four hundred or a thousand years. In the new age proper there is no place for the Messiah as the national king. Instead of him, there emerges a new figure, the supernatural agent of redemption who is to appear at the end of the days to inaugurate the new age. This figure bears the enigmatic title, 'Man'. He is a figure of cosmic eschatology, the archetypal man as the head of a new humanity, entering first into Judaism from the East, and thence penetrating westwards until he is found eventually in the Fourth (Messianic) Eclogue of Vergil. It is possible that the same conception underlies the picture of the Man coming on the clouds of heaven in Daniel 7.13, though here it is transformed into the embodiment of the people of Israel. In later Jewish apocalyptic writings the 'Man' combined the functions of Judge and agent of redemption, thus becoming a rival of God himself. Hence we may easily understand how the figures of the Messiah and the 'Man' coalesced in the Synoptic Gospels.[44]

The Eschatological Preaching of Jesus

The preaching of Jesus is controlled by an imminent expectation of the Reign of God. In this he stands in a line with Jewish eschatology in general, though clearly not in its nationalistic form. He never speaks of a political Messiah who will destroy the enemies of Israel, of the establishment of a Jewish world empire, the gathering of the twelve tribes, of peace and prosperity in the land, or anything of that kind. Instead, we find in his preaching the cosmic hopes of apocalyptic writers. True, he never indulges in learned or fantastic speculation such as we find in their works. He never looks back upon the past epochs of world history or attempts to date the End. He never invites his hearers to look for signs of the end in nature or history. Equally, he eschews all elaboration of detail as regards the judgement, resurrection and future glory. All these elements are absorbed in the single all-embracing thought that God will then reign. Only a few apocalyptic traits appear here and there in his teaching.[45] Jesus clearly believes that the present age is ebbing out. Mark's summary of his preaching ('The time is fulfilled, and the Reign of God has drawn nigh', Mark 1.15) is a fair representation of numerous sayings of Jesus which point to a new future and characterize the present as the time of decision.

Jesus expects the coming of the 'Man' as the Judge and agent of redemption.[46] He looks for the resurrection of the dead and the judgement.[47] He describes the blessedness of the righteous simply as 'life'. True, he sometimes speaks of the heavenly banquet, when the righteous will sit down to meat with Abraham, Isaac and Jacob (Matt. 8.11; Luke 13.28f.), or of the prospect of drinking wine in the Reign of God (Mark 14.25). But it is difficult to be sure how far such sayings are meant to be taken literally, or only figuratively. In any case, when the Sadducees try to reduce the doctrine of the resurrection to an absurdity by a materialistic conception of life in the age of redemption, he counters their arguments by saying: 'When they rise from the dead, they neither marry, nor are given in marriage but are as the angels which are in heaven' (Mark 12.25).

If Jesus takes over the apocalyptic view of the future, he does so with considerable reductions. The unique feature in his teaching is the assurance with which he proclaims that *Now* has the

time come. The Reign of God is breaking in. The time of the
End is at hand.

> Blessed are the eyes which see the things that ye see:
> For I tell you,
> that many prophets and kings have desired to see the things
> which ye see,
> and have not seen them;
> and to hear those things which ye hear,
> and have not heard them (Luke 10.23f.; Matt. 13.16f.).

It is no time now to mourn or fast; the time for joy is breaking
in. It is the time for the 'marriage' (Mark 2.18f.).[48] Hence this
word of encouragement for those who were waiting for God's
Reign:

> Blessed are ye poor:
> for yours is the kingdom of God.
> Blessed are ye that hunger now:
> for ye shall be filled.
> Blessed are ye that weep now:
> for ye shall laugh (Luke 6.20f.).

There are, of course, signs of the times, though not the kind
expected in apocalyptic fantasy: 'The kingdom of God cometh
not with observation: Neither shall they say, Lo here! or, lo
there! for, behold, the Reign of God is (in a trice) in your
midst' (Luke 17.20f.).[49] 'For as the lightning, that lighteneth
out of the one part under heaven, shineth unto the other part of
heaven; so also must the Son of man be in his day' (Luke 17.24).
The people are blind to the true signs of the times:

> When ye see a cloud rise out of the west, straightway ye say,
> There cometh a shower; and so it is. And when ye see the south
> wind blow, ye say, There will be heat; and it cometh to pass.
> Ye hypocrites, ye can discern the face of the sky, and of the earth;
> but how is it that ye do not discern this time? (Luke 12.54-6).

> Now learn a parable of the fig tree:
> When her branch is yet tender, and putteth forth leaves,
> ye know that summer is near:

So ye in like manner, when ye shall see these things come to
pass,
know that he is nigh, even at the doors (Mark 13.28f.).

Who is this 'he'? The 'Man'![50] But what is meant by 'when ye
see these things come to pass'? What are the signs of the times?
Jesus repudiates the Pharisees' demand for a sign: 'Why doth
this generation seek after a sign? verily I say unto you, There
shall be no sign given unto this generation' (Mark 8.11f.).
God does not expose his doings to tangible criteria. They cannot
be discerned by calculation, however ingenious, but only by an
inner receptivity for Jesus' words and works. He himself, his
appearance on the stage of history, his words, and his deeds—
they are the signs of the times.

The blind receive their sight, and the lame walk,
the lepers are cleansed, and the deaf hear,
the dead are raised up, and the poor have the gospel preached
unto them (Matt. 11.5; Luke 7.22).

The predictions of the prophets (for it is in their words that
this saying is couched) are in process of fulfilment.[51] Endowed
with the power of the Spirit, Jesus is beginning to heal the sick
and to cast out demons, to which, in common with his contemporaries, he attributed human suffering.

'If I by the finger of God cast out devils, no doubt the kingdom of God is come upon you' (Luke 11.20; Matt. 12.28).
'No man can enter into a strong man's house, and spoil his
goods, except he first bind the strong man; and then he will
spoil his goods' (Mark 3.27). In the flight of the demons men
can discern already the overthrow of Satan. 'I beheld Satan as
lightning fall from heaven. Behold, I give you power to tread
on serpents and scorpions, and over all the power of the enemy
and nothing shall by any means hurt you' (Luke 10.18f.).

There is no way of expediting the course of events God has
determined—for instance, by a strict observance of the commandments and penitential exercises, as the Pharisees thought,
or by force of arms, as the Zealots imagined.

> For so is the kingdom of God, as if a man should cast seed into the ground; And should sleep, and rise night and day, and the seed should spring and grow up, he knoweth not how. For the earth bringeth forth fruit of herself; first the blade, then the ear, after that the full corn in the ear. But when the fruit is brought forth, immediately he putteth in the sickle, because the harvest is come (Mark 4.26-9).

All man can do is to be ready, to 'turn'. Now is the time of decision. Jesus' preaching is a summons to decision.

'Blessed is he, whosoever shall not be offended in me' (Matt. 11.6; Luke 7.23). The 'Queen of the south' once came to hear the wisdom of Solomon: the Ninevites repented at the preaching of Jonah: 'and behold, a greater than Solomon is here . . . a greater than Jonah is here' (Luke 11.31f.; Matt. 12.41f.). 'Whosoever therefore shall be ashamed of me and of my words in this adulterous and sinful generation; of him shall the Son of man be ashamed, when he cometh in the glory of his Father with the holy angels' (Mark 8.38).

In the last analysis therefore Jesus himself in his person is the 'sign of the time'. This, however, does not mean that he invites men to believe in himself.[52] He does not, for instance, proclaim himself as Messiah. In fact, he points to the Messiah, the 'Man', as the Coming One distinct from himself.[53] He himself is the personal embodiment of the challenge to decision. His word invites men to decide for the Reign of God now breaking in. *Now* is the last hour. *Now* it is Either-Or. *Now* the question is: Do men really want God's Reign? Or is it the world they want? The decision they must make is a radical one.

'No man, having put his hand to the plough, and looking back, is fit for the kingdom of God' (Luke 9.62). 'Follow me, and let the dead bury their dead' (Matt. 8.22). 'If any man come to me, and hate not his father, and mother, and wife, and children, and brethren, and sisters, yea, and his own life also, he cannot be my disciple' (Luke 14.26; Matt. 10.37). 'Whosoever doth not bear his cross, and come after me, cannot be my disciple' (Luke 14.27; Matt. 10.38; Mark 8.34).

This is why Jesus himself left his own family: 'Whosoever shall do the will of God, the same is my brother, and my sister, and mother' (Mark 3.35). This is why he uprooted many others from home and trade and took them with him on his travels. Yet he did not establish a religious order or a sect (still less a church).[54] Nor did he propose that everyone should leave his home and family. But all are challenged to a decision. All must make up their minds what they really want to set their hearts on, whether it is God, or the goods of this world. 'Lay not up for yourselves treasures upon earth. . . . For where your treasure is, there will your heart be also' (Matt. 6.19-21; Luke 12.33f.).

> No man can serve two masters:
> for either he will hate the one, and love the other;
> or else he will hold to the one,
> and despise the other.
> Ye cannot serve God and mammon (Matt. 6.24; Luke 13.13).

'How dangerous it is to be rich! It is easier for a camel to go through the eye of a needle than for a rich man to enter into the kingdom of God' (Mark 10.25). Most men cling to earthly possessions and anxieties; they certainly want to obtain the salvation God prepares for them, but when it comes to making up their minds, they refuse it, like guests who have accepted an invitation to a banquet. When the time arrives they are too preoccupied (Luke 14.15-21; Matt. 22.1-10). They must be quite sure what they really want, just as a man building a tower or going to war must count the cost beforehand (Luke 14.28-34). If men would enter the kingdom of God, they must be ready for any sacrifice, like the farmer who, having found a treasure, gives up everything to gain possession of it, or like the merchant who sells everything in order to acquire one precious pearl (Matt. 13.44-6).

> If thy right eye offend thee,
> pluck it out and cast it from thee:
> for it is profitable for thee that one of thy members should perish,
> and not that thy whole body should be cast into hell.

And if thy right hand offend thee,
   cut it off and cast it from thee:
   for it is profitable for thee. that one of thy members should
     perish,
   and not that thy whole body should be cast into hell (Matt. 5.29f.).

This renunciation of the world represents no escapism or asceticism, but an otherworldliness which is simply being ready for God's command, summoning men to abandon all earthly ties. On the positive side and complementary to it is the commandment of love, in which a man turns away from self and places himself at the disposal of others. In doing this, he has decided for God.

Of course, Jesus was mistaken in thinking that the world was destined soon to come to an end. His error was similar to that of the ancient prophets who believed that God's redemptive act was immediately impending, or like Deutero-Isaiah, who though it was already dawning in the present. Does his message therefore stand or fall with that misconception? It would be better to reverse the proposition and say that this expectation springs from the conviction which lies at the root of his preaching. The prophets are so overwhelmed by their sense of the sovereign majesty of God and the absolute character of his will that they foreshorten the divine act of judgement. Contrasted with God and his will, the world seems such a trivial place that it is already as it were at an end. This sense of crisis in human destiny expresses itself in the conviction that the hour of decision has struck. So it is with Jesus. He is so convinced of God's will and determination, and that it is his business to proclaim it, that he feels himself to be standing on the frontiers of time. His eschatological preaching is not the outcome of wishful thinking or speculation, but of his sense of the utter nothingness of man before God. The understanding of human life implied thereby clearly does not stand or fall with his expectation of an imminent end of the world. It contains a definite judgement upon the world. In other words, it sees the world exclusively *sub specie Dei*.

His claim that the destiny of men is determined by their attitude to him and his word was taken up by the early Church and expressed in their proclamation of Jesus as 'Messiah'—particularly in their expectation that he was to come on the clouds of heaven as the 'Man', bringing judgement and salvation. His preaching was thus taken up in a new form, thus becoming specifically 'Christian' preaching. Jesus proclaimed the message. The Church proclaims *him*.

III

HELLENISTIC JUDAISM

HELLENISTIC JUDAISM,[55] i.e. the Judaism of the Graeco-Roman world, preserved its racial and national unity and remained loyal to Jerusalem as the focal point of national and religious life. The Jews of the Diaspora paid their temple tax, and went on pilgrimage to Jerusalem at the great festivals whenever it was possible for them to do so. At the same time, however, the real basis of Hellenistic Judaism was the synagogue and its worship. The Jews of the Dispersion were ritualistic in their daily life, but not so strictly as the Jews of Palestine. Circumcision and the observance of the sabbath were the chief marks of distinction between themselves and their pagan neighbours, together with certain regulations of purity, of which the most striking was the abstention from pork, so noticeable in a pagan environment.

On the other hand, they had abandoned their native tongue in favour of Greek, the *lingua franca* of the civilized world. Even the scriptures were no longer intelligible in the original Hebrew or the Aramaic translations, and had therefore to be translated into Greek. Scholars like Philo of Alexandria could only read them in Greek. The Greek version of the Old Testament, known as the Septuagint, came out gradually during the third and second centuries B.C. At the same time there was growing up a whole body of Hellenistic Jewish literature. Not only were Greek literary forms adopted, such as historiography, epic, drama, sibylline oracles and the symposium, but even Greek ways of thought.

Though traditionally the Jews regarded their pagan neighbours as sunk in idolatry and lust, acute Jewish minds realized that with the spread of philosophical enlightenment, monotheism had become popular in the Hellenistic world. Greek philosophy encouraged a spiritual conception of God, while in particular the Stoics purveyed a doctrine of virtue, both in academic teaching and popular propaganda, which was on a level with Jewish morality. This, however, raised in a new form the problem of the connexion between pagan religion and morality and their own, including the Old Testament itself. At first there was an easy answer ready to hand. Did not the Greeks themselves believe that their wisdom came from Egypt, if not from Oriental sources? Then the wise men of Greece, claimed the Jews, must have drawn their teaching from Moses. That answer still left undecided the actual relation between the two spheres, but the Jews secured their own cause by trying to discover Greek philosophy in the Old Testament (though in practice, of course, it meant reading Greek philosophy *into* it). Partly, in the conviction that they alone possessed the truth, they indulged in propaganda, offering the Old Testament to the pagan world as the source of its own wisdom.

The method by which they discovered Greek wisdom in the Old Testament was by the use of allegory. This art of interpretation had reached its zenith in Stoicism, where it was employed to read philosophical doctrines into the myths and poetry of ancient Greece. The Jewish religious philosopher, Philo of Alexandria (*ca.* 25 B.C.-A.D. 40), for example, interprets the precept that the sacrificial victim must be without blemish in the following manner:

> For you will find that all this careful scrutiny of the animal is a symbol representing in a figure the reformation of your own conduct, for the law does not prescribe for unreasoning creatures, but for those who have mind and reason. It is not that the victims should be without flaw but that those who offer themselves should not suffer from any corroding passion [πάθος].[56]

When Abraham leaves his fatherland, his kin and his father's house, it means that the soul of man must be purged from the body and its senses, and from speech (σῶμα, αἴσθησις, λόγος).[57] Abraham gazing at the stars in Chaldea is man giving himself up to nature; Abraham marrying Hagar is man pursuing the general education (encyclopaedia and the various departments of science); his marriage with Sarah is the study and practice of virtue and philosophy.[58] The personalities of the Old Testament are embodiments of particular virtues and psychological dispositions or of vices. διδασκαλικὴ ἀρετή, i.e. the gradual growth from knowledge to faith, is embodied in Abraham, while Isaac represents φυσικὴ ἀρετή (the gift of congenital knowledge of God), and Jacob, finally, ἀσκητικὴ ἀρετή (man struggling with his passions and acquiring self-control, or alternatively, man's sufferings and tribulations in the world).[59]

The most important feature of Greek thought taken over by Hellenistic Judaism—and this is particularly clear in the case of Philo—is the Greek idea of the world as a cosmos. The world is a unitary organism. Its strict observance of the laws of cause and effect make it so, and therefore rationally intelligible. For the Greek mind this meant that the world was itself divine. The Jewish thinker, however, regarded it as God's creation, though the original idea of creation has been surrendered with the adoption of the Greek notion of the cosmos. God's transcendence is now reinterpreted in a Greek sense. It becomes his shaping formless matter into a cosmos, and articulating it like a master workman. The Creator has become the Greek τεχνίτης. His work in the world is open to objective scientific observation, and its structure is rationally intelligible.

Above all, the Stoic theology offered a ready instrument for the expression of Israel's faith in God as Creator. Their 'natural theology', with its proof of God's existence from the unity of the world and the purpose behind it, was adopted in Hellenistic Judaism, together with the Stoic theodicy. In the Wisdom of Solomon,[60] we already find the doctrine of the *pneuma* pervading and controlling the world, of the divine breath giving life and structure to it. This *pneuma* is identified with the Old Testament 'wisdom' of God.[61] In particular, the idea of providence (πρόνοια) is adopted. It is the power which guides and controls world events, and leads history to its appointed goal. Similarly, there is the concept of nature (φύσις), the divine law which operates in the cosmos, and with which all the separate parts of the universe, including man himself, must live in harmony, thus finding their proper and salutary place in relation to the whole. Then there was the Stoic doctrine of the Logos, which presented the rational aspect of nature: this was a particularly useful instrument for the representation of certain aspects of Old Testament teaching. It was easy to identify the Stoic Logos with the 'word of God', whose creative power is spoken of in the Old Testament. Thus for Philo God's Logos is the mediator between him and the world, while the separate powers (λόγοι or δυνάμεις) could be identified with the angels of the Old Testament.

The doctrine of man undergoes a similar modification. His creatureliness is now conceived differently from the interpretation it receives in the Old Testament. Man participates in the universal Logos, which is the controlling power in him as in the world at large. In this way he has an affinity with God. Man's worship must be spiritual, and allegorical interpretation discovers just the kind of worship required in the texts of the Old Testament. The essence of that worship is knowledge and the cultivation of the virtues, and therefore the domination of the physical and sensual by the spiritual. In this way the spirit of man is analogous to that of the cosmos at large, where the Logos imparts to matter its spiritual form. Hand in hand with this Greek anthropology, with its fundamental antithesis between body and soul (spirit), Hellenistic Judaism adopts not only the Greek doctrine of virtue, but also their conception of education as training. While Philo naturally accepts the temple worship at Jerusalem as a divine institution, its true, spiritual import is seen only in allegorical interpretation. Ritual purity of the soul is self-knowledge, while the offering of the tithe means the practice of piety and the love of neighbour, and so forth. True sacrifice consists in a right psychological disposition, the offering of a good, obedient will to God. The true temple is sometimes the cosmos ruled by the Logos as its high priest, sometimes the rational soul (λογικὴ ψυχή), in which the 'true man', the reason (νοῦς), is the priest.[62] With such notions as these, the critique

of polytheism and sacrifice worked out in the Greek enlightenment is adopted,[63] together with its system of ethical instruction,
its concept of freedom (i.e. freedom from the emotions) and
virtue, of nature as man's educator, and the conscience, together
with the catalogue of virtues and vices.[64]

Thus for Hellenistic Judaism faith is no longer trusting
obedience and submission to the will of God and his purpose as
the basis of man's relation to him. It is now the goal of the
process of self-training, the stability of a perfect character.
The Old Testament idea of the creatureliness of man also
loses its force. Philo may speak of man's nothingness, but
in a dualistic, metaphysical sense derived from Hellenistic
ideas.

As well as Stoicism, Platonism, or rather Neo-Platonism, had
an effect on Hellenistic Judaism. In some ways this provided
still more serviceable instruments than Stoicism for the expression of certain Old Testament ideas. For Philo, Plato is the
ἱερώτατος, the greatest of the saints, the unsurpassed ally of
Moses. Platonic idealism with its antithesis between the eternal
world of ideas and the phenomenal world of becoming and
decaying seemed to provide a suitable terminology for describing God's transcendence over the world. But, inevitably, the
result was a new version of transcendence: it was now thought of
in terms of the contrariety between spirit and matter. Like
the earlier Wisdom of Solomon, Philo combines Stoic theology
with ideas derived from Platonism. The Logos is not only the
rational law prevading and controlling the universe, but also
the sum of the transcendent world of ideas, the 'spiritual world'
(κόσμος νοητός), at the head of which stands God himself, the
perfect Being devoid of all quality. Hence we can hardly expect
Philo to exhibit complete consistency in his thought. His belief
in creation was inevitably modified by his Platonic idealism,
and his view of the universe as a harmony pervaded and controlled by divine powers. The world and man tend to be regarded in this dualistic light. The world is the sphere of change
and decay, of weakness and disintegration, of the sensual as

opposed to the spiritual, of illusion and evil. The body of man is merely an earthly vessel for the spirit.[65]

Here we have a still loftier conception of worship than we find in Stoicism. It is the idea of worship as communion between the soul and God, reaching its climax in the beatific vision. Here the ideal man is not the Greek, with his resolute nobility, the just man with his virtue, the pillar of the human race.[66] It is the ascetic and the mystic, who by following the way of knowledge and the cultivation of virtue eventually achieves his liberation from the body, in which his soul is imprisoned.[67] Thus he attains the beatific vision.

> For if, O mind, thou dost not prepare thyself of thyself, excising desires, pleasures, griefs, fears, follies, injustices and related evils, and dost (not) change and adapt thyself to the vision of holiness, thou wilt end thy life in blindness, unable to see the intelligible sun. If, however, thou art worthily initiated and canst be consecrated to God and in a certain sense become an animate shrine of the Father (then) instead of having closed eyes, thou wilt see the First (Cause) and in wakefulness thou wilt cease from the deep sleep in which thou hast been held. Then will appear to thee that manifest One, Who causes incorporal rays to shine for thee, and grants visions of the unambiguous and indescribable things of nature and the abundant sources of other good things. For the beginning and end of happiness is to be able to see God.'[68]

In his work on the creation of the world Philo describes the way and its goal. The spirit or reason (νοῦς) of man, the image of the divine spirit is:

> Invisible, while itself seeing all things, and while comprehending the substances of others, it is as to its own substance unperceived; and while it opens by arts and sciences roads branching in many directions, all of them great highways, it comes through land and sea investigating what either element contains. Again, when on soaring wing it has contemplated the atmosphere and all its phases, it is borne yet higher to the ether and the circuit of heaven, and is whirled round with the dances of the planets and

fixed stars, in accordance with the laws of perfect music, following that love of wisdom which guides its steps. And so, carrying
its gaze beyond the confines of all substance discernible by
sense, it comes to a point at which it reaches out after the
intelligible world, and on descrying in that world sights of
surpassing loveliness, even the patterns and the originals of the
things of sense which it saw here, it is seized by a sober intoxica-
tion, like those filled with Corybantic frenzy, and is inspired,
possessed by a longing far other than theirs and a nobler desire.
Wafted by this to the topmost arch of things perceptible to
mind, it seems to be on its way to the Great King Himself; but,
amid its longing to see Him, pure and untempered rays of concentrated light stream forth like a torrent, so that by its gleams
the eye of understanding is dazzled.[69]

Here we have a combination of doctrines derived from the
Hellenistic mysteries with ideas from Platonic philosophy.
Philo welcomes the terminology of the mysteries, because
he is conscious of offering mystery wisdom.[70] Thus Philo's
conception of faith passes through the successive stage of Old
Testament trust in God, the Stoic disposition of fortitude, and
finally unshakable certainty, the reliance on that which alone is
firm, the turning away from the transitory to the eternal in a
Platonic sense, and finally mystical experience. Thus faith comes
to mean unworldliness, culminating in ecstasy.

An obvious result of this transposition of the divine transcendence from futurity to mysticism is a loss of sense for the historical. The personalities of the Old Testament become the types
of particular virtues or psychological dispositions. The history
of the nation becomes an allegorical illustration of religious
psychology and ethics, and loses its sense of movement towards
a goal. In the same way Philo has no eschatology in the Old
Testament sense. Of course he believes that God's promises are
true, but for him they are limited to a brilliant future for
Israel.

THE GREEK HERITAGE

THE GREEK HERITAGE

I

THE GREEK CITY STATE

Its Nature and Basis

IT IS BY THE ADOPTION of a common historical purpose that a group of human beings becomes a nation. It is then that history begins as the history of a nation. In this way human history is distinguished from natural occurrences. The individual human being is no longer exposed to the mysterious and uncanny forces of his natural environment or to the equally mysterious and uncanny impulses in his own breast. The world now becomes a place where he can feel at home, which he can understand, and, within limits, control. He himself is aware of his own purposes and potentialities, and knows that he is free—again, within limits. Up to this point the course of history is everywhere the same. But now the question arises as to the extent his intellectual understanding and technical control of the world have reached. How far is he conscious of knowing himself to be free, and capable of organizing his life to suit his own purposes? And how far, again, does the world, with its phenomena and natural occurrences, retain its mysterious and uncanny character? How far is it beyond his control? How far does it elude his attempts to understand and plan it for himself?

The Old Testament kept alive its awareness of the world as a place beyond man's control. In the Greek world, however, the intellectual understanding and control of nature, as well as the understanding of human nature and the organization of social life, were developed to a degree which has had a lasting impact on western culture. Hence the development of science (τέχνη and ἐπιστήμη) and the State (Πόλις). Here the world was objectified, thus becoming 'nature' in the strict sense of the word, while human society was organized on the basis of positive law.

In Plato,[1] Protagoras relates how in the earliest days men had not yet discovered the art of politics (πολιτικὴ τέχνη), and as a result, individual human beings were dominated by the animal kingdom. 'So they sought to band themselves together and secure their lives by founding cities (ἐζήτουν δὴ ἀθροίζεσθαι καὶ σώζεσθαι κτίζοντες πόλεις)'. But they were not successful until Zeus gave them the art of politics, sending to them Hermes, who brought prudence and justice (σωφροσύνη and δικαιοσύνη). As a result, men now acquired the virtues necessary for the pursuit of politics. In this way the city state arose, depriving nature of its uncanny character. Man had now got the better over nature. Thus the chorus in the *Antigone* of Sophocles sing:

> Wonders are many, and none
> is more wonderful than man.[2]

The uncanny thing about man, as described by the chorus, is his lordship over nature, over the stormy sea through which he pilots his vessels and over that greatest of deities, the earth, through which he draws furrows with his plough; over the birds and fishes; over the hind roaming on the mountains; over horse and steer; over frost and rain and over sickness. He does not stand helpless before the future. Only death eludes his control. It is his skill (τέχνη) which enables him to do all these things. And if he applies himself to virtue, he stands high in the State:

> When he honours the laws of the land,
> and that justice which he hath sworn by the gods to uphold,
> proudly he stands in his city:
> no city hath he who, for his rashness, dwells with sin.[3]

The myths of the gods show the same sense of spiritual forces. After the reign of the old, uncanny 'chthonic' powers, Zeus inaugurated a new regime under a new race of gods, having cast out his father, Chronos, and the Titans. The mighty

gods of pre-Homeric days, earth and death, are suppressed—
Mother Earth and the Eumenides, who pour out her blessings,
and who at the same time are the deities of blood feud and
curse. The old nature demons, like the satyrs and nymphs,
become the playmates of the new gods, who are not nature
deities, but deities of the spirit in its various manifestations.
The Olympian gods are not embodiments of uncanny powers,
but the spiritual forces of moderation and purpose, order, law
and beauty. Zeus is the judge who avenges evil.[4] His consort,
Themis, is the Queen of lawgiving. Apollo is the god of order
and equity. Athene is the goddess of the subtle intellect and
premeditated act. Aphrodite the goddess of beauty and grace,
Hermes the god of the favourable moment and its profitable
use.[5] Thus the gods become representatives and patrons of
man's social institutions and the virtues they require.

The city state was founded on justice ($\delta i \kappa \eta$). Hesiod (*ca.* 700),
and Solon (*ca.* 650-560) are preachers of $\delta i \kappa \eta$, and in this
respect are the counterparts of the Old Testament prophets.

> These things my heart prompteth me to teach the Athenians,
> and to make them understand that lawlessness ($\delta \upsilon \sigma \nu o \mu i \eta$)
> worketh more harm to the state than any other cause. But a
> law-abiding spirit ($\epsilon \upsilon \nu o \mu i \eta$) createth order and harmony and at
> the same time putteth chains upon evil days; it maketh rough
> things smooth, it checketh inordinate desires, it dimmeth the
> glare of wanton pride and withereth the budding bloom of
> wild delusion; it maketh crooked judgements straight and
> softeneth arrogant behaviour; it stoppeth acts of sedition and
> stoppeth the anger of bitter strife. Under the reign of law,
> sanity and wisdom prevail ever among men.[6]

The city state was constituted by certain norms, its constitution providing the characteristically human mode of life.
Hence law ($\nu o \mu o s$) was the greatest good of the citizens. By
being bound to the law, the citizens gained their freedom
($\epsilon \lambda \epsilon \upsilon \theta \epsilon \rho i a$). This is not only because the State, as constituted by
its law, is qualified for action and is therefore able to defend
its freedom against foreign enemies, but chiefly because

it provided each of its citizens with the opportunity of sharing in the functions of government. Freedom did not mean that every man could do as he pleased, or that the law existed to balance the conflicting claims of individuals, thus securing private liberty. Freedom was freedom to serve the commonwealth. The individual found his dignity in political responsibility. It was freedom to do one's duty to the State, which gave the individual a sense of constituting and representing the State.

The Greek was proudly aware of the difference between his own city state and the vast empires of the East. These were not states of free citizens, but masses ruled by despots. Herodotus relates how Xerxes, King of Persia, asked the Greek Demaratus whether he thought the Greeks would dare to resist him and his armies. Demaratus replies: 'Want has at all times been a fellow-dweller with us in our land, while Valour (ἀρετή) is an ally whom we have gained by dint of wisdom and strict laws. Her aid enables us to drive out want and escape thraldom (δεσποσύνη).[7] And in particular he says of the Spartans:

> For though they be freemen, they are not in all respects free;
> Law is the master (δεσπότης) whom they own; and this master they fear more than thy subjects fear thee. Whatever he commands they do; and his commandment is always the same: it forbids them to flee in battle, whatever the number of their foes, and requires them to stand firm, and either to conquer or die.[8]

In Aeschylus' *Persae*, Atossa, Xerxes' mother, dreams that she sees Persia and Hellas as two beautiful virgins on whom Xerxes has laid his yoke to harness them to his chariot:

> ... One with head inclined
> Was glad and plumed her in that harness proud,
> Meek to the curb. The other, all uncowed,
> Struggled, and with both hands tore
> The harness, and away unbridled bore
> The chariot, and at mid-yoke snapt the wood.[9]

Atossa asks:

> What master holds them in the fray, what shepherd's rod to drive the herd?

To which the Leader of the chorus replies:

> To no man living are they slaves, nor bow they before no man's word.
> *Atossa:* Unmastered, how can they endure the onset of an angry foe?
> *Leader:* Methinks Darius knoweth, and his great and goodly armies know.[10]

The Greek was always ready to die for his city. To be expelled from it meant ostracism from society, from all that gave a man justice and dignity. This pride in the democratic city state receives its classical expression in Pericles' funeral oration:

> Our constitution does not copy the laws of neighbouring states; we are rather a pattern of others than imitators ourselves. Its administration favours the many instead of the few; this is why it is called a democracy ($\delta\eta\mu\omega\kappa\rho\alpha\tau\iota\alpha$). If we look to the laws, they afford equally justice to all in their private differences; if to social standing, advancement in public life falls to reputation for capacity ($\dot\alpha\rho\epsilon\tau\dot\eta$), class considerations not being allowed to interfere with merit; nor again does poverty bar the way, if a man is able to serve the state, he is not hindered by the obscurity of his condition.[11]

The city state was not a product of human ingenuity or a social contract. It had been there before the individual and was higher than he. Its constitution was not the result of a balancing out of conflicting claims on the part of its members. Rather, it was of divine origin. 'Those who speak with understanding', says Heraclitus, 'must hold fast to what is common to all as a city holds fast to its law, and even more strongly. For all human laws are fed by the one divine law. It prevails as much as it will, and suffices for all things with something to spare.'[12]

The criterion for all positive law was the 'unwritten law'

(the νόμος ἄγραφος) the 'common law' (the κοινὸς νόμος), which finally could be designated also as the law of nature (νόμος φύσεως).[13] Thus, when Creon seeks to make his own will the law of the state, Antigone retorts:

> Yes; for it was not Zeus that had published me that edict; not such are the laws set among men by the Justice who dwells with the gods below; nor deemed I that thy decrees were of such force, that a mortal could override the unwritten and un-failing statutes of heaven. For their life is not of to-day or yesterday, but from all time, and no man knows when they were first put forth.[14]

The constitution of the city state was thus an empirical manifestation of an eternal principle. The gods watched over it and protected it, punishing the wrongdoer. The State had an aura of sanctity about it, and the relation of the citizen to it was in effect his religion, with its external expression in the official cultus. Unlike the majority of the Semitic deities, the Greek gods were not tied to the land or the soil. Primarily, they were gods of the nation, of the nation constituted as a State. Religion and politics did not develop in watertight compartments, nor was there any conflict between them. There was no problem about the relation of Church and State, no autonomous priestly caste as in the religions of the East. The worship of the gods was a State cultus, the priests State officials.

The Crisis of the City State

Yet all these considerations fail to touch the real problem before the city state. How long would the belief in the divine origin of its constitution survive? Would the State continue to be looked upon as a sacred institution with priority over all individual interests? Would the gods still command reverence for their divinity, or would they be reduced to the level of personifica-tions of man's spiritual and intellectual capacities? True, the doctrine of the divine origin of the State and its laws was still upheld. But, on the other hand, the concrete shape of the laws was determined by the decisions and action of the citizens. Thus there was a very real danger of the gods losing their authority, of the city state and its laws passing increasingly into human control and being subordinated to their private and collective interests. Once this kind of criticism had been brought to bear on the existing constitution, once the democratic assembly could repeal old laws and pass new ones at will, the State became increasingly the scene of party conflict and a scramble for power on the part of individuals. As a result, political life became secularized, and there was no check on self-seeking, greed or avarice. The old, divine sanctions had disappeared.

The tragedians were fully aware of this danger. They recognized that the city state was cut adrift from its moorings when man forgot the transcendent ties which bound him to it. They called for a return to the unwritten law, to reverence for the mysterious (δεινόν) to piety (εὐσέβεια):

> Times there be when fear is good,
>> And the Watcher in the breast
> Needs must reign in masterhood.
>> Aye, 'tis best
> Through much straitening to be wise.
> Who that hath no fear at all
> In the sunlight of his eyes,
>> Man or city, but shall fall
>> From right somewise?[16]

In the *Eumenides*, the third part of Aeschylus' *Oresteia*, Athene, having summoned the assembly of the gods and allotted the judges their tasks and promulgated their ordinance (θεσμός), appoints the Areopagus to be the future place of judgement:

> All things here
> Being holy, Reverence and her sister, Fear,
> In darkness as in daylight shall restrain

> From all unrighteousness the sons of men,
> While Athens' self corrupt not her own law.
> With mire and evil influx ye can flaw
> Fair water till no lips may drink thereof.
> I charge you, citizens, enfold and love
> That spirit that nor anarch is nor thrall;
> And casting away Fear, yet cast not all;
> For who that hath no fear is safe from sin?[16]

In a similar vein Sophocles shows in the *Antigone* how the law of the city state can be upheld only so long as it is not an arbitary human ordinance, but grounded in the 'unwritten and irrefragable ordinances of the gods'. He shows how man perishes when he loses his sense of being hedged around by the transcendent power which constantly threatens him with death, and which is critical of all purely human ordinances.[17]

At the same time the old mythology, with its crude pictures of the gods, ceased to carry conviction. The old Greek religion was εὐσέβεια, an awesome reverence for the divine powers who, high above man, dwelt immortally in eternal light and bliss; who accorded their favours to man, and whose will was not to be measured by human standards. Their claim on man, over and above his worship, was a twofold one. First, they demanded respect for the sacred ordinances of nature and law, over which they presided, avenging perjury and the breach of treaties. Secondly, they required man to know himself and his limitations; to acknowledge their superiority, to adapt himself to his mortal lot and preserve a sense of the gulf between himself and them. When Diomede vents his fury on Aeneas, who is under divine protection, Apollo warns him:

> Think, Tydeides, and shrink, nor desire to match
> thy spirit with the gods; seeing there is no comparison
> of the race of immortal gods
> and of men that walk upon the earth.[18]

> Even as are the generations of leaves
> such are those likewise of men;
> the leaves that be the wind scattereth on the earth,

and the forest buddeth and putteth more forth again,
when the season of spring is at hand;
so of the generations of men
one springeth and another passeth away.[19]

In Olympus the muses

together, voice sweetly answering voice,
hymn the unending gifts the gods enjoy
and the sufferings of men,
all that they endure at the hands of the deathless gods,
and how that they live witless and helpless
and cannot find healing for death
or defence against old age.[20]

Hesiod begins his *Works and Days* with a song in praise of
Zeus and his mighty power:

Muses of Pieria who give glory through song,
come hither, tell of your father and chant his praise.
Through him mortal men are famed or unfamed,
sing or unsing alike, as great Zeus wills.
For easily he makes strong, and easily makes the strong man low;
easily he humbles the proud and raises the obscure,
and easily he straightens the crooked and blasts the proud—
Zeus who thunders aloft.[21]

The same attitude runs all through the odes of Pindar: 'From
thee, O Zeus, cometh all high excellence ($\dot{\alpha}\rho\epsilon\tau\alpha\acute{\iota}$) to mortals':
'Zeus ordereth this or that, Zeus, God of all': 'For from the
gods come all means of mortal valour, hereby come bards and
men of mighty hand and eloquent speech': 'By fate divine
receive men also valour and wisdom': 'Therefore forget not . . .
to set God above every other as the cause thereof.'[22]

The chorus in the Aeschylus' *Supplices* utters similar warn-
ings:

From the high towers of hope on which they stand
He casts men down; they perish utterly.
Yet he takes no sword, he lifts no violent hand.

> Effortless all must be
> That is of God. All things
>   Whereon his thought may light
> Moveless to pass he brings
>   There on the height.[23]

The first commandment therefore is that man should recognize his limitations, lest he succumb to *hybris* and transgress the measure appointed for him. He must be modest and sober (σωφροσύνη). For the gods are jealous of excess, and at the peak of fortune a man is always on the verge of a fall. Hence the proverbs of the sages: 'Know thyself'—'Nothing too much'—'Boast not in your strength.' Herodotus' history is full of the notion that man's *hybris* evokes the vengeance (νέμεσις) of the gods. Homer relates how Ajax, the son of Oileus was saved from shipwreck upon a rock on the coast and boasted at having escaped the gods in defiance of the waves. Whereupon Poseidon smashes the rock in anger, and the wicked braggart sinks.[24] The piles of corpses at Plataea should teach

> that the eye
> Of mortal man lift not his hopes too high.
>
> .   .   .   .   .
>
> Zeus sitteth Judge above us. His it is
> To check the uncurbed dreams of man.[25]

In Sophocles we hear the same warning again and again:

> Man, being mortal, must learn to hide
> Excess of fortune, eschew defiant speech.
> Yet when fate smiles, he never will believe
> That his present prosperity may one day leave him.[26]

In the *Ajax* the poet exhibits the downfall of the proud who boast against the gods and trust in their own strength. The father had already warned his son as he set out for the war:

> My son, seek victory in arms,
> but seek it ever with the help of heaven.

But Ajax replies:

> Father, with the help of gods e'en a man of nought
> might win the mastery;
> but I, even without their aid,
> trust to bring that glory within my grasp.

And when Athene tries to come to his side during the battle he thrusts her away:

> Queen, stand thou beside the other Greeks;
> where Ajax stands, battle will never break our line.

And the seer continues:

> By such words it was that he brought upon him
> the appalling anger of the goddess,
> since his thoughts were too great for man . . .

even as he had said earlier:

> Lives that have waxed too proud,
> and avail for good no more,
> are struck down by heavy misfortunes from the gods . . .[27]

When, at the beginning of the play, Athene had shown Ajax, now his fallen foe, to Odysseus, Odysseus confesses:

> I think of mine own lot no less than his.
> For I see that we are but phantoms,
> all we who live, or fleeting shadows.

at which Athene replies:

> Therefore, beholding such things, look that thine own lips
> never speak a haughty word against the gods,
> and assume no swelling port,
> if thou prevailest above another
> in prowess or by ample store of wealth.
> For a day can humble all human things,
> and a day can lift them up;
> but the wise of heart are loved of the gods,
> and the evil are abhorred.[28]

But it was just this *eusebeia*, so emphatically proclaimed by the tragedians, which disappeared from the city state. The old myth lost its force. Quite early on the gods became vague and indefinite beings, no longer addressed by their proper names. The philosopher said: 'The wise is one only. It is unwilling and willing to be called by the name of Zeus.'[29] And similarly, in the chorus of the *Agamemnon*:

> Zeus! Zeus, whate'er He be,
> If this name He love to hear
> This He shall be called of me.[30]

And in Euripides' *Trojan Women* there is a prayer which runs:

> O Earth's Upbearer, thou whose throne is Earth,
> Whoe'er thou be, O past our finding out,
> Zeus, bide thou Nature's Law, or Mind of Man,
> Thee I invoke; for treading soundless paths,
> To justice' goal thou bring'st all mortal things.[31]

The constraint of fate, the force of human passions, all seem too tremendous and uncanny to be embodied in the gods portrayed in the myths. In Homer, Moira already played a shadowy role over and above the Olympian deities. Now, faith in them becomes more and more belief in fate. It is well expressed in Euripides' *Alcestis*:

> I have mused on the words of the wise,
>   Of the mighty in song;
> I have lifted mine heart to the skies,
> I have searched all truth with mine eyes;
>   But naught more strong
> Than Fate have I found: there is naught
>   In the tablets of Thrace,
> Neither drugs whereof Orpheus taught,
> Nor in all that Apollo brought
>   To Asclepius' race,

When the herbs of healing he severed, and out of their anguish
delivered
The pain-distraught.

There is none other Goddess beside
   To the altars of whom
No man draweth near, nor hath cried
To her image, nor victim hath died,
   Averting her doom,
O Goddess, more mighty for ill
   Come not upon me
Than in days overpast: for his will
Even Zeus may in no wise fulfil
   Unholpen of thee.
Steel is molten as water before thee, but never relenting came
   o'er thee,
Who art ruthless still.[32]

The gods do not hear men's prayer or cries for help. The lot
of man does not suggest that there is any justice with the gods.
Their behaviour as portrayed in the myths now becomes the
subject of human criticism. At first, the intention was to
purify the myths from any ideas unworthy of the gods.[33] But
so successful was this, that the myth itself was completely
destroyed in the process, and criticism was now turned upon
the ritual and cultus, with its atonement usages and ideas of
purity.

The most significant and, for the Greek spirit, typical development was the accentuation of the individualistic tendencies
within democracy and their furnishing with a theoretical
justification at the hands of the sophists. This led to the destruction of faith in the validity of all norms which had come to be
recognized in the course of history and of their attribution to the
gods. The laws no longer derive their sanction from nature
($\phi\acute{v}\sigma\epsilon\iota$), but from positive enactment ($\theta\acute{\epsilon}\sigma\epsilon\iota$). They rest
(according to Antiphon) on contract. They are an imposition
($\acute{o}\mu o\lambda o\gamma\eta\theta\acute{\epsilon}\nu\tau\alpha$, $\acute{\epsilon}\pi\acute{\iota}\theta\epsilon\tau\alpha$), not a product of natural growth
($\phi\acute{v}\sigma\epsilon\iota$). They may, according to Protagoras, Hippias and

Antiphon, be useful, indeed necessary. And, in the view of Critias, they are above all a useful instrument in the hands of governors for keeping the masses under control. But when all this is conceded, they are, according to Hippias and Antiphon, artificial restrictions (δεσμὰ τῆς φύσεως) and are only, in the view of Gorgias, to be respected when they serve man's own interests. For Callicles and Thrasymachus the superman is above such things. Similarly, religion, according to Prodicus, is simply the psychological by-product of human evolution. At first men worshipped the great phenomena and gifts of nature. Later they worshipped the discoverers of the useful arts, while for Critias religion was, partly at least, the opium of the masses, the means by which the ruling classes kept them subservient to their laws.

The city state and all its laws thus came to be judged exclusively from the standpoint of their utility for the individual. They were supposed to be the outcome of rational calculation and of consent, and to exist solely for the benefit of the individual. Justice was no longer the claim of a norm transcending private interest, but the adjustment of conflicting claims, or even what was conducive to individual self-interest (injustice being what was harmful thereto). It is true that some of the sophists like Protagoras endeavoured to appeal to nature as the source of justice, while refraining from attacking the State as such, and in fact providing a theoretical justification for it. But other less scrupulous sophists used the argument to prove the right of the stronger. Protagoras' saying, 'Man is the measure of all things, of the things that are, that they are, of the things that are not, that they are not',[34] was originally intended as an epistemological principle, implying the relativity of all human judgements based on the evidence of the senses and on moral questions, and denying the possibility of absolute truth in such matters. But it could also be exploited in the interests of brutal self-interest. And his principle of rhetoric, 'To make the weaker cause the stronger',[35] could be used to justify ethical nihilism.

Aristophanes' satire, *The Clouds*, was written to show what all this teaching was leading to. Strepsiades, having got involved in debt through the prodigality of his son, Pheidippides, sends him to school with Socrates (whom Aristophanes takes for a sophist), so that he may learn the two 'methods of speaking' (or 'causes', Greek λόγοι), the stronger and the weaker. The two Logoi are brought on to the stage, the one the Just and the other the Unjust, and the latter wins the day. He represents the 'new views' (γνῶμαι καιναί), while all the Just Cause can do is to speak what is just. The Unjust Cause has little difficulty in refuting his adversary:

> Your words I will meet, and entirely defeat:
> There never *was* Justice or Truth, I repeat.

He boasts:

> I am the Lesser Logic? True:
>   these Schoolmen call me so,
> Simply because I was the first
>   of all mankind to show
> How old established rules and laws
>   might contradicted be:
> And this, as you may guess, is worth
>   a thousand pounds to me,
> To take the feebler cause, and yet
>   to win the disputation.[36]

Pheidippides proved a good scholar:

> How sweet it is these novel arts
>   these clever words to know,
> And have the power established rules
>   and laws to overthrow.[37]

He starts beating his father. It is certainly usual (νομίζεσθαι) for it to be the other way round, but though the father protests:

> But Law goes everywhere for me:
>   deny it if you can.

Pheidippides rejoins:

> Well was not he who made the law,
>> a man, a mortal man,
> As I or you, who in old times
>> talked over all the crowd?
> And think you that to you or me
>> the same is not allowed.
> To change it, so that sons by blows
>> should keep their fathers steady? . . .
> Look at the game-cocks, look at all
>> the animal creation,
> Do not *they* beat their parents? Aye:
>> I say then, that in fact
> They are as we, except that they
>> no special laws enact.[38]

In the same play Aristophanes also satirizes the sophists' account of nature and their iconoclastic treatment of the ancient myths. He makes the sophists debate about the distance a flea can jump, and whether gnats buzz through their mouths or through their rumps. Socrates explains to Strepsiades that it is not the gods but the forces of nature which produce natural phenomena. Zeus does not really exist. Rain is a natural product, like thunder and lightning. The whirling ether, which Strepsiades stupidly imagines to be a god, sets the clouds in motion, and they produce thunder like men making noises in their bowels.

II

Socrates and Natural Science

WHEREVER THE SOPHISTS did not try to foster individual ambition and self-seeking, but made a sincere attempt to provide a basis for political government, they substituted the authority of science for that of religion. The supreme court of appeal lay in nature (φύσις), which furnished the criteria for human values and actions. That being so, science was necessary as the handmaid for the investigating and interpreting of nature. First, nature meant reality as opposed to all that was artificial (including positive law). Secondly, it was reality as opposed to outward appearance, which for the Greek mind included everything which belongs to the world of *hic et nunc*, to the world of becoming and decaying. Nature, that which really exists, must be the foundation reality from which all specific phenomena originate, and out of which all such phenomena, in so far as they have any real existence at all, derive their existence in a state of becoming and decaying. Thus we get the problem of the ultimate reality, first raised by Ionian philosophy, and then brought by the sophists to Athens. It was a problem which, as will be seen from the foregoing discussion, had a vital bearing on the basis of political government.

All this applies equally to Socrates. To this extent he is a sophist (as Aristophanes regarded him). He submits all conventional judgements, which are in vogue at the time, to the test of rational criticism. But his intention is not merely to destroy them, or to abandon them, but to inquire into their intrinsic validity. He rejects whatever fails to stand up to this test, whatever is not susceptible of objective proof, whatever has no higher sanction than that of subjective opinion. While the true is the expedient (the συμφέρον), it is what really *is* expedient, and not just what the individual thinks is so. True expediency cannot be discovered by asking what is advantageous to the individual, but only by asking what is conducive to the common weal in the city state. The expedient and the good therefore coincide, thus furnishing a regulative norm for the individual. Socrates does not therefore look for those laws which secure the private rights of the individual, but those which bind him to society. His initial assumption about Law includes its authority over the individual. In looking for just laws this is what men are looking for. Thus the laws in force at any given time require unqualified allegiance, even when they are intrinsically imperfect or wrongly applied. Thus Socrates submits to the unjust sentence passed on himself, scorning the opportunity of escape, and witnessing by his death to his belief in the authoritative character of Law.

The object of Socrates' quest is ultimate reality and the ultimate sanction behind all human judgements and activities. But he approaches it in the opposite way to the Ionian philosophers. They sought to find out the 'beginning' ($\dot{\alpha}\rho\chi\dot{\eta}$) of all things. In this way they sought to reduce the multiplicity of the universe to an ultimate unity, and thus make it rational. Mythology had been concerned with the 'beginnings' in a temporal sense, with the beginning of the world in time. Ionian science, however, was concerned with the original *substance* out of which all things were made, and thus attempted to make change and decay rationally intelligible. This 'beginning' is not what was once, but what always is, the constant reality behind all phenomena. Thales proposed that the *arché* was water. It was water that gave all things their coherence. For 'that which gives everything its origin naturally holds it together as well'.[39] Similarly Plato defines the philosopher as one who is always striving to attain a knowledge which will reveal to him 'something of that reality which endures for ever and is not always passing into and out of existence'.[40]

But what is the ultimate reality thus discerned? What is the unchangeable element, not subject itself to development, but providing an intelligible explanation of all development and change? Thales maintained it was water, Anaximenes air

(πνεῦμα or ἀήρ). Anaximander postulated a basic element underlying all existent matter, which he called the 'Boundless'
(ἄπειρον). But these proposals give no satisfactory solution to
the problem of the underlying unity or purpose in the structure
of the universe. Any theory which tries to ascertain this
structure without accounting for the origin of purpose is
clearly doomed to failure from the outset.[41] A more satisfactory
approach seemed to offer itself in the fact that the universe and
its constituent phenomena confront the observer in a particular
form. It is this form which imparts to formless matter its
existence. Here we have the characteristic Greek dualism.
The world is a duality consisting of matter and form. Thus the
universe is conceived of as the analogy of a work (ἔργον) of art
(τέχνη). The constitutive principle of the universe is not matter,
but form. No work can become reality until it has taken
shape in the artist's mind. The ultimate reality must therefore be the archetypal pattern or image in the artist's mind.
The 'beginning' is not material, but spiritual. And if it is form
which imparts meaning and purpose to the work of art, the
archetypal pattern must also be the 'Good' (ἀγαθόν). Thus in
the last analysis the origin of the universe must be Absolute
Good.

The problem of reality is ultimately the problem of meaning.
Greek idealism sprang from the conflict of various competing
theories. First, there was the Eleatic school, which maintained
that change was illusory, and that only that which was at rest
was real, though in order to account for the world of illusion
Parmenides was obliged to introduce a spiritual principle which
he called Eros. Then there was Heraclitus, who identified reality
with change itself. Change for him was controlled by the law
of reason (λόγος). Then came the atomists, for whom the only
reality was mechanical force which set the material particles in
motion. Finally, there were cosmologies, such as that of Empedocles. According to him, the four material elements (earth,
fire, air and water) are set in motion by the forces of Love
(φιλότης) and strife (νεῖκος), and that of Anaxagoras, who

postulated 'seeds' (σπέρματα) controlled purposefully by the power of reason (νοῦς).

Here Socrates represents a decisive turning-point. Up to now, philosophy has been mainly concerned with physics. Socrates recalls it to the study of man. Nature does not offer him what he is looking for, the 'reason why', that is to say, the 'Good'. The Delphic oracle had told him, 'Know thyself'. He turns his gaze inward upon himself, not in order to find there, in his own subjectivity, the meaning of life, but to discover the norms which define his subjectivity. He who turns to myths about Centaurs, Chimeras, Gorgons, Pegasus, and other fabulous creatures 'and with a rustic sort of wisdom (ἀγροίκῳ τινὶ σοφίᾳ) undertakes to explain each in accordance with probability, he will need a great deal of leisure. But I have no leisure, for them at all; and the reason, my friend, is this: I am not yet able, as the Delphic oracle has it, to know myself; so it seems to me ridiculous, when I do not yet know that, to investigate irrelevant things. And so I dismiss these matters and accepting the customary belief about them, as I was saying just now, I investigate not these things, but myself, to know whether I am a monster more complicated and more furious than Typhon or a gentler and simpler creature, to whom a divine and quiet lot is given by nature.'[42]

But what is the clue he finds to the meaning of life when he looks into himself? It is the Logoi.[43] He forsakes the natural philosophy of Anaxagoras, which he had studied, and turns to the Logoi. Anaxagoras could only explain the process of causation, thus demonstrating the *conditio sine qua non* for an occurrence, but not the real grounds which lay bare its meaning. 'So I thought I must have recourse to conceptions (=Logoi) and examine in them the truth of realities.' It is by the method of dialogue that one man convinces another by reason. It must therefore always be possible by discussion (διαλέγεσθαι) to find out the most convincing case (ἐρρωμενέστατος λόγος), and so end up in agreement (συμφωνεῖν). This is the famous 'dialectical method'. In the process of the dialogue the truth is bound to come to light. Men must then see what 'virtue', 'justice' and the 'Good' really are. This was the work to which Socrates devoted his life. In so doing he was acting as a servant of the State, though he never held any official position. The subject of his quest was the basis of the State. He never engaged in commerce or entered politics or joined the scramble for political office or honour. 'For I tried to persuade each of you to care for himself and his own perfection in goodness and wisdom rather than for any of his belongings, and for the state itself rather than for its interests, and to follow the same method in his care for other things.'[44] Thus he deserved to have his meals provided in the Prytaneum like a victor in the Olympic Games.[45]

Plato and Idealism

Plato's fundamental concern was exactly the same. He too wanted to determine the genuine establishment of the State.[46] Philosophy and individual education were the only means for the recognition and proper application of these principles. In the *Republic* (*Πολιτεία*), Plato counters the theories of the sophists by painting a picture of the ideal State, the archetypal image of the city state. This, though existing only in heaven, must be the constant object of contemplation for all true statesmanship. The eternal reality is the 'Good', and those who want to realize the Good in politics must give their allegiance to it. Plato has no theoretical or academic purpose in writing the *Republic*, but the thoroughly practical purpose of teaching the individual the nature of justice. It is the inner harmony of the soul. This is necessary for politics because the State is constituted by human activity. Constant attention to the ideal archetype teaches man to understand himself as a political animal.[47] Plato reduces to an absurdity the sophists' theory of the State as a product of 'nature' and of the normative significance of natural law by picturing a State consisting of pigs.[48] Such a State needs no laws. Not being constituted by men, it has no real history; there is no justice because there is no injustice. Whereas the State as we know it in history requires justice, because it consists of men. Justice is not a natural endowment (φύσει). It must be acquired by the study of the ideal archetype and assimilated by the individual. At this point Plato differs from Socrates. Socrates goes to the Logoi in order to discover ultimate reality. Plato however looks beyond the world of becoming and decaying to the eternal world of ideas. Here is the ultimate reality 'existing ever in singularity of form independent by itself' (αὐτὸ καθ' αὑτὸ μεθ' αὑτοῦ μονοειδὲς ἀεὶ ὄν).[49] Man participates in the world of ideas through the Logoi which apprehend the ideas. His rational faculty (λογιστικόν) is the pre-existent part of the soul. But this vision of the ideal world is not a matter of theoretical speculation or detached contemplation. For the highest of the Ideas is the 'Good'. Being and meaning are identical. Man's cognitive participation in the Good is also conative, acting as a stimulus to the will. This urge for knowledge is identical with Eros, the quest for the Good. The wise man turns away from the confusion of human striving to the kingdom of the Idea. 'He contemplates a world of unchanging and harmonious order, where reason governs and nothing can do or suffer wrong; and like one who imitates an admired companion, he cannot fail to fashion himself in its likeness.'[50] In the perfect harmony of the movements of the heavenly bodies the world of Ideas is open to intuitive perception. This perception is the proper nourishment for human nature; for

> the motions which are naturally akin to the divine principle within us are the thoughts and revolutions of the universe. These each man should follow, and correct those corrupted courses of the head which have to do with generation, and by learning the harmonies and revolutions of the whole, should assimilate the perceiver to the thing perceived, according to his original nature, and by thus assimilating them, attain that final perfection of life, which the gods set before mankind as best, both for the present and the future.[51]

To become 'religious' ($\theta\epsilon o\sigma\epsilon\beta\acute{\eta}s$), it is necessary to perceive the nature of the soul (i.e. the primary, divine and imperishable element in all things) and the reason ($\nu o\hat{v}s$), which governs the harmonious movement of the stars. And to this end a man must 'observe the connection therewith of mathematics. He must perceive its relationship to music, and apply it harmoniously to the institutions and rules of ethics'.[52]

The vision of the world of Ideas may be called Plato's new religion. Eros is a divine power, and those who can no longer believe in the ancient myths can become aware of this power. Eros is the force which inspires a man to seek the vision of the Beautiful and the Good. Plato goes on to describe this vision as a mystery. In the knowledge of the Good the reason is freed from the limitations of the myth and acquires a sense of direction and obligation, so that it is no longer confined to the interests of the individual. In this way, the doctrine of the Ideas, which is intended to provide a new basis for the life of the city state, can also be expressed in the form of myth.[53] Myth is necessary as a means of freeing the individual from his own whims and fancies. After the dissolution of the old myth and the disintegration of accepted law, the individual is thrown back upon himself. But can he really be his own master? Life is turned in upon itself and anxious about itself when it loses its sense of security against the external world and feels overwhelmed by its environment. Hence it must learn anew its origin and goal and the road from one to the other as something beyond its own control. This explains Plato's adoption of the teaching of the mysteries on the journey of the soul, its pre-existence and fall. Yet this myth is not a dogma, but only an expression of the conviction which cannot be expressed in rational terms, of man's obligation towards the transcendent Good.

Myth does not exclude the necessity of reason, but demands it. The Good and the really existent are One, and the way to the Good is also the way to the knowledge of the truth. In inquiring into the principles of government, philosophy is at the same time obliged to investigate the origin of the world. For while the origin exists 'on the other side of that which is' it is not inaccessible to reason.[54] The question as to whether the end of philosophy is abstract knowledge or practical virtue (ἀρετή) is irrelevant to Platonism. The knowledge of the Good is not the means to a practical end, as though the Good were a criterion, which once discovered could thereafter be employed as a ready instrument for the shaping of the city state. Rather, the knowledge of the Good is an end in itself, and knowledge of it is conducive to happiness. But it is just this that makes a man a real statesman, i.e. a citizen. For the city state is not an institution, but it lives in the persons who combine together to make it. In the knowledge of the Good a man apprehends himself as a political animal. Thus he finds his proper place in the universe, which is: to be a citizen. The theoretical and practical problems coincide. Science, or philosophy, is not simply the theory of politics. It is not, as the sophist imagines, a closed body of knowledge, enabling the statesman to get to work without bothering his head about the transcendent Good. Rather, the true statesman serves the State by his constant search for the Good. His primary and fundamental duty is in fact to seek the knowledge of the Good.

The Greek View of Life: Its Basic Principles

The theoretical and practical problems coincide only so long as it is presupposed that human existence means existence in the city state. With the progressive decay of the city state to a point beyond cure men who are concerned with the riddle of human existence lose all interest in it. Science and philosophy become divorced from politics. In answering the riddle of the origin of the universe man tries to find out the meaning of his own existence by working out a view of life (*Weltanschauung*). Naturally, this has certain implications for everyday life. But the invariable assumption is that such a view of life can be worked out theoretically or scientifically. Its insights are formulated in a series of dogmatic propositions (δόγματα; Latin, *placita*). It is then man's duty to carry them out. The operative assumption here is the idea of detached scientific observation. Aristotle thought that philosophy originated in wonder and amazement.[55] This shows that he thought it ought to be pursued for its own sake, quite apart from its practical utility. The existential motive at work here is that by under-standing the universe, a man comes to understand himself. Thus for Aristotle philosophy, the queen of sciences, is no longer interested in practical causation or with human behaviour (πρὸς τὰ ἀναγκαῖα, πρὸς διαγωγήν), but with first causes and origins (πρῶτα αἴτια, ἀρχαί). It is detached observation and contemplation (θεωρία). Much earlier on, Anaxagoras, when asked what he lived for, answered, 'To contemplate the sun, the moon and the sky',[56] and he laid down that the end of life was contemplation and the freedom it brings.[57] Similarly, Aristotle finds perfect happiness in contemplation.[58] The life of contemplation is superior to that of pleasure or that of states-manship (βίος ἀπολαυστικός, πολιτικός, θεωρητικός.) What, then, are the basic principles of the Greek view of life? What will this period hand on as a heritage to the future? Principles which have been implicit all along, but are now becoming clear in a way they have never been before.

Man finds himself in the universe and seeks to understand his existence in it by objectifying it in rational thinking. As he inquires into its origin, he comes to regard it as a har-monious unity. That is exactly the meaning of the word 'cosmos'. The wise men say:

> Heaven and earth and gods and men are held together by communion and friendship by orderliness, temperance, and justice; and that is the reason why they call the whole of this world by the name of order [Kosmos], not of disorder or dissoluteness. Now you . . . have failed to observe the great power of geometrical equality amongst both gods and men.[59]

The soul of the universe is harmony, and music is 'the ultimate revelation of reality, the primal cosmic force which is the source of all things'.[60]

The implication of this is that the universe is regarded as a closed system. Since it is a unity, it must in the last analysis lie within the range of observation. Its unity embraces gods and men.[61] There is no place for any transcendent sphere, no room for miracles, or any other interference with the rational laws of cause and effect. Authentic existence is for the Greek mind limited on every side, a closed system with a well-defined shape of its own.[62] True, the universe, or the series of events which take place in it, is regarded as unlimited in time. But it is definitely limited in space. The unlimited, space and matter—where these are reckoned with—is not really existent. It is the indefinable, unknowable, the 'non-existent' ($\mu\dot{\eta}$ $\ddot{o}\nu$), which acquires existence only when it is given definition and form. Since the sphere is regarded as the perfect figure, the universe itself must be spherical in shape.

A further characteristic is that the universe is conceived after the analogy of a 'work of art', and therefore in terms of form and matter.[63] In a work of art matter ($\ddot{v}\lambda\eta$) is given shape and acquires form. The use of this analogy explains why $\ddot{v}\lambda\eta$ (wood) was adopted as the designation of matter. Of course, when we come down to detail, there are many different views as to the relation between matter and form. Sometimes they are regarded as contrarieties, sometimes as complementary. Sometimes *hyle* is thought to be really material and the shaping principle immaterial, and so forth. However that may be, it is the business of reason to discover the formative principles and laws which govern the acquisition of form. Indeed, as a result of the prevalent idealism, the law of reason and the law of cosmic events are actually identified.

Man, however, understands himself as a part, or a member, of the universe, organically incorporated in the objective world. Here he feels at home and secure. He apprehends himself by objectifying himself for his own observation like the phenomena of nature. He understands the individual as a case of the universal. Thus he is able to solve the riddle of his own being in discovering the rationality of the universe at large. What imparts existence, meaning and law to the universe must do the same for him too. The reality which constitutes the universe must equally constitute human existence. This reality is reason or spirit (λόγος, νοῦς). It is this that gives the universe its form. It is this which on the one hand, in the human mind, apprehends the universal reason, and on the other, is the universal reason which legislates for human behaviour.

A rational ethic and an ideal of education are worked out on the basis of this view of life. Man is a microcosm. Just as the harmony of law constitutes the universe at large, so must harmony, i.e. a right relation between the various elements of the soul, constitute the soul of man, if it is to attain to its proper happiness. For Plato, this harmony is the supreme virtue, justice. But Plato and Democritus are substantially in agreement on this point. For Democritus also declares: 'The beautiful is in all things moderation. Excess and deficiency I reject. Cheerfulness in man is conduced by moderation in desire and symmetry of life.'[64] Hence music is regarded as 'the true foundation of all education and the formation of human character'; all Greek philosophies 'see in music the means whereby we are able to work with immediate effect on the souls of men, and exercise a profound influence on the characters by our choice of rhythms and harmonies'.[65]

Man must form himself into a work of art. He must shape his life in the light of an ideal, the Beautiful and Good (καλὸν κἀγαθόν). The idea of education, of the perfection of character, determines a man's whole manner of life. The guiding virtue of all his actions, is simply efficiency in the performance of his work. The man who models himself on the ideal is 'orderly', 'gentlemanly', 'graceful', 'harmonious' (κόσμιος, εὐσχήμων, εὔρυθμος, εὐάρμοστος, ἔμμετρος) and so on; these are the ethical characteristics. Education means 'bringing oneself to order', 'equipping oneself'. (διακοσμεῖν, σκευάζειν ἑαυτόν). In this way ethical terminology is taken over from art and craft.[66]

It is possible here to develop a system of ethics in which specific actions are the expressions of virtues. One can draw up a complete list of virtues, which taken together form a unity. They describe the perfect gentleman (the καλὸς κἀγαθός). Thus in Plato we have three virtues—wisdom, courage and moderation (σοφία, ἀνδρεία, σωφροσύνη), corresponding to the three parts of the soul, viz. intellect, will and emotions (λογιστικόν, θυμοειδές, ἐπιθυμητικόν). The unifying principle behind these virtues is justice (δικαιοσύνη).

The image of the Ideal has the further function of differentiating between the various forms of life (βίος) which grow out of the historical and social conditions, or from man's specific endowments. These provide the framework for the development of the gentlemanly character. There is no idea of the concrete situation providing in encounter the challenge to choose the Good, a challenge to be heard ever anew, and never recognized once for good and all. Every man has a prearranged part to play in life (βίος—the βιολόγος is an actor on the stage). Thus it is possible to systematize the various possibilities in life in accordance with a definite, though restricted scheme. What matters is the extent to which the individual conforms to the scheme and exemplifies it in his life. As a result, the Greeks never developed biography in the proper sense of the word, still less autobiography, which only appeared later in the course of Christian development with its new understanding of the individual and of his place in the world.[67]

Human society is similarly understood in the light of the Ideal. The philosophers produce their blueprints of the ideal State. Just as the purpose of education is to produce good citizens, so too all personal relationships are subsumed under the aspect of training and education. If perfection of character is the aim of all moral effort, and not openness for the claim of others in each successive concrete encounter, the relation of the I and Thou must similarly find its meaning in their ability to lead one another to perfection of character. Eros, the impulse of love, which, in its lower phases represents the individual attraction of men for one another, is sublimated into the sphere of education for social life. It is not 'love' in the Biblical sense, the force which binds men together in mutual devotion, but a purely individualistic urge to achieve perfection of character. The dialogue, in which the search for truth is pursued, is therefore the appropriate mode of intercourse between persons.

We are now in a position to understand a characteristic feature of the Greek mind. That is, that history never became a department of study distinct from the physical world. The Greeks never developed a philosophy of history. The beginnings of such a philosophy might perhaps be discerned in Herodotus, with his view of history as the interaction of human *hybris* and divine retribution. But in Thucydides history is subject to the same rational observation as physics. He seeks to exhibit the psychological impulses and passions and the political and economic factors which are the real motive behind historical events. But just as the transcendence of God (i.e. his transcendence over the world of becoming and decaying) is a metaphysical transcendence of spirit (immanent in the cosmos) over matter, and not the transcendence of constant futurity, so the historical process is conceived as the movement of cosmic events, in which the rule is, *plus ça change, plus c'est la même chose*.[68] Historical knowledge seeks to ascertain the constant factor in history, the eternally valid truth, the exemplary. For Platonic idealism empirical history is a story of decline and fall, not an occasion for the exercise of responsibility, in which new situations present man with new duties. If—and this, when all is said and done, is the aim of education—the spiritual became the dominant factor in human society, then history would be brought to a standstill. The constant changes ($\mu\epsilon\tau\alpha\beta\omega\lambda\alpha\iota$) which make history the realm of becoming ($\gamma\epsilon\nu\epsilon\sigma\iota\varsigma$) would come to an end.[69]

Thus the duty of man is to realize in himself the universal and eternal. All empirical reality is matter requiring to be given shape. Man's encounters with his neighbour, like fate itself, are pressed into the service of self-perfection. Now, if all this be so, man has the chance to solve the greatest riddle of all, death itself. Death must be divested of its fatal, irrational character. This can be achieved in either of two ways. First, it may be accepted as a purely natural phenomenon. Then the individual can submit to it willingly, knowing that thereby he is conforming to the rhythm of a universe in which all things grow and decay. Secondly, death can be made the crown of a noble life. Man must learn to die a noble death (καλῶς ἀποθνῄσκειν). Thus for Plato, the philosophic life is a life of constant preparation for death (μελετᾶν ἀποθνῄσκειν). It is a life in which man strives to free himself from his entanglements with empirical reality, from the bonds that tie him to the particular and transitory. Thus he may cultivate a spiritual life transcending the realm of becoming and decaying. The particular, the *hic et nunc*, must be viewed in the light of the laws which give form and make the universe a work of art. All specific duties must be performed in the light of these laws. Thus man has to mould himself into the unity of the cosmos, and live in the realm of timeless, eternal reality. Man has the freedom to do so, for he is essentially spirit.

HELLENISM

HELLENISM

I

THE STOIC IDEAL OF THE WISE MAN

WITH THE DECLINE OF THE CITY STATE, the Greek view of life underwent a further modification at the hands of the Stoics. Their achievement was to have momentous consequences.[1] Their aim was to work out a rational understanding of the world and human nature in such a way as to insure man's security in the world. The world itself, as in the Greek tradition as a whole, is conceived as a unity, permeated and governed by the divine power immanent within it and by a rational divine law. This conviction offers man a sense of security. The universal law is the law of his own being. Man has his own appropriate place in a universe of which he himself is a part.

But there are also new elements in the Stoic conception of the unity of the world. A new solution is offered to the old problem of the dualism of form and matter. The Stoics identify reason, the Logos, which imparts form to matter, with the vital force of nature, *physis*. The cause and energy behind physical events is identical with reason as the legislative power which shapes things in accordance with a purpose. The Logos is also conceived as breath ($\pi\nu\epsilon\hat{\upsilon}\mu\alpha$), or as an air-like substance (as $\sigma\hat{\omega}\mu\alpha$). It is 'air in motion' ($\dot{\alpha}\grave{\eta}\rho\ \kappa\iota\nu\sigma\acute{\upsilon}\mu\epsilon\nu\sigma\varsigma$), 'ether' ($\alpha\grave{\iota}\theta\acute{\eta}\rho$), 'fiery reason' ($\nu\sigma\hat{\upsilon}\varsigma\ \pi\upsilon\rho\iota\nu\acute{\sigma}\varsigma$), 'rational and fiery breath' ($\pi\nu\epsilon\hat{\upsilon}\mu\alpha\ \nu\sigma\epsilon\rho\grave{\sigma}\nu\ \kappa\alpha\grave{\iota}\ \pi\upsilon\rho\hat{\omega}\delta\epsilon\varsigma$), 'Form-imparting fire' ($\pi\hat{\upsilon}\rho\ \tau\epsilon\chi\nu\iota\kappa\acute{\sigma}\nu$), permeating the universe and giving it articulation. It is the 'breath which passes through all things' ($\pi\nu\epsilon\hat{\upsilon}\mu\alpha\ \delta\iota\hat{\eta}\kappa\sigma\nu\ \delta\iota\grave{\alpha}\ \pi\acute{\alpha}\nu\tau\omega\nu$), giving unity to the whole. 'For', in the words of Chrysippus, 'the whole of reality forms a unity, because a breath permeates it throughout, and by it the universe is held together and stays together and forms an organic unity.'[2] This breath is the 'tension-giving power' ($\tau\sigma\nu\iota\kappa\grave{\eta}\ \delta\acute{\upsilon}\nu\alpha\mu\iota\varsigma$), the 'seminal reason' (λόγος σπερματικός). Articulating law and physical energy are identical. The seminal rational forces (λόγοι σπερματικοί) into which the one Logos is distributed, operate like 'winds' (πνεύματα) or forces (δυνάμεις) in all things, giving them 'as airy tensions' (τόνοι ἀερώδεις) their quality and form. Thus the universe is a living organism with a soul (ζῷον ἔμψυχον). Indeed, it is the deity itself. Alternatively, the deity is the 'universal law of nature' (κοινὸς νόμος φύσεως), and as such it is 'necessity' or 'fate' (ἀνάγκη and εἱμαρμένη). It is the 'providence which prevails throughout the universe' (πρόνοια), and whose rule is discernible in the order (τάξις) and purpose which prevail both on the cosmic and the individual level. The problem of theodicy has been apparently solved. There is no room for evil as a reality: evil is only apparent. Everything has its necessary place and purpose within the whole, and all that is necessary is to recognize it. Above all, man must understand himself in this universal context.

For the individual the Logos is a pointer, showing him the direction in which he must go (λόγος ὀρθός), the *nomos* or law. Man is essentially a Logos-being. It is important for him to recognize his identity with the universal Logos and give his 'assent' to it (συγκατάθεσις). The Logos must hold the reins of government in him if he is to achieve his end, which is happiness. That means, first and foremost, that his life must be lived as a unity. He must live 'according to an unequivocal norm, according to the principle of inner harmony' (ζῆν καθ᾽ ἕνα λόγον, κατὰ σύμφωνον). He must strive for 'consistency throughout his life' (ὁμολογία τοῦ πάντος βίου), and must 'live consistently' (ὁμολογουμένως ζῆν). This, however, means 'being at one with nature' (ὁμολογουμένως τῇ φύσει); for the individual Logos is also the universal Logos of nature.

This fundamental principle can be applied positively. Man is by nature a political animal (φύσει ζῷον πολιτικόν). He is destined for society (φύσει κοινωνικός). He must do his duty within the natural orders of society—to his family, his friends, subordinates, superiors and so forth. These duties can be tabulated. The Logos is the basic principle of justice (τὸ δίκαιον). It exists by nature (φύσει), not by enactment (θέσει). The law of nature does not depend on human whims and fancies, but is the norm of society, on which all positive law must be based. Positive law is never actually identical with natural law, but it has to realize it progressively. The Stoic idea of natural law was taken up by the Roman jurists and used as a basis for statutory legislation. Thus it continued to exercise an influence through the Middle Ages, and right down to modern times. Like positive law, the empirical State enjoys a relative validity. It is an expression of 'human providence, the human counterpart of the Law' (πρόνοια ἀνθρώπων κατὰ νόμον). Not only God, but men also, partaking as they do of the Logos, can exercise providence. As a human system (σύστημα ἀνθρώπων), the empirical State represents a limitation of the universal commonwealth of nature (κοινωνία πάντων ἀνθρώπων). The true constitution of the State (πολιτεία) is the constitution of the universe. It is the city of God, whose law is the Logos. The constitution of all empirical States is on the one hand an approximation to the 'cosmopolity', on the other a denial of it. Fundamentally, man is 'cosmopolitan,' a truth which he realizes when he lives according to nature. Thus all the accidental differences of history, the differences between one man and another, are unimportant. All distinctions of rank and dignity are unreal, and must be set aside, even the distinction between free man and slave. All men are equal by nature, and all have the capacity for freedom.

Since man is essentially Logos, reason, another consequence can be drawn—namely, an individualistic and negative ethic. For man, it is argued, attains happiness when he withdraws wholly into his inner life, thus achieving freedom and independence from the impingements of the outside world. The ethical ideal here is freedom (ἐλευθερία). Man attains it by recognizing the fundamental differences between what lies within his power and what is beyond it (τὰ ἐφ' ἡμῖν and τὰ οὐκ ἐφ' ἡμῖν). He must recognize what lies beyond his choice and decision,

seeing them as ἀπροαιρετικά. He must see that these things are
no concern of his (they are not πρὸς ἡμᾶς), and must therefore
be regarded as 'alien' (ἀλλότρια).

What lies within our power, and what does not? The only
thing that does is our inner life—our imagination, our desire
and will. Everything else is beyond our control, all that confronts us from outside, even our own bodies, every external
situation in life, every blow of fate that strikes us. If man would
be free, he must free himself from all conventional judgements
about good and evil. There is only one good and one evil—
what promotes inward freedom, and what destroys it, respectively. All earthly goods are 'indifferent' (ἀδιάφορα), though this
is to some extent modified by the Stoics of the middle period,
who recognized distinctions here: some things were to be pre-
ferred, others rejected, some things were worthy, others unworthy (προηγούμενα and ἀπροηγούμενα, ἄξια and ἀπάξια).

Above all, however, man must free himself from his emotions (πάθη). For these seek to attach him to 'alien things'. He
must strive after self-sufficiency (αὐτάρκεια), both within and
without. He must cultivate renunciation and endurance
(ἀπέχεσθαι and ἀνέχεσθαι). For then he will be free and happy,
and nothing can assail him. Those who become slaves to their
own bodies and to the powers and persons to which bodies are
subject, are vulnerable to misfortune and suffering. If, however,
they are inwardly free, nothing can assail them. All external
evils are reduced to the level of indifference, like all external
goods. Those who have renounced the goods are unconcerned
with the evils. Health and sickness, riches and poverty, honour
and dignity or ostracism and scorn—the wise man treats them
all as grist to his mill, as aids for the maintenance of his moral
strength and spiritual freedom. He withdraws into himself
and with clarity of mind perceives the divine, universal law,
which, when all is said and done, he cannot alter. He gives it his
assent and lets fate do with him what it will. In this way,
however, he possesses inner freedom and rejoices in the magnificent spectacle of the divine government of the world:

Lead me, O Zeus, and thou, O fate,
To the goal which you have ordained for me.
I will follow without shrinking. Were I a miscreant,
And would not follow, I should have to none the less.[3]

Therefore 'you must give up all, body, possessions, fame, books, tumults, power, exemption from power. For to whichsoever your propension is, you are a slave, you are under subjection, you are made liable to restraint, to compulsion; you are altogether the property of others.'[4]

> We should enter upon a course of education and instruction not to change the constitutions of things, which is neither put within our reach nor for our good; but that, being as they are, and as their nature is with regard to us, we may have our mind accommodated to what exists.[5]

Everything that happens happens in accordance with the law of nature, the law of God. And man has an inner affinity with God. God is his Father. And as for the man who is mindful that he is a son of God:

> why shall he fear anything that happens among men? Shall kindred to Caesar, or any other of the great at Rome, enable a man to live secure, above contempt, and void of all fear whatever; and shall not the having God for our Maker, and Father, and Guardian free us from all griefs and terrors?[6]

Thus does Epictetus speak to God:

> Make use of me for the future as thou wilt. I am of the same mind; I am equal with thee. I refuse nothing which seems good to thee. Lead me whither thou wilt. Clothe me in whatever dress thou wilt. Is it thy will, that I should be in a public or a private condition, dwell here, or be banished, be poor or rich? Under all these circumstances I will make thy defence to men.[7]

After drawing a picture of 'providence', which makes itself known in the purposeful ordering of nature, Epictetus cries:

> Are these the only works of providence, with regard to us? And what words can proportionately express our applauses and

praise? For, if we had any understanding, ought we not both in public and in private incessantly to sing hymns, and speak well of the Deity, and rehearse his benefits? Ought we not, whether we are digging, or ploughing, or eating, to sing hymns to God? Great is God, who has supplied us with these instruments to till the ground: great is God, who has given us hands, a power of swallowing, a stomach: who has given us to grow insensibly, to breathe in sleep. Even these things we ought on every occasion to celebrate; but to make it the subject of the greatest and most divine hymn, that he has given us the faculty of apprehending them, and using them in a proper way. Well, then: because the most of you are blind and insensible, was it not necessary that there should be someone to fill this station, and give out, for all men, the hymn to God? For what else can I, a lame old man, do but sing hymns to God? If I was a nightingale, I would act the part of a nightingale: if a swan, the part of a swan. But, since I am a reasonable creature, it is my duty to praise God. This is my business, I do it. Nor will I ever desert this post as long as it is vouchsafed me; and I exhort you to join in the same song.[8]

One ought to leave this life gratefully.

Do not you know that both sickness and death must overtake us? At what employment? The husbandman at his plough; the sailor on his voyage. At what employment would you be taken? For, indeed, at what employment ought you to be taken? If there is any better employment at which you can be taken, follow that. For my own part, I would be taken engaged in nothing, but in the care of my own faculty of choice; how to render it undisturbed, unrestrained, uncompelled, free. I would be found studying this, that I may be able to say to God, 'Have I transgressed thy commands? Have I perverted the powers, the senses, the preconceptions which thou hast given me? Have I ever accused thee, or censured thy dispensations? I have been sick, because it was thy pleasure; and so have others, but I willingly. I have been poor, it being thy will, but with joy. I have not been in power, because it was not thy will; and power I have never desired, Hast thou ever seen me out of humour upon this account? Have I not always approached thee with a cheerful countenance, prepared to execute thy commands and the significations of thy will? Is it thy pleasure that I should depart from this assembly? I depart. I give thee all thanks that thou hast thought me worthy to have a share in it with thee; to behold thy works, and to join with thee in comprehending thy administration. Let death overtake me while I am thinking, while I am writing, while I am reading such things as these.'[9]

It is only the way we take things that makes them good or evil. 'Neither death nor exile, nor pain, nor anything of this kind is the cause of our doing, or not doing, any action; but our opinions and principles.'[10] 'Remember that this holds universally; we squeeze ourselves; we straiten ourselves: that is, our own principles (δόγματα) squeeze and straiten us.'[11] 'What if you throw money in his way? He will despise it. What if a girl? What, if in the dark? What, if he be tried by popular fame, calumny, praise, death? He is able to overcome them all.'[12]

Just as Hermes could turn all to gold with his magic rod, so the wise man turns all evil to good. 'Bring sickness, death, want, reproach, capital trial. All these, by the rod of Hermes, shall turn to advantage.'[13]

Thus the wise man lives in detachment from history and the world. He shuts his eyes to all external reality, and thus arms himself against the blows of fate. He has nothing to lose and nothing to gain. He cannot have any fresh experiences, for nothing is new to him. There is no future. There is a sameness about everything that happens. The world moves according to predetermined laws which he knows and accepts from the outset.

The ideal of society and the ideal of the wise man who minds his own business, the positive and the negative ethic—these are capable of being fused into a unity when the wise man submits to the duties imposed by society in a spirit of inner freedom. That is how Epictetus understands it, and the Stoic Emperor Marcus Aurelius put it into practice. For educational purposes, this freedom and mastery over the emotions can be described in terms of the traditional pattern of the 'virtues'. These are classified under the headings of temperance, prudence, justice and fortitude (σωφροσύνη, φρόνησις, δικαιοσύνη, ἀνδρεία), while the specific duties (τὰ καθήκοντα) may be developed in detail.

The ideal of the wise man concentrating on his self-education may however lead to the ascetic, monastic ideal of 'solitude' and tranquillity (ἐρήμωσις and ἡσυχία). In this way Stoicism provided an outlook and even a terminology for Christian monasticism. This process was facilitated by the later Stoics, such as Seneca and Marcus Aurelius, who assimilated certain tendencies derived from a dualistic anthropology. Such tendencies are already discernible in Plato, where they are clearly taken over from the so-called Orphic religion. The body is regarded as a vessel, as the prison of the soul, as a burden from which the spirit strives to get free. It is often called by the contemptuous diminutive σωμάτιον, or alternatively, 'flesh', again often with the equally contemptuous diminutive σαρκίδιον. Its antithesis is the rational part of man, his 'daemon', which is even called *spiritus sacer*.

But this does not entail any essential modification of Stoic monism or pantheism. The spirit dwelling in the body is not really an alien element. It is neither a divine spark fallen from the world of light, as in Gnosticism, nor is it a supernatural gift, as in Christianity. It is the Logos of man, identical with the universal Logos, his intellect and will. It is the divine element in him, which lies within his own control. There is no doubt about the harmony between the purpose of individual life and the course of the world at large. The world is still a unity governed by divine providence. Therefore man is still at home in it.

The freedom of the Stoic wise man provides a striking analogy to the Pauline conception of Christian freedom. A preliminary comparison of the two will throw even further light on it. There is a curious inconsistency inherent in the Stoic view of life, arising from the double sense in which the term 'Law' is used. First, it means physical law or natural forces, and secondly, rational norm. If everything that happens is due to the operation of the universal Logos, what is the source of emotion (πάθος), which opposes the Logos? Must it not also have its seat in human nature? Yet the fact is that the Logos does not work in man with the inevitability of a natural force, predetermining human actions like those of animals and plants. Rather, the Logos confronts human subjectivity as a norm which makes a demand upon him, and the harmony between the human subject and the universal Logos can only be realized by an interior assent. Why is this assent so difficult, and why is it so seldom achieved?

The problem is obscured by a rationalistic optimism. Rational thought is regarded as autonomous. It is a law unto itself, governing the desires and the will. In the last resort man desires and wills only what is to his own good. Reason shows man what this is, and the will obediently follows its behests. Failure is attributed to error. When that happens, a man is not really doing what he wants to do. All that is necessary is for reason to point where he is mistaken, and he will forthwith rectify his mistake. All that is needed is a change of 'opinions' (δόγματα)![14] Since he is capable of rational thought, man is in control of himself and inwardly free. In other words, freedom for the Stoics means independence of all reality, external to the human subject. For the Christian on the other hand, the problem of freedom raises the whole question of human nature. Is man left to himself really capable of the Good?[15] Paul can also agree that when a man does evil he is not really doing what he wants to do. But that does not mean that his wrongdoing is simply a mistake. It means that man is radically incapable of doing what he wants to do. His will is corrupted from the outset—led astray and perverted by evil. Hence it is useless to appeal to the reason by telling a man what he ought to do.

> Thus for the Stoics, spiritual autonomy is the coveted prize of security of being (and that *is* what they mean by freedom). In Christianity, on the other hand, spiritual autonomy is the threshold of the abyss—the abyss of absolute moral subjectivity. This subjectivity is required to give an account of itself, and incurs guilt.[16]

For the Stoic, the way to peace and security is to turn away from the world, whereas for the Christian this is precisely to plunge oneself into the disquietude of guilt. For by turning our backs on the world we find ourselves face to face with God. In a similar way, to turn to the world is to look for peace where there is none. Christianity calls men *out* of the world, not to find peace in their own hearts, but to realize their responsibility towards God. This fact of responsibility, which differentiates man from all 'worldly' things, drives him to despair. Freedom must therefore be freedom from self, and the only way to attain it is to accept it as a gift.

All this can be expressed in another way. The Stoic believes that it is possible to escape from his involvement in time. By detaching himself from the world he detaches himself from time. The essential part of man is the Logos, and the Logos is timeless. So the Stoic concentrates exclusively upon his Logos-being, thus rising superior to all obligations and denying himself any future. But in thus repudiating the future, he deprives the present and the past of their temporal character as well. His present is unreal, for the essence of the present is that it is the moment of decision for the future. The only decision he has to make has been anticipated already. Of course, that decision must be maintained, which means that it must be constantly renewed. But it is never a concrete decision in the moment, made in responsibility for a definite act or disposition. It is in a paradoxical way always the same decision, a decision that the moment is devoid of significance. It cannot be a concrete decision made *hic et nunc*, for the man involved in it is not man *in concreto* (i.e. man qualified by his past for his present responsibility), but abstract Logos-man, whose past is not really his at all, since he is obliged to divest himself of all ties with the past, from its joys as well as its sorrows. Only so can he ascend to the timeless, eternal existence of the life of the Logos. For Christianity, existence in time is essential to human nature. His present is a present of decision for a future which is ever new. Man enters his present from his past, and the past is unalterable, whether for good or evil. It is the past which determines his being. Hence the question can only be: How far is man bound to his past? Is he really free to decide in face of the future? If so, it would mean that he is free to decide over against his past. Paul maintains that it is just this freedom that man lacks. Such freedom would be the freedom of man from himself. A man *is* his past. Hence freedom can only be received as a gift of grace.

II

STAR WORSHIP

FATALISM AND ASTROLOGY

THE GREEKS HAD ALWAYS BELIEVED that the stars were supernatural beings, but they had never actually worshipped them
during classical times.[17] In the Hellenistic age, however, star
worship penetrated into the Mediterranean lands from the Near
East and gradually conquered the Roman world. And although
the Greek gods proved intractable to any attempt to convert
them into astral deities, popular Hellenistic philosophy was
influenced by ideas picked up from star worship in a number of
different ways. It was the Syrian Baals ('Lords') which lent themselves most readily to this process. Originally gods of vegetation,
they became astral deities under Chaldean influence. Syrian
merchants, slaves and mercenaries introduced them into the
West, e.g. as Jupiter of Doliche or Jupiter of Heliopolis, and
even before the end of the Republic such cults had found their
way into Italy. In the age of the Empire their influence grew
apace, especially under the Severi. Julia Domna (= Martha), the
wife of Septimius Severus (193-211), was the daughter of the
high priest of Baal of Emesa. Heliogabalus, who became
Emperor in 218, was himself a priest of this same deity. Aurelian
(270-5) promoted the Syrian sun god, whose picture he had
stolen from Palmyra, to the status of an imperial deity with the
title, *Sol Invictus*. Mithraism, a cult which was particularly
popular with the army, contributed greatly to the propagation
and development of the worship of *Sol Invictus*.

More important, however, than the worship of these Syrian
deities was the theology which came along with it. The Oriental
deities of the sky and sun naturally offered a congenial soil for
the development of a belief in a supreme God. The tendency
towards monotheism already existing within philosophical
enlightenment, particularly among the Stoics, was thus rein-
forced by this sacerdotalist theology from the Orient, where the

sun had become an omnipotent deity pervading the world with its vital force. So it came about that solar pantheism conquered the entire Roman world during the age of the Empire.

The last formula reached by the religion of the pagan Semites, and in consequence by that of the Romans, was a divinity unique, almighty, eternal, universal and ineffable, that revealed itself throughout nature, but whose most splendid and most energetic revelation was the sun.[18]

The historical significance of this influx of Oriental star worship was not however exhausted in this development of a solar pantheism. Along with it there came a development of a belief in the transcendence of the deity combined with fatalism, the symptom of which is astrology. This was one of the consequences of the invasion of the Oriental religions, though it was by no means exclusively a result of them. For in the Hellenistic world the Greek view of life was in any case undergoing a profound change, making it receptive to Oriental ideas. The latter simply added fuel to the fire.

This sense that man was simply the plaything of fate became very prevalent among many classes of society, particularly in the ever increasing population of the great cities. The political upheavals which had destroyed the ancient city states as well as the Roman Republic left the individual utterly bewildered and helpless. Everything was now on such a large scale that he could no longer understand what it was all about or see any law at work behind it. He could no longer, as in the old days of the city state, with its much smaller scale, contribute effectively to politics, and thus to his own personal destiny. He had become simply the plaything of fate. The continuous upheavals, the triumphal processions, the foundation and collapse of one empire after another, party strife and civil war at home—all of these left the individual with a sense of utter helplessness. In great men, men of daring and action unhampered by inhibitions or scruples, generals and despots, and even adventurers, this feeling takes the form of a proud conviction of being the instruments of fate. The capricious goddess Tyche ($\tau \acute{\upsilon} \chi \eta$, 'chance'; Latin, *fortuna*), who governs world events, is for them a propitious deity who brings good luck. But for the countless myriads who feel themselves to be the slaves of fate, she is stern necessity ($\mathring{\alpha}\nu \acute{\alpha}\gamma \kappa \eta$), ineluctable fate ($\epsilon \mathring{\iota}\mu \alpha \rho \mu \acute{\epsilon}\nu \eta$).

> Everywhere in the whole world at every hour by all men's voices Fortune alone is invoked and named, alone accused, alone impeached, alone pondered, alone applauded, alone rebuked and visited with reproaches; deemed volatile and indeed by most men blind as well, wayward, inconsistent, uncertain, fickle in her favours and favouring the unworthy. To her is indebted all that is spent and credited, all that is received, she alone fills both pages in the whole of mortals' account; and we are so much all at the mercy of chance that Chance herself, by whom God is proved uncertain, takes the place of God.

So wrote the elder Pliny.[19] But can fate, with all her caprice, still be conceived as a deity? We can understand how she acquired the name of 'Spontaneity' ($\tau \grave{o}$ $\alpha \mathring{\upsilon} \tau \acute{o}\mu \alpha \tau o\nu$). 'Spontaneity seems to be a god', runs a saying of Menander,[20] and to Spontaneity there is dedicated an inscription from Pergamum in the age of the Empire.[21]

This sense of helplessness in the hands of fate, of living in a world where it is impossible to plan their future, makes men wonder whether it is possible to be at home in the world at all. The world becomes a hostile, alien place. It was just this mood that led men to turn to star worship, where they found just what they wanted. For that worship implied that the universe was not a harmonious unity, but that it was split into two spheres, the lower, sublunary world, and the world of the stars. Moreover, the lower world was not centred in itself, but was under the control of the stars. Everything that happened in this lower world was determined by what went on in the world of the stars. Hence, in the last resort all activity here is trivial and meaningless, and if it seems to be independent, that is a mere illusion.

But the consequence of radical dualism was not invariably

drawn. The late Stoics endeavoured to combine their fatalism and star worship with the traditional Greek conception of the cosmos. They maintained the discredited feeling for the world with a kind of defiance. Man must, they contended, make no attempt to resist fate, but accept it. Fate is also providence, and can be traditionally understood. Thus the unity of the cosmos was preserved.[22] Epictetus calmly asserts his conviction to this effect.[23] Seneca's attempt to maintain it is more of a *tour de force*.

> Fate [*fata*] guides us, and it was settled at the first hour of birth what length of time remains for each. Cause is linked with cause. . . . Therefore everything should be endured with fortitude, since things do not, as we suppose, simply happen—they all come [*non, ut putamus, incidunt cuncta, sed veniunt*]. Long ago it was determined what would make you rejoice, what would make you weep, and although the lives of individuals seem to be marked by great dissimilarity, yet is the end one—we receive what is perishable, and shall ourselves perish [*accipimus peritura perituri*]. Why, therefore, do we chafe? Why complain? For this were we born [*ad hoc parti sumus*]. Let Nature deal with matter, which is her own, as she pleases: let us be cheerful and brave in face of everything, reflecting that it is nothing of our own that perishes. What then is the part of the good man? To offer himself to fate [*praebere se fato*]. It is a great consolation that it is together with the universe we are swept along [*cum universo rapi*]; whatever it is that has ordained us so to live, so to die, by the same necessity it binds us also to the gods. One unchangeable course [*cursus*] bears along the affairs of men and gods alike. Although the great creator and ruler of the universe himself wrote the decrees of fate, yet he follows them. He obeys for ever, he decreed but once.[24]

But this kind of fatalism can just as easily degenerate into superstition. The world of the stars, in whose law and order the divine government of the universe is more clearly manifest than in the sublunary world, becomes the object of veneration. The wise man—and not only the Stoic—strives frantically to attain the vision of this world. He turns his back on this life with its wild ambitions and lusts. 'The contemplation of the sky has become a communion.'[25] By contemplating the harmonious movements of the stars the devotee himself 'participates in their immortality, and already, before his appointed hour, converses with the gods'. Thus Vettius Valens, an astrologer of the second century A.D.[26] But this kind of absorption in the contemplation of the world of the stars is already to be found in Seneca. Writing to his mother Helvia, he says:

> Inside the world there can be found no place of exile; for nothing that is inside the world is foreign to mankind. No matter where you lift your gaze from earth the heaven, the realm of God, and man are separated by an unalterable distance. Accordingly, so long as my eyes are not deprived of that spectacle with which they are never sated, so long as I may behold the sun, and the moon, so long as I may fix my gaze upon the other planets, so long as I may trace out their risings and settings, their periods, and the reason for the swiftness or the slowness of their wanderings . . . so long as I may be with these, and in so far as it is permitted to a man, to commune with celestial beings, so long as I may keep my mind directed ever to the sight of kindred things on high, what difference does it make to me what soil I tread upon?[27]

Similarly, in his letter of consolation to Marcia he describes the vision which the soul will some day enjoy when it ascends to heaven after death:

> You will see the gleaming of countless stars, you will see one star flooding everything with his light and the sun that marks off the spaces of day and night in his daily course, and in his annual course distributes even more equably the periods of summer and winter. You will see the moon taking his place by night, who as she meets her brother borrows from him a pale, reflected light, now quite hidden, now overhanging the earth with her white face exposed, ever changing as she waxes and wanes, ever different from her last appearance. You will see the five planets pursuing their different courses and sparkling down to earth from opposite directions; on even the slightest motions of

these hang the fortunes of nations, and the greatest and smallest happenings are shaped to accord with the progress of a kindly or unkindly star.[28]

Finally, in his correspondence with Lucilius, Seneca portrays the day of a man's death, the 'birthday of eternity', when the spirit leaves its earthly body and returns to the gods. Then:

the secrets of nature shall be disclosed to you, the haze will be shaken from your eyes, and the bright light will stream in upon you from all sides. Picture to yourself how great is the glow when all the stars mingle their fires: no shadows will disturb the clear sky. The whole expanse of heaven will shine evenly; for day and night are interchanged only in the lowest atmosphere. Then you will say that you have lived in darkness, after you have seen, in your perfect state, the perfect light— that light which now you behold darkly in a vision that is cramped to the last degree. And yet, far off as it is, you already look upon it in wonder; what do you think the heavenly light will be when you have seen it in its proper sphere?[29]

In such visions or phantasies men still cling to the old idea of the unity of the cosmos. This was possible so long as the Stoic attitude of the freedom of the wise man from everything that happens in the outside world and the idea of the independence of the inner Ego and its relationship to the divine, universal law are not allowed to go by the board. Once that happens, however, the law which prevails in the world of the stars is seen in a different light. It is no longer the law whose writ runs throughout the universe, and which even the stars themselves obey. It is the law which is defied by the stars, which are now regarded as the omnipotent despots of the universe. That is just how they appear in Oriental astrology. Here the astral deities have lost their personal nature and have become cosmic powers of an abstract kind. They operate on strictly causal lines, and are susceptible of mathematical calculation. This kind of science, which can predict the future from the movement of the planets, is astrology.

It penetrated from the East, and gained a powerful hold on

all classes of society, no matter whether it was practised by pundits or by charlatans. It became fashionable to have one's horoscope read, and to consult the Chaldeans about the favourable moment for any undertaking, whether great or small.[30] Augustus had his horoscope published, and coins were minted inscribed with the sign of his birth—Capricorn. Astrology also played a fateful role in the life of Tiberius.[31] Manilius wrote an astrological poem of a didactic nature in Rome and dedicated it to Tiberius. It was intended as a Stoic refutation of Lucretius. In the second century A.D. Vettius Valens wrote a book on the interpretation of the stars, while his Alexandrian contemporary, Claudius Ptolemaeus, sought to combine astrological superstition with scientific astronomy in his *Tetrabiblos*. Firmicus Maternus (fourth century A.D.) was an astrologer before his conversion to Christianity, when he became a doughty opponent of pagan religion.

An essential feature in the view of life of which these developments are symptomatic is, first, that as a result of the depreciation of the sublunary world at the expense of the world of the stars the idea of transcendence was modified in a sense foreign to Greek thought. God's transcendence is no longer his spirituality, which man, since he participates in it, can understand by rational thought as the power in the universe which imparts form to matter. A new dualism replaces the old dualism of form and matter, of spirit and sensuality. It is the dualism of the two worlds, the sublunary, and the world of the stars. It is symptomatic that whereas the classical Greeks regarded light as the light of day, articulating the universe in its fullness, and enabling man to find his way in it, it now becomes the object of direct vision for those who have turned their backs on the sublunary world.[32] A symptom of this is that the deity is now characterized by attributes foreign to the classical mind. Thus God becomes the 'Most High' (ὕψιστος) and the 'Almighty' (παντοκράτωρ), a term which eventually found its way into the Christian creed. Theology develops the concept of omnipotence and eternity.

Further, it is of the utmost significance that astrology produced a wholly new attitude to time. The stars are the world rulers because they are the lords of time. World events move with their motion, in periods. History is not governed by its own immanent laws, proceeding automatically at every moment of time, as a harmonious process. It is subjected to the changes of time governed by the motions of the stars. It runs in periods, each of which—days, weeks or epochs—is under the control of a particular planet. Another symptom is the spread from the East during the age of the Empire of the idea of planet weeks. The division of time into periods provides a congenial soil for the development of an eschatology. Men begin to look for an age of redemption which will follow the confusions and disasters of the present. This kind of belief offers a clue to the understanding of the political upheavals which are going on in the world. The end of the civil wars and the reign of Augustus can be hailed as the dawn of a new era, as the Golden Age, the age of redemption, ushered in by the appearance of a new star, which Virgil in his fourth Eclogue, celebrating the birth of the Saviour of the world, identifies with Apollo. The conception of omnipotent time finds its symbol in the Aeon, a figure of Iranian mythology, further developed by Chaldean theology.[33]

Finally, star worship introduces an eschatology of the individual. The soul of man, which derives from the star world, will, after death, reascend to its native world, a belief which originally applied to the souls of kings, but which was later made 'democratic'—that is, it was applied to all human souls.[34] Heaven is the home of the souls, and they long to return thither all through their sojourn in their earthly prison.

Of course, at the outset this belief was far from being universally accepted. It was only a comfortable promise preached by a few sects to the myriads who felt themselves to be the slaves of fate. Sometimes it competed with other redemptive religions, sometimes it was combined with them. For there were many religions which offered deliverance from fate and from the tyranny of the stars.

Among these were the mysteries. In them the initiate becomes the master of his own destiny.

> Let fortune go and fume with fury in another place [cries the priest of Isis, pointing to Lucius, whom the goddess has summoned]. For fortune (*casus infestus*) hath no puissance against them which have devoted their lives to serve and honour the majesty of our goddess. . . . Let such, which be not devout (*inreligiosi*) to the goddess, see and acknowledge their error: 'Behold, here is Lucius that is delivered from his former so great miseries by the providence of the goddess Isis, and rejoiceth therefore and triumpheth of victory over his fortune.'[35]

Among these too, was Gnosticism. Those who have 'knowledge' are not only secure from the attacks of demons, but are no longer prisoners of fate (*fatum*).[36] For of the Gnostic it may be said:

> In truth, Mind (νοῦς), the soul belonging to God (ἡ τοῦ θεοῦ ψυχή), is Lord over all things, over fate (εἱμαρμένη), over the law and over all else. And nothing is impossible to it, whether it be to lift the human soul above fate, or to subject it to fate, indifferent as it is towards whatever happens.[37]
>
> The pneumatic man, who has attained to the knowledge of himself, has no need to resort to magic for the sake of advantage, though magic in itself is a good thing. Nor need he make any attempt to get Ananke into his power. He lets everything take its natural or determined course. He goes his own way, seeking himself alone. And when he comes to know God, he holds fast to the ineffable [divine] triad, and lets fate (εἱμαρμένη) do what it will with his mortal clay—that is to say, his body.[38]

Among these finally, is the Christian gospel. Paul takes for granted that this is what the gospel promises when he writes to the Galatians:

> Even so we, when we were children, were in bondage under the elements of the world (τὰ στοιχεῖα τοῦ κόσμου). But when

the fulness of time was come, God sent forth his Son . . . to redeem them that were under the law, that we might receive the adoption of sons. . . . But now, after that ye have known God, or rather are known of God, how turn ye again to the weak and beggarly elements, whereunto ye desire again to be in bondage? (Gal. 4.3f., 9).

Christian Gnosticism provides us with the statement:

But both the stars and the powers (οἱ ἀστέρες καὶ αἱ δυνάμεις) are of different kinds: some are beneficent, some maleficent, some right, some left. . . . From this strife and battle of the powers the Lord rescues us and supplies peace from the array of powers and angels, in which some are arrayed for us and others against us.[39]

III

The Mystery Religions

With the oriental cults and the world of thought which went with them, there was also a simultaneous influx of demonology into the West. Of course, the Greeks and Romans had long believed in ghosts and evil spirits, though such things had played only a minor role. Now, however, they acquired a new popularity and influence, being enriched by Oriental motives. In addition to Egyptian and Chaldean influences, others derived from Iranian dualism played a particularly important part. Thus, there was the figure of the devil, at the head of a host of evil spirits, battening on the flesh and smoke of burnt sacrifices, and seeking to creep into men's bodies and bring sickness and all manner of evil. Such ideas not only became popular among the uneducated masses, but, what was more important, were taken up by the Neo-platonists.[40]

Like astrology before it, demonology brought in its train all kinds of practices connected with exorcism and necromancy. Magic also became very popular.[41] There is no need for us to describe these tendencies in detail. They are symptoms of the age, and contributed to the recovery of the sense of the mysteriousness and even hostility of the universe, which reason and science seemed to have gone so far to understand and control. Reason and action—so at least many thought were futile. They could not help man to become master of his fate. Rather, man felt himself to be the victim of elusive, malicious powers which lay in wait for him. Hence he looked for superhuman powers to deliver him. He was ready to listen not only to professional exorcists and magicians, who were able to subdue the spirits and reduce them to servitude, but also to the propaganda of religions which offered supernatural powers and even promised him divinity. These were the so-called mystery religions.

When we speak of mystery religions[42] we mean a series of new cults coming in from the Near East and acquiring a new form in the Graeco-Roman world. Originally tribal religions, they were introduced into the West by slaves, merchants and soldiers, and the natives increasingly joined the congregations thus founded. Thus there arose worshipping communities whose religion was quite distinct from the city state cults, and which represented in essentials a homogeneous type of piety. The most important of these new cults were those which came from Asia Minor and Phrygia, especially the cult of Attis, then the Egyptian cult of Isis and Osiris, and the Syrian religion with its cult of Adonis. Mithraism should also be included among the mystery religions though it differs from the others in that only men were admitted to it. This religion, whose austerity made it alien to the Greek world, is the typical soldier's religion. It does not, like the other mystery religions, offer redemption, but aims at promoting the ethical and military efficiency of its devotees by a process of education.[43] There is no need to go into any further detail about it here.

The mystery religions were originally national or tribal cults. By the time they had become mystery religions they were completely divorced from their native soil. They produced worshipping communities constituted by the voluntary adherence of their devotees. In these communities the class distinctions of the secular world, difference of nationality and race, of economic and social position, were abolished. Free men and slaves, the important and insignificant were all brethren there, and women associated freely with men (except of course, in Mithraism). The community was organized on a hierarchical pattern, the priest or mystagogue being the father of the community.

Thus far the mystery communities form a parallel to the Christian congregation. At the same time, however, there are important differences. In the first place, they were not exclusive. True, their rites and ceremonies were, partly at least, held in secret, a fact which tended to make them secret societies. But membership of a particular community did not prevent its adherents from joining in the official cultus of the city state, or even from seeking initiation in other mysteries. Moreover, the mystery societies were not, like the Jewish or Christian congregations, united in a single Church.

The following features are common to all the mysteries (including, in the first instance, Mithraism as well). Admission to the community was by a rite of initiation, taking the form of a solemn consecration (τελετή). This was, of course, held in secret, which explains why they were called mysteries. The consecrated were joined together by the mystery, which separated them from the unconsecrated, and they were bound by an oath to keep it secret. The actual initiation was preceded by numerous rites of purification. There were fastings, lustrations and baptisms, and occasionally (in Mithraism at least) castigation. After these preliminaries, there followed the delivery (παράδοσις) of the sacred formula (σύνθημα, σύμβολον), culminating in the vision of the deity (ἐπόπτεια), in which the appearance of lights played a part. In this vision union with the deity was attained, the initiate being thus endowed with immortality. In many of the mysteries this union was symbolically effected by sexual intercourse (συνουσία). Other symbolic rites, regarded as possessing sacramental efficacy, are the vesting with the robe of the deity, in which the initiate 'put on' the deity, and sacred banquets which effected or sealed his communion with the deity.[44]

The general sense of the mysteries may be defined as the imparting of 'salvation' (σωτηρία). Hence the deities are called 'saviours' (σωτήρ, e.g. Serapis, or σώτειρα, e.g. Isis). This salvation includes all the blessings it is possible to desire; deliverance from all the perils of life, such as storm and shipwreck, protection from sickness and misfortune. But above all it includes the salvation of the soul and immortality (ἀθανασία, ἀφθαρσία).

As we might expect, the central figure in the cultus is, with the exception of Mithraism, the youthful god who dies and rises again. For these deities were originally vegetation deities which had lost their former associations. The cultic union with them identifies the initiate with their fate. He shares the death of the god and his rising again to immortal life. The mystic utterance preserved by Firmicus Maximus provides a good illustration of this:

> Take courage, ye initiates! As the god was saved,
> So too for us comes salvation from suffering.[45]

Hence also—in many of the mysteries at any rate—the rite in which the initiate dies and rises again from death. This process is also described as rebirth. The initiate is 'born again', 'changed', 'deified', and 'enlightened'. He now possesses the 'medicine of immortality' in his soul.[46] To make things sure, the consecration may be repeated. It is difficult to be sure to what extent a deeper spiritual experience was associated with the consecration. But at least it is clear that, given certain conditions, it could establish a real personal union with the deity. The Isis cult in particular seems to have produced a really living and spiritual type of piety. Isis becomes the sum of all deity, the Queen of Heaven. She is also the Mother goddess, who, like the Christian Madonna in later times, nurses the holy child in her bosom.[47] The initiate's prayer of thanksgiving recorded by Apuleius may serve as an illustration of the devotion to Isis:

> O holy and blessed dame, the perpetual comfort of human kind, who by thy bounty and grace nourishest all the world, and bearest a great affection to the adversities of the miserable as a loving mother, thou takest no rest night or day, neither art thou idle at any time in giving benefits and succouring all men as well on land as sea; thou art she that puttest away all storms and dangers from men's life by stretching forth thy right hand, whereby likewise thou dost unweave even the inextricable and tangled web of fate, and appeasest the great tempests of fortune, and keepest back the harmful course of the stars. The gods supernal do honour thee; the gods infernal have thee in reverence; thou dost make all the earth to turn. Thou givest light to the sun, thou governest the world, thou treadest down the power of hell. By thy mean the stars give answer, the seasons return, the

gods rejoice, the elements serve: at thy commandment the winds
do blow, the clouds nourish the earth, the seeds prosper, and
the fruits do grow. The birds of the air, the beasts of the hill,
the serpents of the den, and the fishes of the sea do tremble at
thy majesty: but my spirit is not able to give thee sufficient
praise, my patrimony is unable to satisfy thy sacrifices; my
voice hath no power to utter that which I think of thy majesty,
no, not if I had a thousand mouths and so many tongues and
were able to continue for ever. Howbeit as a good religious
person, and according to my poor estate, I will do what I may:
I will always keep thy divine appearance in remembrance, and
close the imagination of thy most holy godhead within my
breast.[48]

Clearly, among the mystery religions, especially in those which
hailed from Egypt, there grew up a form of worship and devotion hitherto unparalleled in Graeco-Roman antiquity.[49] They
also provided a fertile soil for a type of mysticism in which the
rites and ceremonies were interpreted as mere outward symbols
of psychical appearances achieved in meditation and ecstasy.[50]

In view of the varieties of religious experience offered, it is
impossible to say that the mystery religions represent any one
type of theology. Those who took part in them did so from
varying motives. It is therefore difficult to discern in them any
one type of philosophy of life. Yet it would be true to say that
the spread of the mystery religions is symptomatic of the change
in the general view of life which had come over the Graeco-
Roman world. They show how uncertain men had become
about their relation to the world in which they lived. It could
no longer give them what they wanted if they were to be really
themselves, if they were to live a life in which they could understand the world and their place in it. The performance of civic
duty offered no real satisfaction, nor, except that a general
attitude of Stoic self-sufficiency was possible, did it help to retreat
to the inner recesses of the spirit, to indulge in intellectual
contemplation of the world and its unity, or to appreciate man's
oneness with the universal Logos. For the average man the only

possible explanation of the universe is in terms of fate. He knows he is the slave of fate. It makes no difference whether he turns to astrology, or if, in a naive and primitive fashion he regards himself as the plaything of chance (Tyche). He knows that he is exposed to the vicissitudes of good and evil. He knows finally, that he is subject to the gloomy prospect of death, and that enemy he can never hope to conquer. If any god can help him, it is not the patron deity of the city state and its constitution, nor even the Logos, the rational law of nature which makes the world a unity and shows the individual his rightful place within it. It must be a deity above the world, on whose caprice or grace he is utterly dependent. He knows he is in the hands of a power beyond his own control. His experience of fate does not suggest that it is a divine power to which he can surrender as a power in whose hands his salvation rests. From this predicament he is delivered by the grace of the deity which comes to him in the mystery.

However, one cannot speak of an explicit dualism as the underlying assumption of the mysteries. For the majority of their devotees clearly do not regard the world in itself as evil, or as the devil's handiwork. Religion here does not mean a thoroughgoing renunciation of the world. The mystery worshippers would fain find their security *in* the world and its blessings. And if the principle function of the mysteries is to enable men to acquire immortality, they are also expected to provide protection and salvation in *this* life. But there is a strong sense that the world is a very untoward place with hostile demonic powers at work in it. The presuppositions for a dualistic interpretation of the world are present here, and the logical conclusion is drawn in mysticism, which grows up out of the mystery religions. Where that conclusion is drawn, we are already in the presence of Gnosticism.

IV

GNOSTICISM

GNOSTICISM[51] IS THE NAME given to a phenomenon which appears in a variety of forms, but always with the same fundamental structure. It first appeared and attracted the attention of scholars as a movement within the Christian religion, and for a long time it was regarded as a purely Christian movement, a perversion of the Christian faith into a speculative theology, the 'acute Hellenization of Christianity'.[52] Further research has, however, made it abundantly clear that it was a really a religious movement of pre-Christian origin, invading the West from the Orient as a competitor of Christianity. Since it appropriated all sorts of mythological and philosophical traditions for its expression, we may call it a synthetic phenomenon.[53] Yet it would be wrong to regard it only as such. All its forms, its mythology and theology, arise from 'a definite attitude to life and an interpretation of human existence derived therefrom'.[54] In general, we may call it a redemptive religion based on dualism. This is what gives it an affinity to Christianity, an affinity of which even its adherents were aware. Consequently, Gnosticism and Christianity have affected each other in a number of different directions from the earliest days of the Christian movement. True, Christianity gradually came to draw a line of demarcation in its struggle against Gnosticism, and although certain features in the Gnostic imagery claimed a rightful place within the Church, other Gnostic ideas were not only ignored, but bitterly resisted.

We shall make no attempt to describe the various Gnostic images which developed on Oriental and Greek soil, both within and outside the Christian movement, or its very scanty literature.[55] Gnostic sects, building up their rites and doctrines under various influences, including, in the Greek world, the philosophical tradition, arose partly in the form of 'baptist' movements in the region of the Jordan.[56] Elsewhere they assumed the form of mystery cults, where, by a process of syncretism, the Gnostic motives took on concrete form in one of the mysteries. Sometimes, for instance, the Gnostic redeemer is identified with the Phrygian Attis. But Gnosticism as a tendency was not confined to the religious sects.[57] It even penetrated to religious philosophical literature of Hellenism, and is also found in Philo, the Jewish philosopher of religion, while it influenced Neo-platonism, despite Plotinus' polemic against it.[58]

The Gnostic myth recounts—with manifold variations—the fate of the soul. It tells of its origin in the world of light, of its tragic fall and its life as an alien on earth, its imprisonment in the body, its deliverance and final ascent and return to the world of light. The soul—or, more accurately in the language of Gnosticism itself, man's true, inner self, is a part, splinter, or spark of a heavenly figure of light, the original man. Before all time this figure was conquered by the demonic powers of darkness, though how that came to pass is a point on which the various mythologies differ. These powers tore the figure of light into shreds and divided it up, and the elements of light thus produced were used by the demons as cohesive magnetic powers which were needed in order to create a world out of the chaos of darkness as a counterpart of the world of light, of which they were jealous. If these elements of light were removed, this artificial world of ours, the cosmos, would return to its primordial state of chaos. Therefore the demons jealously watch over the sparks of light which they stole. Naturally, interest is concentrated on these sparks of light, which are inclosed in man and represent his innermost self. The demons endeavour to stupefy them and make them drunk, sending them to sleep and making them forget their heavenly home. Sometimes their attempt succeeds, but in other cases the consciousness of their heavenly origin remains awake. They know they are in an alien world, and that this world is their prison, and hence their yearning for deliverance. The supreme deity takes pity on the imprisoned sparks of light, and sends down the heavenly figure of light, his Son, to redeem them. This Son arrays himself in the garment of the earthly body, lest the demons should recognize him. He invites his own to join him, awakens them from their sleep, reminds them of their heavenly home, and teaches them about the way to return. His chief task is to pass on the sacred passwords which are needed on the journey back. For the souls must pass the different spheres of the planets, the watch-posts of the demonic cosmic powers. The Gnostic redeemer delivers discourses in which he reveals himself as God's emissary: 'I am the shepherd', 'I am the truth', and so forth. After accomplishing his work, he ascends and returns to heaven again to prepare a way for his own to follow him. This they will do when they die and the spark of light is severed from the prison of the body. His work is to assemble all the sparks of light. That is the work he has inaugurated, and it will be completed when all the sparks of light have been set free and have ascended to heaven to rejoin the one body of the figure of light who in primordial times fell, was imprisoned and torn to shreds. When the process is complete, this world will come to an end and return to its original chaos. The darkness is left to itself, and that is the judgement.[59]

This myth testifies to a definite philosophy of life. It represents a discovery of the radical difference between man and the world in which he lives. Thus it is the exact opposite of the Greek understanding of human nature. It has a sense of the radical otherness of man, of his loneliness in the world. The world, for man, is not only an alien abode, but a prison, a dark, noisome cave. He has been flung into this cave without any fault of his own, and before he was capable of any conscious choice. It is this view of life which the doctrine of the pre-existence of the soul is intended to secure.

> Who flung me into Tibil? (=the earthly world)
> Into Tibil who flung me?
> Who sealed up in the walls,
> Who hurled me into the stocks

Which this world resembles?
Who bound me with this chain,
So intolerable to bear?
Who arrayed me in this robe,
Of many a varied hue and shape?

.   .   .   .

Who has cast me into the abode of darkness?

.   .   .   .

Why have ye snatched me away from my home, and brought
me into this prison, and incarcerated me in this stinking body?

.   .   .   .

How far are the frontiers of this world of darkness?

.   .   .   .

The way we have to go is far and never-ending!

Such lamentations are constantly repeated.[60] In the *Song of the Naassenes* the human Self—here actually called the soul—is depicted as a stag in flight, seeking in vain the way to freedom from earthly fate:

Now she wears the crown and beholds the light,
now she is cast down into the depths of misery;
now she weeps, now she recovers her joy;
now she weeps and laughs at the same time;
now she is judged and passes away in death;
now she is born anew;
and without hope of escape, the hapless, wandering soul
is shut up in a labyrinth of woe.[61]

Man is the lonely victim of a dreadful fear—fear of infinite space and time, fear of the turmoil and hostility of the world, or rather, fear of the demonic powers at work in it, seeking to lead him astray and alienate him from his true self. He is also afraid of himself, for he feels he is in the clutches of the demonic powers. He is no longer his own master, but the playground of the demons. He is estranged from his own spiritual life, the impulses of his desire and will. Gone is the old idea of education, of the development of personality towards an ideal. Physical and sensual life is not matter needing the mind to give it form. Nor is it merely something ἀλλότριον, alien, as the Stoics held, something the wise man can turn his back on and retreat from to his inmost being, his reason, the organ of thought and knowledge.[62] No, it is the enemy of his Self, and even his soul can be his enemy, insofar as it subdues and overpowers him. 'The abyss of the Self conceals within its own darkness the forces which rise up from it and oppose it.'[63] It is impossible to abandon the vital faculties of desire and will and seek refuge in the rational life of the mind. Every step we take is infected with the poison of the demonic. Man's true Self is differentiated not only from the body and its senses, but also from his soul. The anthropology of Gnosticism is therefore trichotomous, It distinguishes body, soul and Self. The designation for the Self may vary. Greek-speaking Gnosticism calls it πνεῦμα, 'spirit', though in a sense which must be distinguished from the classical idea of the spirit. The adjective ψυχικός, 'of or belonging to the soul', thus acquires the pejorative significance which it bears in the New Testament.[64] But it is impossible to state in positive terms what the true self really is. It can be defined only in negative terms. Since it is a pre-existent spark of heavenly light, it is an entity of absolute transcendence. It is as it were the postulate behind all yearning and faith. Gnosticism is incapable of defining transcendence in positive terms. Having abandoned the Greek idea of the spirit (and the conception of transcendence which goes with it), it cannot get rid of the notion that the Self must be placed in the category of substance (as a spark of light), or cease to place the fate of the Self in the category of natural events. A comparison with the Christian understanding of the Self will make this clear. For Christianity abandons not only the Greek conception of the spirit, but also its accompanying doctrine of transcendence. Consequently it is able to do justice to the radical distinction between human personality and its objective environment, while its transcendence is conceived in terms of pure futurity. My real Self is always a future possibility. It is realized ever anew in each successive decision, whether active or receptive.

The Self is no longer an instance of the universal which finds its peace by turning away from the particular and contemplating the universal. Thus man's philosophy of the universe has undergone a complete change since classical times. In Greek Gnosticism, it is true, the outward form of the Greek view of the universe is retained. It is still thought of as a harmonious structure, as unity of law and order. But it is just the cosmos so conceived which undergoes a radical depreciation. Its very law and order are now the source of its terror. This harmony is a prison.[65] The stars, whose brilliant lustre and orderly movement were once contemplated as symbols of the divine nature, now become satanic powers, in whose prisons the sparks of light are bound. The separation between God and the world has become complete. God's transcendence is conceived in radical terms, and therefore eludes all definition.[66] His transcendence is purely negative. He is *not* the world (the world being deprived of all divinity). This view of the world, so typical for the decay of antiquity, is developed to an extreme which will prove of decisive significance for the future. After the decay of the mythological view of the world, the world will now be left in its 'pure, indifferent objectivity', thus offering free scope for a purely secular scientific observation, whereas for the ancient world theology and physics had never been divorced from one another.[67]

If transcendence is simply the negation of everything in this world, how can it have any relevance for human life? What more can it be than a criterion by which to judge this life, or an object of yearning? What about the God who can only be defined as 'Not-world'? How can he be made relevant to real life? How can the true Self, if it be the bare negation of the empirical, psychic Self, get to grips with itself and come into its own? In mythological language, how can the imprisoned spark of light be liberated?

This liberation can only come in the form of redemption.

It must be a redemption which frees man from his prison by freeing him from himself. It is out of the question that man should redeem himself, e.g. by reforming himself or undergoing an inner change. Redemption cannot be conceived as a real event in this world at all. For in this world the only visible events are physical or psychological. Hence redemption must be an absolutely eschatological event, a breach, a dissolution or separation of the real Self from the body and soul. It can only be realized mythologically as the separation of the constituent elements in the human personality which ensues upon death. On leaving the body and soul, the real Self, the pre-existent spark of light, ascends to its home, the heavenly world of light. Both the real Self and its redemption are objects of faith. Such redemption can only be secured by the preaching of a word which comes as a message from the other world, by a message brought by the emissary from the world of light. In the last resort, this is the only way in which the transcendent can become a present experience. It is the only possible way of realizing the other world in this. In mythological language this also means that when the Self becomes aware of its otherworldliness, it is at the same time conscious of its absolute superiority over the world. It interprets the discovery of its true Self as a revelation from the other side. Thus awakened, the Self becomes conscious of its 'calling'.

This faith in the reality of the calling which comes to the individual through the medium of the tradition is thus the true Gnostic existence. It is belief in a message which combines cosmological information with a summons to repentance or a call to awake and detach oneself from this world. It is a faith which at the same time includes the hope of an eschatological deliverance and the ascent of the soul.

'O ye peoples, earth-born men who have abandoned yourselves to drunkenness and sleep and to ignorance of God, be sober, and bring your carousals to an end—ye who are bewitched by unspiritual sleep.' Thus exhorts the prophet, and continues:

Why, ye earth-born men, do ye abandon yourselves to death,
ye who have the power to become partakers of immortality?
Change your minds, ye consorts of illusion and comrades of
ignorance. Free yourselves from the light that is darkness, claim
your share in immortality, and leave corruption behind.

Whither are ye fleeing, O men, ye drunken ones, who have
drunk to the full the wine of ignorance . . .? Stand still, be sober,
look up with the eyes of your hearts. And if all is not possible
to you, at least do what ye can. . . . Seek the Leader, who
guideth you to the gates of knowledge, thither, where the
radiant light shineth, there, where none is drunk, but all are
sober, and in your hearts look upon him who will grant you
the vision of himself. For he cannot be heard or named, nor
seen with the eyes, but only with the mind and the heart.
But first thou must rend the garment that now thou wearest,
the attire of ignorance, the bulwark of evil, the bond of corruption, the dark prison, the living death, the sense-endowed
corpse, the grave thou bearest about with thee, the grave, which
thou carriest around with thee, the thievish companion who
hateth thee in loving thee, and envieth thee in hating thee . . .
that thou mightest not hear what thou must hear, and see what
thou must see.[68]

In practice, the Gnostics were organized as mystery communities. In them the traditional formulae were handed on
which were needed by the Self for its ascent. There were also
sacraments, baptisms and sacred meals, for the purifying and
strengthening of the Self. In the life of the community the
transcendent destiny of the soul was manifested (in a way which
was fundamentally illogical) by ascetic practices (rites of purification). Of course, it is impossible to be sure at this distance
how far in any given case their basic ideas were carried through
to their logical conclusion. Sometimes, no doubt, Gnosticism
was little better than magic, while at other times miracles were
regarded as a proof of mastery over the world. Sometimes this
superiority was displayed in the miraculous odours or radiant
light which exuded from their persons, symptoms which became very important later on in monastic mysticism. In another

direction the same superiority over the world might be shown in a libertinism emancipated from all moral obligations.

The assurances of the Gnostic are typical. In the first place his true self is invisible. It is not the self which is visible to others, or which the painter can portray.[69] No less typical are the statements assuring the Gnostic that this present world has ceased to be of any importance.[70] It is just this which gives rise to libertinism. Once he has attained to liberty, the Gnostic cannot be affected by anything from the outside. Any kind of abstinence is out of the question, and indeed would be meaningless. There is no point in doing any work, no point in trying to make the world a better place, no point in training the soul for bliss. Such activity as there is is purely negative in character: abstinence from certain kinds of food, purifications, giving up sleep, and so forth. Yet even these things, except in so far as they spring from primitive fears of defilement, are only meant as exhibitions of the pneumatic's detachment from the world. Such Gnostic virtues (ἀρεταί) as there are have ceased to be capabilities for an ἔργον; they are simply ascetic or cathartic modes of behaviour.

The Gnostic feels himself to belong not to the nation or the city state, or even the world. He is no cosmopolitan. True, the unity of the human race is taken for granted. All men are fundamentally endowed with the divine spark. The preaching of conversion is directed to all. Yet in practice, mankind is divided into two classes, the pneumatic and the 'hylic' (sometimes we find a middle class, the 'psychic'), according as to whether they have the pneuma or spark of light alive in them or not, or whether they do not have it at all. The fellowship realized among the pneumatics is not like that of a natural, human or political society. It is based exclusively on a common detachment from the world. All earthly distinctions and all earthly ties are disregarded. Fundamentally, there is an invisible community which can only be seen by faith. Social life is not encouraged, as in any earthly society. The aim is simply to help men to achieve otherworldliness or redemption.

Despite this, however, in the last resort the Gnostic has no real need for cultus or community. It is significant that Gnosticism tends to produce an individualistic type of mysticism, in which the redemption, the ascent of the Self, is anticipated in meditation and ecstasy.[71] Gnosis, which in its initial stages stood for the knowledge of man's predicament, ends with the vision of God. The purpose of all spiritual endeavour is to achieve the experience of the true Self, and that can be defined only in negative terms. This is illogical and contradictory, for all experience must take place in this world.

There is a hymn of thanksgiving which provides a good illustration of Gnostic spirituality:

I was delivered from my bonds,
   and am escaped to thee, my God.
For thou didst stand by to champion my cause,
   didst redeem me and succour me.
Thou didst keep back mine adversaries
   that they showed their faces no more.
For thy Person was with me,
   and It saved me in thy grace.
I was despised and rejected of many
   and was in their eyes as base metal.

But I received strength and succour from thee.
Thou didst set lights on my right and my left,
   that there might be no darkness round about me.
I was bedecked with the covering of thy Spirit
   and stripped off the garments of hide.
For thy right hand hath exalted me,
   thou hast removed sickness from me.

I became whole in thy truth
   and holy in thy righteousness.
All mine adversaries yielded before my face;
   I became the Lord's in the name of the Lord.
I was justified by his loving kindness,
   and his peace endureth for ever and ever. Amen.[72]

PRIMITIVE CHRISTIANITY

I

PRIMITIVE CHRISTIANITY AS A SYNCRETISTIC PHENOMENON

PRIMITIVE CHRISTIANITY AROSE from the band of Jesus' disciples, who, after their Master had been put to death by Pontius Pilate on the Cross, had seen him as one risen from the dead. Their belief that God had raised him from the dead gave them at the same time the assurance that Jesus had been exalted to heavenly glory and raised to the dignity of the 'Man' who would very shortly come on the clouds of heaven to set up the Reign of God. The growing company of those who awaited his coming was conscious of itself as the Church of the last age, as the community of the 'saints' and 'elect', as the true people of God, for whom the promises were now being fulfilled, as the goal and end of the redemptive history of Israel.

The eschatological community did not split off from Judaism as though it were conscious of itself as a new religious society. In the eyes of their contemporaries they must have looked like a Jewish sect, and for the historian they appear in that light too. For the resources they possessed—their traditions about Jesus, which were carefully preserved, and the latent resources of their own faith, led only gradually to a new form of organization and new philosophy of human life, the world and history.

The decisive step was taken when the good news of Jesus, crucified and risen, the coming Judge and agent of redemption, was carried beyond the confines of Palestinian Judaism, and Christian congregations sprang up in the Graeco-Roman world. These congregations consisted partly of Hellenistic Jewish Christians, partly of Gentiles, wherever the Christian mission sought its point of contact in the Hellenistic synagogues. For here, without going farther afield, it was possible to reach many of the Gentiles, who had joined the Jewish community, sometimes closely, sometimes more loosely. On other occasions the Christian missionaries went direct to the Gentile population, and then, in the first instance, to the lower classes in the cities. There were probably churches of Gentiles only, but few, if any, of the churches could have been purely Jewish. In any case Christianity found itself in a new spiritual environment: The Gospel had to be preached in terms intelligible to Hellenistic audiences and their mental outlook, while at the same time the audience themselves were bound to interpret the gospel message in their own way, in the light of their own spiritual needs. Hence the growth of divers types of Christianity.

By and large, the chief difference between Hellenistic Christianity and the original Palestinian version was that the former ceased to be dominated by the eschatological expectation and the philosophy of life which that implied. Instead, there was developed a new pattern of piety centred in the cultus. The Hellenistic Christians, it is true, continued to expect an imminent end of the world, the coming of the Judge and Saviour from heaven and the resurrection of the dead and the last judgement. But there were also Christians who became sceptical of the primitive Jewish Christian eschatology and rejected it. Indeed, some tried to get rid of it altogether. Above all, the Gentile Christians found the idea of a redemptive history foreign to them, and as a result they lost the sense of belonging to the community of the last days. They could no longer feel that they were standing at the culmination of redemptive history directed by the providence of God. This was the case wherever the tradition of the Synagogue and Christian catechetical instruction had failed to implant the idea of redemptive history. The speedy disappearance of the apocalyptic title 'Man' is symptomatic; even Paul himself refrains from using it. It was no longer understood that 'Christos' was a translation of 'Messiah', and meant that Jesus was the Lord of the age of redemption: the title simply became a proper name. Other titles took its place, such as 'Son of God' and 'Saviour', titles which were already current in the Gentile world to designate agents of redemption. It was however the title 'Kyrios' which became the most popular designation of Jesus. It characterizes him as the cult deity who works supernaturally in the worship of the Church as a cultic body. Hellenistic pneumatology, with ecstasy and speaking with tongues, find their way into the churches. The Kyrios Jesus Christos is conceived as a mystery deity, in whose death and Resurrection the faithful participate through the sacraments. Parallel with this sacramental cultus piety we very soon find Gnostic ideas of wisdom affecting the churches. Ideas originating from the Gnostic redemption myths are used to describe the person and work of Jesus Christ and the nature of the Church, and, accompanying these, ascetic and even libertinist tendencies.

At the same time, however, the Hellenistic Christians received the gospel tradition of the Palestinian churches. Admittedly, the importance attached to this tradition varied from place to place. Paul himself seldom refers to it. Yet almost everywhere the Old Testament asserts itself, being accepted as canonical scripture by all except extreme gnosticizing circles. This adoption of the Old Testament followed as a matter of course in those congregations which grew out of the Synagogue. The latter was also the medium by which Hellenistic Christianity adopted conceptions emanating from philosophical enlightenment, conceptions which the Synagogue itself had assimilated at an earlier stage. Christian missionary preaching was not only the proclamation of Christ, but, when addressed to a Gentile audience, a preaching of monotheism as well. For this, not only arguments derived from the Old Testament, but the natural theology of Stoicism was pressed into service. Quite early on the Christian churches adopted a system of morality, with its pattern of catechetical instruction derived in equal proportions from the Old Testament Jewish tradition and from the ethics of popular philosophical pedagogic, shortly to be enriched by the moral ideals of the Hellenistic bourgeoisie.

Thus Hellenistic Christianity is no unitary phenomenon, but, taken by and large, a remarkable product of syncretism.[1] It is full of tendencies and contradictions, some of which were to be condemned later on by orthodox Christianity as heretical.[2] Hence also the struggles between the various tendencies, of which the Pauline Epistles give such a vivid impression.

Yes, at first sight we are bound to agree that Hellenistic Christianity is the outcome of syncretism. The world is the creation of God, who cares for the birds and decks the grass of the field with its beauty (Matt. 6.26, 30). Yet at the same time it is the realm of Satan, the 'god of this world' (II Cor. 4.4), the 'prince of this world' (John 12.31). The earth is the Lord's and all the fulness thereof (I Cor. 10.26). Yet creation is subject to vanity and corruption ($\mu\alpha\tau\alpha\iota\acute{o}\tau\eta\varsigma$ and $\phi\theta o\rho\acute{a}$), yearning for the day of its deliverance (Rom. 8.19-22). The terms in which this deliverance is conceived are derived partly, and indeed mainly, from the Jewish tradition. The old age is already coming to an end, and the new age is about to dawn soon with the coming of the 'Man', the resurrection of the dead and the judgement. But side by side with these conceptions we get the eschatology of the Fourth Gospel, which uses not the Jewish dualism of the two ages but the Gnostic dualism of the two realms of light and darkness, truth and falsehood, above and below, and which asserts that the judgement and resurrection have already been realized, or at least have been inaugurated because 'the light is come into the world' (John 3.19).[3] Now that Jesus has come, those who believe in him have already passed from death unto life (John 5.24f.). The person of Jesus is sometimes defined in terms of Jewish and apocalyptic categories, sometimes as the 'Lord' of the cultus, as a mystery deity, sometimes again as the Gnostic redeemer, the pre-existent being from the heavenly world, whose earthly body is only an outward garb. This explains why the 'rulers of this world' failed to recognize him, as only 'his own' can. The Christian community is sometimes described in Old Testament categories as the people of God, the true seed of Abraham, sometimes in Gnostic categories as the 'body of Christ', in which individuals are incorporated by means of the sacraments of baptism and the Lord's Supper.[4] Of course, some of these concepts are confined to particular writings or groups of writings in the New Testament (which varies a great deal in its language and thought). But they are also to be found side by side or in combination in the same author, especially in Paul and the Epistle to the Hebrews.

Is Christianity then really a syncretistic religion? Or is there a fundamental unity behind all this diversity? A comparison of primitive Christianity with the various traditions and religious movements in which it was cradled and which influenced its growth should help us to answer this question. Does primitive Christianity contain a single, new and unique doctrine of human existence? The comparison may best be conducted by selecting certain main subjects as test cases. In doing this, we shall rely chiefly on the Pauline and Johannine writings, because they provide the clearest evidence for the Christian attitude to existence.

II

MAN AND HIS RELATION TO TIME

IT IS CLEAR that the early Christian doctrine of man is diametrically opposed to that which prevailed in the Greek tradition. Man is not regarded as an instance of universal human Being, which in its turn is seen to be an instance of cosmic Being in general. There is no attempt to escape from the questionableness of man's own individuality by concentrating on the universal law or the cosmic harmony. Like Gnosticism, primitive Christianity was totally uninterested in education or training. It had no use for the Greek dualistic anthropology, with its tension between spirit and sensuality, or the view of life which that implied, viz. the realization of the ideal of the 'gentleman' as a 'work of art'. Man's essential Being is not Logos, reason or spirit. If we ask primitive Christianity where the essential Being of man resides, there can only be one answer: in the *will*. To be a man or to live a human life, means to strive for something, to aspire after something, to will.

Of course, the Greeks and the New Testament are equally aware that man's will can lead him into disaster. But in the Greek view this is due to the failure of reason to control the will. All that is necessary is to train the reason, and then the will should automatically obey it. It is assumed that the will itself always wills what is the good, the best for man. Reason perceives what is best, communicates its insight to the will, and the will automatically obeys its promptings. Such was the teaching of the Stoics, loyal as they were to the Socratic and Platonic tradition.[5]

Such reflection is alien to the New Testament. Not that it was ignorant of the Logos or reason as the organ of the knowledge of good and evil. The category of conscience was taken over from Hellenism, and is employed by some of the New Testament writers, especially Paul, who believes that reason enables man to distinguish between good and evil (Rom. 2.14f.; Phil. 4.8). But in saying this, we have by no means indicated how radical is the New Testament doctrine of man, and explicit reflection on the origin of the knowledge of good and evil is far beyond the range of primitive Christianity.

But the chief point is that the New Testament does not regard the will of man in purely formal terms. It does not automatically aspire to the Good. It is not a clean slate, whose character of good or evil is acquired by the ideas which direct it, ideas which may be right or wrong, and just because of that require the direction of the reason. Rather, the will is regarded as good or evil in itself. It is from the 'heart', i.e. the will, that good or evil deeds proceed (Luke 6.43-5, etc.). And here we may for the moment leave open the question whether there can actually be such a thing as a good 'heart'. However that may be, man is not lord of his will in such a way that the Logos or reason enables him to transcend his will and direct it according to rational thinking. No, a man and his will are identical. If his will is in bondage to evil, which is what the New Testament always assumes, the whole man is in bondage to evil. He cannot therefore dissociate himself from his will, or summon it back from evil. In Romans 7.15-25 Paul unfolds the contradiction between what a man wills and what he actually does—'what I would, that I do not; but what I hate, that do I'. Here the will which wills the 'good' is not man's empirical will, but the basic impulse which lies behind all actual acts of will, the desire for life as something that is good. If this basic impulse is incapable of realization, it means that the empirical will cannot will what it really wills. Consequently education or training of the will is useless. What is needed is to bring home to the will its utter impotence; so that it can cry: 'O wretched man that I am! who shall deliver me from the body of this death?'

Apart from this assertion of the utter impotence of the will, the New Testament doctrine of man keeps close to that of the Old Testament. Here too the nature or essence of man is not his reason. There is nothing like the Greek anthropology with its dualism of spirit and sensuality, or its ideas on education. Here again the knowledge of good and evil is not conceived along rationalistic lines. The New Testament follows this tradition. It is also diametrically opposed to the Greek view on a further point. Evil is not a merely negative thing, a defect which will be put right later. It is something positive, disobedience against God, rebellion, 'sin'. This results in a different conception of becoming free from evil. For the Greek mind the way lay in education and instruction. Evil was simply a survival from an earlier stage of development. Teach man about the Good,[6] inculcate the ideal of nobility, and it will mould his character. By striving after the ideal, he approximates ever more closely to what he already is in the light of the ideal. The rule is: 'become what you are.'

Now all this implies a view of man's relation to time which is in striking contrast to that of the Old and New Testaments. The Bible knows nothing of the development of man, in which evil is left behind as a survival from an earlier stage. Rather, it insists that a man is always what his past has made him. He always brings his past along with him into his present. He can never make a fresh start with a clean sheet. He has no real future in the sense of something entirely new. Since evil is sin, it throws man's relation with God entirely out of gear, just as the relations between man and man are thrown out of gear by the wrongs they do to one another. Just as when one man has wronged another the only way out is for him to own up to it and receive forgiveness, so it is with man's relation to God. Only confession and forgiveness can make him a new man and give him a fresh start. This does not mean that he becomes morally better. In the language of the Old and New Testaments he is now 'righteous', 'justified'. That is to say, God has pronounced him free.[7]

Thus far the New Testament agrees with the Jewish tradition. But it goes further in asserting the impotence of the human will. Man is in radical bondage to evil and cannot will the good. This is not just ordinary pessimism about human nature. There are plenty of examples of this in Greek literature, and still more in the Old Testament. Indeed, Judaism can offer parallels to Paul's theory of the fall of Adam as the cause of sin and death entering the world and bringing men into bondage.[8] But Judaism never supposes that man is totally incapable of good works. On the whole, the best he can hope for, it is true, is to hold the balance, to compensate for his transgressions by fulfilling the law. But since no man does only what is good, every man needs God's forgiveness, although to some extent he can make amends for his transgressions by 'good works', which are not demanded by the law and are therefore supererogatory.[9] Paul thinks otherwise. In his very attempt to obtain righteousness from God through his works, the original sin of man is latent. It shows that what man really is after is something to boast about before God. He imagines he can live in his own strength and earn his acceptance with God. This is simply the Jewish form of a tendency inherent in all men. The Greek form of it is boasting of one's wisdom. This hankering after something to boast about is the root of all other evils. It is sin, rebellion against God. Man is simply blind to the fact that he can only live by the grace of God. 'What hast thou that thou didst not receive? now if thou didst receive it, why dost thou glory, as if thou hadst not received it?' (I Cor. 4.7). This is just what man must own up to. He must make an absolute surrender to the grace of God. That is what is meant by 'believing'. And that is the stumbling-block for natural man, with his hankering after recognition. That is what makes the gospel message for him a scandal and foolishness (σκάνδαλον and μωρία) (I Cor. 1.23). It is a scandal because it is the message of the Cross. For by causing Christ crucified to be proclaimed as Lord, God crushes human pride. That is why Paul refuses to boast any more 'save in the cross of our Lord Jesus Christ, by whom the world is crucified unto me, and I unto the world' (Gal. 6.14).

Here the Old Testament view of man as a being open to the future reaches its logical conclusion. This is achieved by means of a paradox. While humanity is essentially openness for the future, the fact is that man bars his own way to the future by wanting to live unto himself. He boasts in what he has, in what he is, in what he has made out of himself, in what he can control, in what he takes to be a ground for pride, in what he imagines he can offer to God. When he boasts he lays hold upon what he already has and is—upon his past. But to renounce such boasting, to surrender all his gain and count it but loss, indeed as 'dung' (Phil. 3.7f.), to surrender unreservedly to the grace of God, to believe—all this is simply radical openness for the future. It is to realize that we are always in via, that we have never reached the end:

> Not as though I had already attained, either were already perfect: but I follow after, if that I may apprehend that for which also I am apprehended of Christ Jesus. . . . I count not myself to have apprehended: but this one thing I do, forgetting those things which are behind, and reaching forth unto those things which are before, I press toward the mark . . . (Phil. 3.12f.).

This radical openness for the future in absolute surrender to the grace of God is prepared to accept all encounters as tokens of his grace. Incidentally, this provides the answer to the problem of suffering. We may, it is true, still find in the New Testament, including the Pauline writings, the Jewish belief in transcendent glory as the compensation for suffering in this world (e.g. Rom. 8.18; II Cor. 4.17f.); but for Paul such a belief has lost its motive power. The real reason why Paul triumphs over suffering is that he who has died with Jesus has the grace of God alive in him as the resurrection life of Christ. 'For though he was crucified in weakness, yet he liveth by the power of God. For we also are weak in him, but we shall live with him by the power of God toward you' (II Cor. 13.4). Thus Paul is constantly offering himself 'for Jesus' sake' to death, that the life of Jesus might be made manifest in his mortal flesh (II Cor. 4.11). 'For which cause we faint not; but though our outward man perish, yet the inward man is renewed day by day' (II Cor.

4.16). Suffering is thus converted into a blessing, and once he realizes this man becomes free from the world, from all that is transitory and belongs to the past, and becomes open to the transcendent future. When Paul prays that God may deliver him from his bodily sufferings, the answer he receives is not the consoling promise of bliss in heaven as a compensation. Instead, he hears the Lord saying to him: 'My grace is sufficient for thee: for my strength is made perfect in weakness', to which he replies: 'Most gladly therefore will I rather glory in my infirmities, that the power of Christ may rest upon me. Therefore I take pleasure in infirmities, in reproaches, in necessities, in persecutions, in distresses, for Christ's sake; for when I am weak, then am I strong' (II Cor. 12.9f.).

This radical openness for the future is the Christian's freedom. Such a conception of freedom seems to bring Paul very close to Stoicism. Indeed, the very fact that he defines genuine human existence in terms of freedom, a concept unknown to the Old Testament and Judaism, is itself sufficient to suggest an affinity between Paul and the Stoics, to say nothing of the actual vocabulary he uses. The Stoic wise man is, like Paul, free from all external necessities and claims from the outside world, its conventions, judgements and values.[10] Epictetus speaks just as triumphantly about his victories over fate, distress and death as Paul himself.[11] And when Paul says, 'All things are lawful to me', the Stoic can heartily agree, even when he adds the reservation: 'but I will not be brought under the power of any' (I Cor. 6.12: πάντα μοι ἔξεστιν, ἀλλ' οὐκ ἐγὼ ἐξουσιασθήσομαι ὑπό τινος). And when Paul says, 'Be not ye the servants of men' (I Cor. 7.23)—that is to say, 'Do not make yourselves dependent on the value judgements of men'—that is perfectly good Stoicism. So is the Pauline paradox, that the slave is a free man (for the Stoics, through wisdom, for Paul, through Christ), although when Paul goes on to say that the free man, since he is 'called', i.e. a Christian, is a slave, viz. of Christ, they begin to part company. The Stoic would say that if the free man is a slave he is a fool. Yet even this could be translated into Pauline terms without much difficulty by saying that the free man who is not called is a slave, viz. of sin (I Cor. 7.22f.). Like Paul, the Stoic could say: 'I know both how to be abased, and I know how to abound: every where and in all things I am instructed both to be full and to be hungry, both to abound and to suffer need.' But he would not continue: 'I can do all things through Christ who strengtheneth me' (Phil. 4.12f.). This is just where the difference lies. The Stoic is free because of his reason. He concentrates on reason by turning his back on all encounters and claims from the outside world. This makes him free *from* the future. He is enabled to escape from the toils of life in time.[12] Paul, on the other hand, is free because he has been made free by the grace of God, and has surrendered freely to his grace. He has been freed from all the claims which seek to bind him to all reality, present, transitory and already past. He has become free *for* the future, for encounters in which he will experience God's grace ever anew as a gift from outside. The Stoic shuts the door to all encounters and lives in the timeless Logos. The Christian opens himself to these encounters, and lives from the future.

The understanding of Christian existence as a life in which God is always One who comes, and as a life which is always a future possibility is, of course, not always fully explicit in the New Testament in all its ramifications. In fact, there was at the outset a serious obstacle to its full realization. That obstacle was the eschatology which the early Church took over from Judaism, with its expectation of an imminent end of the world, and the ushering in of ultimate salvation by a cosmic catastrophe. Only the author of the Fourth Gospel has emancipated himself from this eschatology. But when Paul says that faith, hope and love 'abide', even when 'that which is perfect' ($\tau\grave{o}$ $\tau\acute{\epsilon}\lambda\epsilon\iota o\nu$) is come (I Cor. 13.13), he is bringing an important truth to light. This is that if real life means being open to the future, it can never be regarded as a definitive state of bliss. Faith and hope are the dispositions of those who are always looking for the grace of God as a future possibility.

In another respect, however, the early Christians were quite clear about the implications of freedom. With their sense of being the eschatological people of God, of standing at the end of redemptive history, they no longer identified the redemptive history with the empirical history of Israel. It is, of course, true that the New Testament sometimes uses the history of Israel as a type for admonition or exhortation (e.g. I Cor. 10.1-11; Heb. 3.7-19). The saints of the Old Testament may be regarded as pioneers and examples for the Christians, like Abraham and the heroes of faith enumerated in Hebrews 11. But the history of Israel is no longer their own history. They ceased, for instance, to regard the Jewish festivals as re-enactments 'for us' of the events of the past. When he speaks of the foundation of the Church, Paul no longer points to the exodus from Egypt. The event by which the Church is constituted is the death of Christ. But unlike the giving of the law on Mount Sinai, the death of Christ is not an event in the history of the nation. The sacraments of baptism and the Lord's Supper do not cement the Christians into a nation, but into an eschatological community, which, since it is eschatological, transcends the limits of nationality. The wine of the Lord's Supper is the blood of the 'new covenant' promised by the prophet Jeremiah in the age to come.[13] This idea of an eschatological covenant—that is to say, a covenant which is removed from empirical history, and removes men from it—is now treated seriously. Of course the Christian community is the 'people of God', the 'seed of Abraham', but not as the 'children of the flesh', but as the 'children of promise' (Rom. 9.8; Gal. 3.29). The Old Testament is still the word of God, though not because it contains his word spoken to Israel in the past, but because it is directly typological and allegorical. The original meaning and context of the Old Testament sayings are entirely irrelevant. God does not speak to men through history[14] but through Christ, who is the end of history, and through the word which proclaims him. In the light of this the Old Testament begins to speak with a new meaning.

But this means that God's grace is not an historical pheno-menon. It is not the possession of an historical nation, member-ship of which guarantees the security of the individual. If it were that, trust in grace would be trust in the 'flesh'. That is why Paul counted all that had once been his pride to be but loss (Phil. 3.4-8). In the Christian Church there is neither male nor female, for all are 'one in Christ Jesus' (Gal. 4.28; I Cor. 12.13; Col. 3.11). This also means that man becomes absolutely alone before God. Of course, in belonging to Christ he is a member of his body, and is therefore bound to the other members in the unity of the Church. But before God he stands, in the first place at any rate, in utter loneliness, extricated from his natural ties. The fundamental question which is asked of man, 'Are you ready to believe in the word of God's grace?' can only be answered individually. This individualizing of man's relation to God has its roots in the psalms and Wisdom literature, and above all in Jeremiah. But its full implications were never realized until the time of Paul with his radical conception of the grace of God.

III

THE SITUATION OF MAN IN THE WORLD

FREEDOM FROM THE PAST, openness for the future—that is the essence of human existence. But it is the conviction of the New Testament that man needs first to be restored to his true nature through the event of redemption accomplished in Christ. Until this event has taken place, until man has appropriated the grace of God manifested in that event, he is alienated from his own true nature, alienated from life, enslaved under hostile powers and in bondage to death.

The situation of natural man in the world appears to Christian eyes very much as it does to Gnosticism. In fact, Christianity may employ Gnostic ideas and terminology to describe it. Impotence and fear mark the life of pre-Christian man. When he assures the Roman Christians, 'Ye have not received the spirit of bondage again to fear; but ye have received the Spirit of adoption', Paul is taking for granted that the Romans, as Gentiles, had lived in the bondage of fear. The same idea of man's enslavement is presumed by the Jesus of the Fourth Gospel, when he says: 'If ye continue in my word, then are ye disciples indeed; And ye shall know the truth, and the truth shall make you free' (John 8.31f.), though his audience cannot make head or tail of what he is saying, as the ensuing dialogue shows. For this is the worst feature of man's plight. He is totally unconscious of his enslavement. He has not the least notion what he is doing when he strives to attain life by himself, by his own efforts. The Jew imagines he can do this by his observance of the law. But his zeal in the service of God is futile: it only leads him into death (Rom. 7.14-24, 10.2). When the law is read in the synagogue, there is a veil over their hearts. They are hardened in thought and action, just as the 'god of this world' has blinded the thought and action of those who do not believe (II Cor. 3.14, 4.4). Thus the constant misunderstandings to which the sayings of Jesus are exposed in the Fourth Gospel show that men are in darkness and love the darkness rather than the light (John 3.19).

The powers under which man is enslaved are, as in Gnosticism, the cosmic powers. They are the elements of the world, the astral spirits (τὰ στοιχεῖα τοῦ κόσμου, Gal. 4.3, 9), the 'dominions, principalities and powers' (Rom. 8.38; Col. 1.16, etc.). They are the 'rulers of this world' or even the 'god of this world' or the 'prince of this world' (I Cor. 2.6; II Cor. 4.4; John 12.31, etc.). All these terms are mythological, and are derived from Gnosticism. There is no reason to doubt that the early Christians regarded these powers as real demonic beings. Paul is using mythological concepts derived from Gnosticism when he states that the Old Testament law does not come from God, but was given by angelic powers. If the Gentile Christians adopt the Jewish law, they will be turning again to the 'weak and beggarly elements' (Gal. 3.19f., 4.9). He is equally using the language of mythology when he says that the 'rulers' (ἄρχοντες), deceived by the secret wisdom of God, crucified Christ, the 'Lord of glory', because they did not know him. This was because he was disguised in the form of a servant (I Cor. 2.9; Phil. 2.6ff.).

Primitive Christianity never adopted the Gnostic doctrine of the pre-existence of the soul.[15] Paul did indeed make use of the Gnostic myth of the archetypal Man in order to make man's situation in the world intelligible. The fall of the archetypal man (which Paul naturally identifies with the fall of Adam as related in Genesis 3) has determined the fate of all men since. Adam brought sin and death into the world, and until Christ their sway has been unquestioned (Rom. 5.12ff.). Paul is drawing even more heavily on Gnostic mythology when he attributes the burden of man's sinful past to the nature of Adam:

> The first man is of the earth, earthy: the second man is the Lord from heaven. As is the earthy, such are they also that are earthy: and as is the heavenly, such are they also that are heavenly. And as we have borne the image of the earthy, we shall also bear the image of the heavenly (I Cor. 15.47f.).

And in describing the nature of Adam as 'psychic' and that of Christ as 'pneumatic' (I Cor. 15.44-6) he is again using the language of Gnosticism. Neither classical Greek nor the language of the Old Testament furnishes any precedent for the pejorative sense in which the adjective 'psychic' is used here.[16] Like the Gnostics, Paul distinguishes between 'psychic' and 'pneumatic', the latter meaning those who have 'gnosis', which enables them to fathom the 'deep things of God' (I Cor. 2.10-16).

In this conception of man's situation in the world as a bondage to the hostile cosmic powers, as a fate brought upon him by the fall of the archetypal man, there is a close affinity between Christianity and Gnosticism. But there is also a crucial difference. Both systems agree that empirical man is not what he ought to be. He is deprived of authentic life, true existence. Nor can he ever achieve that existence by his own strength. But according to the Gnostics, this is due to fate or destiny, whereas for primitive Christianity it is due not only to fate, but to man's guilt as well. This is at once apparent from the way Christianity dropped the doctrine of the pre-existence of the soul. It is further apparent in the refusal to abandon the Old Testament doctrine of creation (or the identity of the Creator and Redeemer) and of man's responsibility before God. Now it is true that the exact connexion between fate and guilt is never submitted in the New Testament to theological analysis. Man's enslavement to the cosmic powers and his personal responsibility, his impotence and his guilt are allowed to stand side by side without any attempt to reconcile them. In Romans 5.12ff. sin and death are attributed to the fall of Adam. They are a malignant destiny which has come upon man. In Romans 1.18ff., on the other hand, mankind incurred guilt and continues to incur it by its refusal to perceive God in the works of his creation. Romans 2.1ff. takes it for granted that man is responsible for his plight, for it speaks of judgement hanging as a threat over him—over Gentile as well as Jew. Indeed, Paul feels obliged to give an explicit proof of the responsibility of the Gentiles: although they did not have the Mosaic law, they had the conscience, and the conscience taught them the law of God (Rom. 2.14f.).

The solution of this contradiction is that man's guilt has become his fate. It is essential to see how Paul (and John likewise) conceives the way in which these cosmic powers in actual practice work in the historical existence of man. They make themselves felt in practice as the powers of the flesh, the law, sin and death.

By 'flesh' Paul means in the first instance the whole realm of concrete, tangible reality. It denotes not merely the sphere of the material or sensual, but equally life under the law, with its tangible achievements in keeping the letter of the commandment. This whole realm becomes a demonic power when man makes himself dependent upon it and lives 'after the flesh'. This may take the form of frivolity and licentiousness (Gal. 5.19ff.), which are thought to offer true life. Or it can be quite serious—scrupulous observance of the law (Gal. 3.3; Phil. 3.6), which again is thought to offer true life. In either case the thing man supposes he can control, whether it be pleasure or serious moral effort, becomes a power which controls him and drags him into the clutches of death. For by supposing that he can attain life from transitory things he makes himself dependent upon them, thus becoming himself a victim of transitory reality. Thus sin results in death, for sin is just this attempt of man to attain life through his own efforts. Sin does not, however, become explicit until man is confronted by the law. This awakens man's desire. This may happen either by his transgressing the law through his lustful impulses, or by his misusing the law in order to be able to 'boast' before God[17]—that is to say, in order to attain life by his own strength (Rom. 5.20, 7.7-11). Thus the law, which is intrinsically holy, righteous and good, and comes from God, becomes a lethal power. That is why at times Paul can speak of it in quite a Gnostic way.[18] Thus the rule is: 'The sting of death is sin, and the strength of sin is the law' (I Cor. 15.56). Once man has set out on this road, there is no turning back. He does not know what he is doing. While fondly supposing he is attaining life, he is on the road to death.

Flesh, law, sin and death have become ineluctable powers. Man's guilt has become his fate.

The same truth is expressed in the dominant sense in which the term 'world' is used in the New Testament, often in a typically depreciating manner called 'this world'. Of course, the world, as in the Old Testament and in Judaism, is the creation of God. Yet at the same time it is an alien place for man. Only Christians, it is true, know that they are 'strangers and pilgrims' (I Pet. 2.11; cf. 1.1, 17), that their 'citizenship' is in heaven (Phil. 3.20), that here they have 'no continuing city, but seek one to come' (Heb. 13.14). But they are only realizing what is true of all men. That is what the gospel summons men to realize. It bids them awaken out of sleep, to stop being 'drunk' and to become sober, just as in the preaching of the Gnostics. For this world lies under the thrall of the 'rulers' (ἄρχοντες). Its god is Satan. Hence 'the whole world lieth in the evil one' (I John 5.19). Further, hence, 'the world passeth away, and the lust thereof' (I John 2.17; I Cor. 7.31). The world, like the law, drags the man who has surrendered to it into the clutches of death. It, too, is a demonic power, embodied in Satan, who inspires the world with a spirit opposing the Spirit of God (I Cor. 2.12). Yet the world is not a mythical entity; in the last resort it is an historical one. This is shown by the way in which the world is generally an all-inclusive term for the environment in which men live, and is sometimes used in an even more restricted sense, meaning human society, with its aspirations and judgements, its wisdom, its joys and its sufferings. Thus every man makes his contribution to the 'world'. It is the world in just this sense which becomes a power tyrannizing over the individual, the fate he has created for himself. There is therefore no ultimate cosmological dualism such, as we find in the Gnostics. This is proved by the way in which, for those who have been freed by Christ, the world recovers its character as creation, although even now it is not their home: 'The earth is the Lord's, and the fulness thereof.' 'Every creature of God is good, and nothing to be refused, if it be received with thanksgiving.' Thus the Christian is lord of the world (I Cor. 10.26; I Tim. 4.4; cf. Tit. 1.15; Rom. 14.14, 20; I Cor. 3.21f.).

Finally both the affinity between Christianity and Gnosticism and the difference between them are illustrated by the Christian conception of God's transcendence. In both systems that transcendence is conceived radically. There is nothing to suggest the classical view that God is immanent in the world, no suggestion that the orderly, law-abiding process of nature and course of history are proofs of the divine immanence. The New Testament knows nothing of the Stoic conception of providence. There is a great gulf between God and the world. The world is the 'lower region'; the place of darkness. God is 'above'. He is the light and the truth. 'No man hath seen God at any time' (John 1.18), He 'dwelleth in the light which no man can approach unto' (I Tim. 6.16). The admonition 'Love not the world, neither the things that are in the world' is justified by the assertion that 'all that is in the world . . . is not of the Father, but is of the world' (I John 2.15f.). The Christian receives the Spirit of truth, whom the world cannot receive, because it does not see him or know him (John 14.17).

But this transcendence is not conceived ontologically as in Gnosticism. The gulf between God and man is not metaphysical. Light and darkness are not cosmic forces of a material kind. Nor is the transcendence of God confined to the pure negativity of the 'not worldly'. In the first place, it is his glorious sovereignty, which refuses to tolerate the pride of man or his forgetfulness of his creaturely status. 'God resisteth the proud, but giveth grace to the humble' (Jas. 4.6; I Pet. 5.5, after Prov. 3.34). All human planning must be qualified by the proviso, 'If the Lord will, and we live' (Jas. 4.13-15). God treats man as a potter treats his clay: he has mercy on whom he will, and whom he will he hardens (Rom. 9.18, 20f.). It is 'a fearful thing to fall into the hands of the living God' (Heb. 10.31).

> Let no man deceive himself. If any man among you seemeth to be wise in this world, let him become a fool, that he may be

wise. For the wisdom of this world is foolishness with God. For it is written, He taketh the wise in their own craftiness. And again, The Lord knoweth the thoughts of the wise, that they are vain (I Cor. 3.18-20).

No flesh may glory before God: 'He that glorieth, let him glory in the Lord' (I Cor. 1.29, 31; II Cor. 10.17).

Up to this point we are still moving within the orbit of the Old Testament tradition. But at this point it acquires an entirely new sense through the New Testament recognition that God, precisely by shattering all human boasting, reveals himself as the God of grace. The transcendence of God and his grace are one and the same thing. The Cross of Christ, which is God's judgement over the world and the means by which he makes the wisdom of this world foolishness, is the revelation of his grace. The man who accepts the Cross as God's judgement upon himself is delivered from the world. 'God forbid that I should glory save in the cross of our Lord Jesus Christ by whom the world is crucified unto me, and I unto the world' (Gal. 6.14). As God's judgement is his grace, so is his grace his judgement. For to be judged is simply to shut our hearts to grace (John 3.18).

The grace of God is not visible like worldly entities. His treasures are hidden in earthly vessels (II Cor. 4.7). The resurrection life is manifested in the world in the guise of death (II Cor. 12.9). Only in human weakness is the power of God made known. Once again, this means that the grace of God is never an assured possession. It is always ahead of man, always a future possibility. As grace, the transcendence of God is always his futurity, his constant being ahead of us, his always being where we would like to be. He is always there already as the gracious God for those who are open to the future, but as the judge for those who shut their hearts against the future.

IV

MAN IS INCAPABLE of redeeming himself from the world and the powers which hold sway in it. Of these powers, the most important are the flesh, sin, the law and death. Man's redemption —and at this point Primitive Christianity and Gnosticism are in agreement—can only come from the divine world as an event. It is something that must happen to man from outside. Now Christian faith claims that this is precisely what has happened in Jesus of Nazareth, in his death and resurrection. The significance of his person may be expressed in terms derived from many different sources, though it is not long before one particular interpretation of his person and work becomes the accepted norm. For the original Palestinian Church Jesus is the 'Man' exalted by God, whose impending advent is the subject of eager expectation. Through his past activity on earth, Jesus had gathered around him the community of the last times. Apparently, a redemptive significance was attached to his death. It was regarded as an atoning sacrifice for sin, perhaps also as the sacrifice by which God inaugurated the new covenant with his people. In the Hellenistic churches terms derived from the mysteries had to be used to describe the redemptive significance of Jesus. He is the Lord worshipped in the cultus. The initiated participate in his death and resurrection through the sacraments of baptism and the Lord's Supper.[19] The most important development, however, was the interpretation of the person of Jesus in terms of the Gnostic redemption myth. He is a divine figure sent down from the celestial world of light, the Son of the Most High coming forth from the Father, veiled in earthly form and inaugurating the redemption through his work.[20]

Even before Paul this interpretation of the person of Jesus had found its way into the churches. For Paul is quite obviously quoting a traditional Christological hymn in Philippians 2.6-11, when he relates how Christ, a pre-existent divine being, left the celestial world and appeared on earth in the form of a servant, and after his death was exalted as Lord.[21] The same Gnostic myth lies behind the allusions of Paul to the mysterious divine wisdom, which the 'rulers of this world' did not recognize; for had they done so they would not have crucified the Lord of glory. In his earthly disguise he was invisible to them, and as a consequence, by crucifying him they brought about their own destruction (I Cor. 2.8f.). With these Gnostic concepts Paul combines quite naïvely the already traditional interpretation of the death of Jesus as an atoning sacrifice, which came partly from the Jewish cultus, partly from the juridical notions prevalent in Judaism (Rom. 3.25, etc.). He can just as easily interpret the death and Resurrection of Jesus in terms of the mysteries and their sacramentalism (Rom. 6.2ff.). But the dominant interpretation of the death and Resurrection of Jesus is the Gnostic conception of it as a cosmic event through which the 'old things' have been done away and the 'new' inaugurated (II Cor. 5.17). For Paul, Christ has lost his identity as an individual human person. He knows him no longer 'after the flesh' (II Cor. 5.16). Instead, Jesus has become a cosmic figure, a body to which all belong who have been joined to him through faith and baptism (I Cor. 12.12f.; Gal. 3.27f.). For it is 'into him' that men are baptized (Gal. 3.27), and 'in Christ' that the Christian lives henceforth. The Pauline 'in Christ' is often wrongly interpreted in a mystical sense, whereas it is a Gnostic cosmic conception. It may also be called an *ecclesiological* formula, since the 'body' of Christ is the Church, or an *eschatological* formula, since with the establishment of the body of Christ the eschatological event has been inaugurated.

The most thorough-going attempt to restate the redemptive work of Jesus in Gnostic terms is to be found in the Fourth Gospel. Here Jesus is the pre-existent Son of God, the Word who exists with him from all eternity. He is sent from God, sent into the world, as its light, to give sight to the blind, and to blind those who see (John 9.39). He is not only the light, but also the life and the truth. As the agent of revelation, he brings all these blessings and calls to his side his 'own', those who are 'of the truth'. After accomplishing his Father's mission, he is exalted from the earth and returns to heaven to prepare a way for his own, that they may join him in the heavenly mansions. Indeed, he is himself the 'way' (14.6). 'I, if I be lifted up, from the earth, will draw all men unto me' (12.32).

It is easy to see why the Christian Church took over these ideas from the Gnostic redemption myth. That myth offered a terminology in which the redemption wrought in the person and work of Jesus could be made intelligible as a present reality. The eschatological event was already being realized in the present. This sense of being the eschatological community, of being already raised from this world by the grace of God, of deliverance from its powers, could not be adequately conveyed to the Hellenistic world in terms of the Jewish eschatological hope, which looked for redemption in the future. Indeed, a thinker of Paul's calibre was already sensitive to the difficulty. The eschatological event must be understood as a process already inaugurated with the coming of Jesus, or with his death and Resurrection, and the Gnostic redemption myth lay ready to hand as a vehicle for its expression.

In Paul the Gnostic ideas are still combined with the Jewish apocalyptic element. He still uses the apocalyptic conception of the two ages[22] thus: 'When the fulness of time came, God sent forth his Son' (Gal. 4.4). But the real point is that the coming of Christ is thus designated as the inauguration of the eschatological event. Isaiah's prediction of the day of redemption is now being fulfilled: 'Behold, now is the accepted time; behold, now is the day of salvation' (II Cor. 6.2).

The man in Christ is already a 'new creature', for 'old things are passed away; behold, all things are become new' (II Cor. 5.17). Hence the triumphant cry:

> Death is swallowed up in victory.
> O death, where is thy sting?

> O death, where is thy victory? . . .
> Thanks be to God, who giveth us the victory through our Lord
> Jesus Christ (I Cor. 15.54-7).

The cosmic powers have already been dethroned:

> When we were in the flesh, the motions of sins, which were
> by the law, did work in our members to bring forth fruit unto
> death. But now we are delivered from the law, being dead
> [with Christ] to [the power] wherein we were held: that we
> should serve in newness of spirit, and not in the oldness of the
> letter (Rom. 7.5f.).

Or:

> But before faith came, we were kept under the law, shut up
> unto the faith which should afterwards be revealed. . . . But
> after that faith is come, we are no longer under a schoolmaster.
> For ye are all the children of God by faith in Christ Jesus.
> For as many of you as have been baptized into Christ have
> put on Christ . . . for ye are all one in Christ Jesus (Gal. 3.23-8).
>
> When we were children, [we] were in bondage under the ele-
> ments of the world; but when the time was fulfilled, God sent
> forth his Son . . . to redeem them that were under the law, that
> we might receive the adoption of sons (Gal. 4.3ff.).

With all this, Paul still combines the apocalyptic picture of
the parousia, the resurrection of the dead and the judgement.
But for the Fourth Gospel, the redemption is exclusively a
present process.

> And this is the condemnation, that light is come into the
> world. . . . (John. 3.19).
>
> Verily, verily, I say unto you, He that heareth my word,
> and believeth on him that sent me, hath everlasting life, and
> shall not come into condemnation; but is passed from death
> unto life. Verily, verily, I say unto you, The hour is coming,
> and now is, when the dead shall hear the voice of the Son of
> God: and they that hear shall live (John. 5.24f.).
>
> I am the resurrection, and the life: he that believeth in me,
> though he were dead, yet shall he live: And whosoever liveth
> and believeth in me shall never die (John. 11.25f.).

> Now is the judgement of this world: now shall the prince
> of this world be cast out (John 12.31).[23]

Christianity thus agrees with Gnosticism in placing the
eschatological event in the present. It is inaugurated by the
appearance of the redeemer on earth. Hence it follows that for
Christianity, as well as for Gnosticism, the present salvation is
not visible like an event in history.[24] Indeed, some of the sayings
which express this have quite a Gnostic ring. 'Ye are dead, and
your life is hid with Christ in God' (Col. 3.3). Or: 'Now are
we the sons of God, and it doth not yet appear what we shall
be' (I John 3.2). The believers are, in principle, no longer 'in the
flesh',[25] though, of course, in practice they are still in it (II Cor.
10.3; Gal. 2.20). The outward man is decaying while the inner
man is being renewed, but this process is no more visible to the
outward eye than the glory of Christ which far outshines
the glory which once covered Moses' face (II Cor. 3.7ff.), or the
transformation of the believers into this same glory as they
behold it (II Cor. 3.18). We live by faith, not by sight (II Cor.
5.7), and the knowledge we have at present is as problematical
as an image reflected in a mirror. We shall not see face to face
until the end (I Cor. 13.12).

Yet as in Gnosticism, the event of redemption is exhibited in
certain phenomena, which somehow or other represent it.
Indeed, at first sight it would seem that this is truer of Christianity than it is of Gnosticism. For in Gnosticism the mission and
advent of the redeemer and the inauguration of the eschatological
event were relegated to a mythical age before history began,
while in Christianity these things are events of the recent past.
It is the appearance of Jesus of Nazareth and his crucifixion,
events whose historicity is vouched for by eye witnesses and by
the tradition of which they are the source. All the same, it
would be wrong to lay too much stress on this. For to begin
with the historical person of Jesus was very soon turned into a
myth in primitive Christianity. Furthermore, the Gnostics also
believed that the advent of the redeemer was a real event, and

the source of the tradition enshrined in their worship and doctrine.

The really important point is that for both Christianity and Gnosticism the tradition is itself the presence of the spiritual world in this world. Or, to put it more precisely, the redeemer is present in the word of preaching, the message from above. In the proclamation the eschatological event is bodied forth into the present. According to Paul, when God inaugurated the event of redemption in the death and Resurrection of Christ, he simultaneously established the word of preaching, the ministry of reconciliation. Where this word is heard, the eschatological redemption becomes a present reality (II Cor. 5.18f., 6.2). Similarly, the Fourth Gospel ascribes to Jesus the title of Logos or Word. Originally, this had been a mythological term. According to John Jesus is the Word because he has received from the Father the commission to proclaim the message with which he has been entrusted to the world, and is fulfilling it (8.26, etc). His words are 'spirit and life' (6.63). They bring both purification and judgement.

In conjunction with the word there are also the sacraments, as in the Gnostic systems. Christian sacramental theology differs little from that of Gnosticism, if at all. But its conception of the word is different, and that is decisive. It is true that in both systems the word is a call to awake, a summons to repentance and a challenge to decision. But in Gnosticism this call could only be a summons to become conscious of one's alienation from the world and to detach oneself from it. That it also meant something positive, a real turning to the grace of God, was something that Gnosticism could only make clear by cosmological instruction, by the myth of the archetypal man and the fate of the spark of light, which was man's true Self. Such mystagogic instruction could hardly have the urgency of a call to decision. Primitive Christian preaching had no use for cosmological instruction or for the doctrine of the pre-existence of the soul. And although it presents the Cross and Resurrection of Jesus in mythological terms, the preaching of the Cross is nevertheless a decisive

summons to repentance. This is because the redemptive significance of the Cross (and therefore of the Resurrection also) can only
become apparent to those who submit to being crucified with
Christ, who accept him as Lord in their daily lives. Adherence
to the gospel message is called 'faith', and faith involves a new
existential understanding of Self. In it man realizes his creatureliness and guilt. It is an act of obedience,[26] in which man sur-
renders all his 'boasting', all desire to live on his own resources,
all adherence to tangible realities, and assents to the scandalous
fact of a crucified Lord. Thus he is freed from the world by
being freed from himself. It is true that both primitive Christianity and Gnosticism agree in attributing man's liberation to the
act of God. But in Gnosticism what was freed was the true
self, the spark of light in man, whereas for Christian faith man
is freed *for* his authentic self by being freed from himself—from
the self which man, qualified as he is by his guilty past, brings
along with him into the present. The Gnostic is one 'saved by
nature' ($\phi\acute{v}\sigma\epsilon\iota$ $\sigma\omega\zeta\acute{o}\mu\epsilon\nu\sigma s$), the Christian through his faith.
Hence the typical designation for the Christian religion is not
knowledge ($\gamma\nu\hat{\omega}\sigma\iota s$), but faith ($\pi\acute{\iota}\sigma\tau\iota s$).

This shows that the New Testament understands human
existence as an historical existence. The Gnostics, on the other
hand, attribute everything to fate, and therefore they understand human existence in the categories of natural Being. This
is made abundantly clear in the doctrine of the pre-existence of
the soul. For an existence which lies behind me, but must nevertheless be accepted as my own, despite the fact that it lies outside
the range of my experience, and I can never be responsible for it,
belongs not to history, but to nature. The discovery of the
absolute distinction between humanity and its objective
environment, the discovery made in the experience of the blows
of fate, is nullified when that distinction is interpreted in
ontological terms, as can be seen by the use of the phrase 'being
saved by nature'.

There is a similar difference when we compare the Gnostic
conception of the body of the redeemer with the Pauline

doctrine of the body of Christ. Paul, of course, makes use of cosmological categories when he expounds the doctrine of the body of Christ. But in practice he always transposes it into an historical key. For although he does not reject the view that the sacraments of baptism and the Lord's Supper are the means by which men are grafted into the body of Christ, the decisive point is that membership of the body of Christ is acquired by faith. And faith after all is genuine historical decision. Hence Paul can use the Gnostic conception of the body of Christ in combination with the metaphor, common in Graeco-Roman literature, of the body as the social organism of the state in order to describe the solidarity of the Christian community (I Cor. 12.14ff.). The body of Christ thus acquires shape in an historical context founded on preaching and faith, in which the individual members belonging to it are bound together in mutual care for one another, sharing each other's sufferings and joys.

Finally, the affinity and difference between Gnosticism and Christianity are illustrated from their conception of the pneuma or Spirit. The Gnostics identified the pneuma with the spark of light which has its abode in the inward man. When the agent of revelation came, he quickened the divine spark to newness of life, or if it was dead, restored it. This is similar to the Christian idea that the Spirit is imparted to the baptized and that it operates in them as a divine vital power. In popular Christianity, the Spirit was naïvely regarded as the source of miraculous phenomena. As in Gnosticism, such phenomena were, in an illogical manner, accepted as visible demonstrations of the supernatural otherworldly, character of the baptized. We are referring, of course, to prophecy, ecstasy and speaking with tongues. But neither for Paul nor for the author of the Fourth Gospel, nor even for the New Testament as a whole is ecstasy the high water mark of the Christian life, or the visible manifestation of the transcendent. This is all the more remarkable in the case of Paul, for he knows all about such things as ecstasy, and if he wanted to could boast about ecstatic experiences of his own. But that is just what he refuses to do. He prefers to glory in his 'infirmities'. It is here that he sees the divine power at work in himself (II Cor. 12.1-10). But while Paul does not reject the popular view, he gives it a new turn. He finds real evidence of the Spirit's working in Christian moral behaviour, in victory over lust and passion, and in simple, everyday acts of love. Here of course the operation of the pneuma loses its evidential value. This is shown by the way the Gnosticizing Corinthians criticize Paul for not displaying visible evidence of his pneumatic endowments. It is against such criticism that Paul is directing his polemic in II Cor. 10-13.[27]

According to Paul, the pneuma—and here he determines the line of all future development—is not a magic power working in the hearts of the believers, but the norm of practical behaviour. Whereas in the past Christians had lived after the flesh—that is to say, they had centred their lives on visible, tangible realities —they must now orientate their lives on the Spirit. But since the Spirit is already enjoyed as a gift, it is in the last resort equivalent to the new possibility of life opened up by the grace of God, the life of freedom.[28] Just because it is a gift, freedom is power ($\delta\acute{v}\nu\alpha\mu\iota s$). It is man's own capacity freed from the cosmic powers. And this power is at the same time the norm of behaviour, because freedom means openness for the future— openness, that is, for every fresh claim of God both to action and to the acceptance of his fate. To possess the pneuma does not mean therefore that once a man has made the decision of faith and has been baptized he is now perfect, and need make no further decisions. On the contrary, he is now free as never before for each successive genuine decision in life. His life has become historical in the true sense of the word. Hence the Pauline paradox: 'Work out your own salvation with fear and trembling. *For* it is God which worketh in you both to will and to do of his good pleasure' (Phil. 2.12f.).

Every decision in life involves a renewal of the decision of faith. It means a determination to live 'after the Spirit'. To be 'led by the Spirit' ($\pi\nu\epsilon\acute{v}\mu\alpha\tau\iota$ $\mathring{\alpha}\gamma\epsilon\sigma\theta\alpha\iota$) is something realized in the accomplishment of such decisions. It is obedience to the imperative, 'walk in the Spirit' (Rom. 8.12-14; Gal. 5.16f.). So far from being abrogated, the divine imperative is now grounded on the indicative of freedom; 'If we live by the Spirit, let us also walk in the Spirit' (Gal. 5.25; cf. Rom. 5.12-23; I Cor. 5.7, 6.11). The fulfilment of the law is now no longer the way to salvation, for salvation has already been granted as a gift. Rather, it is the outcome of that gift. The law as the way to salvation has been abrogated. But in so far as it is an expression of the good and holy will of God (Rom. 7.12), it is fulfilled as never before 'in us, who walk not after the flesh, but after the Spirit' (Rom. 8.4), and that means the commandment of love, which comprehends all the precepts of the law. Paul, is of course, thinking here only of the ethical precepts of the law. 'For all the law is fulfilled in one word, even in this; Thou shalt love thy neighbour as thyself' (Gal. 5.14). 'For he that loveth another hath fulfilled the law. Love worketh no ill to his neighbour, therefore love is the fulfilling of the law' (Rom. 13.8-10). If there is any demonstration of faith to the world, any proof of the new life, it is love. 'By this shall all men know that ye are my disciples, if ye have love one to another' (John 13.35). Love is the only criterion by which the believer can know that he has ceased to belong to the old world. 'We know that we have passed from death unto life, because we love the brethren' (I John 3.14).

It is those who share the Spirit and are bound in mutual love who make up the body of Christ, the Church. Since it is a fellowship of the Spirit, it is essentially invisible to the world. In one sense, of course, it is visible, like the Gnostic communities. It consists of real men and women, who still live 'in the flesh'. But here we are faced with a paradox. This conglomeration of believers is also the eschatological community, the 'body of Christ', whose existence is not subject to objective proof. Those who are united in the Church are not bound together by any worldly interests or motives. They are not joined by a common nationality, or even by an Idea, but by the Spirit which dwells in each of them. And just because of this, just because the Church depends for its existence, not on worldly motives or resources, but on the power available through the grace of God, Paul can describe it as that cosmic entity, the 'body of Christ'.

The practical behaviour of the Church and its members in the world resembles that of the Gnostics in that it rests upon a sense of superiority over the world, in an awareness that 'neither death, nor life, nor angels, nor principalities, nor powers, nor things present, nor things to come . . . shall be able to separate us from the love of God, which is in Christ Jesus' (Rom. 8.38f.). This absolute independence from the world, however, produces a certain detachment from all worldly interests and responsibilities. Primitive Christianity is quite uninterested in making the world a better place, it has no proposals for political or social reform. All must do their duty to the State. But they have no direct political responsibilities. After all, the Christian is a 'citizen of heaven' (Phil. 3.20). The slave who is 'in the Lord' has become free from the world, but he must not therefore suppose that he ought to seek sociological freedom: 'Let every man, wherein he is called, therein abide with God' (I Cor. 7.17-24). Freedom might in itself breed licence, but against that the Old Testament, the Jewish tradition and the words of the Lord are a surety. Where such tendencies appear, they are vigorously resisted (I Cor. 6.12-20). Instead, this negative attitude to the world tends to find its outlet in asceticism. Such tendencies appear very early in Christian history, even in Paul himself, when he allows marriage as a necessary evil, and regards celibacy as a special charisma. Ritualistic asceticism, which appears here and there, he tolerates as an infirmity (Rom. 14; I Cor. 8; 10), but he knows that 'there is nothing unclean of itself: but to him that esteemeth anything to be unclean, to him it is unclean' (Rom. 14.14). 'All things are pure; but it is evil for that man who eateth with offence' (Rom. 14.20). The fundamental principle behind such questions is: 'Whatsoever is not of faith is sin' (Rom. 14.23). Paul's own standpoint is not one of legalistic asceticism, but a dialectic of participation and inward detachment:

> It remaineth that both
> they that have wives be as though they had none;
> And they that weep, as though they wept not;
> and they that rejoice, as though they rejoiced not;
> And they that use this world, as though they had no dealings
> with it (I Cor. 7.29-31).

This interior detachment is described in that saying of Paul about his knowing how to be filled and to be hungry, to abound and to be in want (Phil. 4.11-13).[29] And when he exhorts his readers to 'Rejoice with them that do rejoice, and weep with them that weep' (Rom. 12.15), he is, of course, taking it for granted that the faithful share in the ordinary experiences of life.

Yes, in a certain sense action and experience in this world is not a matter of indifference, but vital and essential. It is the action and experience of the free man borne along by love. True, the Spirit is not a principle which can be applied to the improvement of the world. In this respect, it is the Christian's duty to be indifferent to the world. But just because he has no definite programme, the Christian must be always discovering new duties. He is a new man, and by 'the renewing of his mind' he has been given the capacity to 'prove what is that good, and acceptable, and perfect, will of God' (Rom. 12.2). Hence it was possible for the early Church to develop a pattern of catechetical instruction, in which it adopted many ethical concepts of Hellenism (Phil. 4.8), the lists of duties formulated in the 'household codes', and finally, in the Pastoral Epistles, the ideals of the Hellenistic *petit bourgeoisie*.

It would therefore be true to say—and without questioning its fundamentally dialectic attitude to the world—that Christian detachment from civic duty and from political and social responsibility is not one of principle, but only a temporary exigency forced upon the Church by its historical situation. It was due partly to the expectation of an imminent end of the world, partly to the social composition of the earliest Christian

communities. It would never have occurred to their members
that they might assume social, still less political responsibilities.

In their experience of the Spirit and their knowledge that the
grace of God makes men free to love, the problem which was so
fatal for Gnosticism, i.e. the problem of the unworldliness of
the Self, finds its solution.[30] In Gnosticism the unworldly self
could only be described in negatives. It could only be a matter of
faith. It was a point from which every possible human action
and experience was denied. In primitive Christianity, on the
other hand, that same problem found a positive solution. It was
still an object of faith, for it always lay in the future. It could
never be present as an objective datum. Yet in the moment of
action it was a present reality. For in the moment of action man
is always grasping at the future, always being translated anew
into the future. In the love which is grounded on faith (Gal. 5.6)
the unworldly always becomes a present, objective reality, while
in hope it is still in the future. Every act of love, though performed in the objective world, is paradoxically an eschatological
event.

In the last analysis, however, the future can never, as in
Gnosticism, be conceived in fantastic cosmic terms, despite all
the apocalyptic imagery which has found its way into the New
Testament. It can only be understood in the light of God's grace
as the permanent futurity of God which is always there before
man arrives, wherever it be, even in the darkness of death.
Paul can certainly speak of a glory which is ready to be revealed
for us (Rom. 8.18), of the eternal 'weight of glory' which awaits
us (II Cor. 4.17). But at the same time he speaks of faith, hope
and love as things which will not cease, even when that which
is perfect is come (I Cor. 13.13).[31] In other words he can con-
ceive no state of perfection in which the unworldly is a mere
possession. The openness of Christian existence is never-ending.

BIBLIOGRAPHY AND NOTES

TRANSLATOR'S NOTE

Bibliographies are provided, as in the original, for each part. In this translation they are divided into English and non-English. The English bibliographies list those works cited in English by the author himself and works in foreign languages cited by him and available in an English translation. The translator has added a few English works not noted by the author, for the benefit of English-speaking readers; these additions are indicated by an asterisk (*). They should not be regarded as exhaustive.

One abbreviation should be noted:

Z.N.W.—Zeitschrift für die neutestamentliche Wissenschaft.

THE OLD TESTAMENT HERITAGE

Bibliography

ENGLISH

Joh. Pedersen, *Israel, Its Life and Culture*, I-II, 1946; III-IV, 1947.
Stanley A. Cook, *The Old Testament, a Reinterpretation*, 1936.*
N. H. Snaith, *The Distinctive Ideas of the Old Testament*, 1944.*
H. H. Rowley, *The Rediscovery of the Old Testament*, 1945.*
Walter Eichrodt, *Man in the Old Testament*, 1950.*
C. A. Simpson, *The Early Traditions of Israel*, 1948.*

OTHER LANGUAGES

Ludwig Köhler, *Theologie des Alten Testaments* (Neue theol. Grundrisse), 3rd Ed. 1953.
Wolf Wilhelm Graf Baudissin, *Kyrios als Gottesname im Judentum und seine Stelle in der Religionsgeschichte*, Part III, 1929.
J. Hempel, *Gott und Mensch im Alten Testament*, 2nd Ed., 1936.
Idem, *Das Ethos des Alten Testaments*, 1938.
A. Causse, *Du Groupe ethnique à la communauté religieuse. La problème sociologique de la religion d'Israel*, 1937.
A concise conspectus is offered by Gustav Hölscher, *Geschichte der israelitischen und jüdischen Religion* (Sammlung Töpelmann, I, 7), 1922.
A fuller presentation in Walther Eichrodt, *Theologie des Alten Testaments*, 3 vols., 1933, 1935, 1939.

Notes

1   Cf. Baudissin, op. cit. (see above), III, pp. 667-74.

2   Cf. Baudissin, op. cit., III, pp. 624ff., 650ff.

3   For a comparison, see the definitions of the cosmos in the Stoic Chrysippus (H. v. Arnim, *Stoicorum veterum fragmenta*, II, p. 168, fr. 527): Κόσμον δ' εἶναί φησιν ὁ Χρύσιππος σύστημα ἐξ οὐρανοῦ καὶ γῆς καὶ τῶν ἐν τούτοις φύσεων. ἢ τὸ ἐκ θεῶν καὶ ἀνθρώπων σύστημα καὶ ἐκ τῶν ἕνεκα τούτων γεγονότων= Chrysippus defines the cosmos as 'the structure which consists of heaven, earth, and all that exists therein', or as 'the structure which consists of gods and men and the things that exist, which have been brought into being for their sake'.

4   Cf. Baudissin, op. cit., III, pp. 457ff.

5   Cf. Baudissin, op. cit., III, pp. 631ff.

6   Later Judaism expresses this idea by the proposition that man was not created for the sake of the world, but the world for man (Syr. Baruch 14.18). Cf. George Foot Moore, *Judaism in the First Centuries of the Christian Era*, I, pp. 449f.

7   Cf. Gustav Hölscher, *Die Anfänge der hebräischen Geschichts-schreibung* (Sitzungsbericht der Heidelberg. Akademie der Wissenschaften, Phil. hist. Kl., 1941-2, 3. Abh), 1942, p. 110. Gustav Hölscher, *Geschichtsschreibung in Israel* (Skrifter utgivna av Kungl. Humanistika Vetenskapssamfundet i Lund, L.), 1952.

8   Cf. Baudissin, op. cit., III, pp. 665f.; B. contrasts the ethical monotheism of the prophets with the monotheism of the Egyptian King Amenophis IV. For the latter, God is the life-force embodied in the sun, for the former he is the ethical will behind all history.

9   Cf. L. Köhler (see above), p. 71.

10   Cf. Karl Löwith, *Friedrich Nietzsche* (*Church History*, XIII, 3, 1944), p. 18.

11   Old Testament historiography exhibits singularly little interest in the history of culture (for an exception, see Hölscher, *Die Anfänge*, etc.; see n. 7). 'The Jahweh of Mosaic religion is completely indifferent to secular culture' (Baudissin, op. cit., III, p. 451). It should be added that this does not imply any actual hostility to culture.

12   Adolf Bauer, *Vom Judentum zum Christentum* (Wissenchaft und Bildung, 142), Leipzig, Quelle u. Meyer, 1917, p. 19.

13 Cf. Hölscher, *Die Anfänge*, etc. (see n. 7), p. 102. Also his *Geschichtsschreibung in Israel*, p. 134. Cf. also Ed. Meyer, *Die Israeliten und ihre Nachbarstämme* (1906), pp. 486f.

14 On the invisibility of God cf. W. W. Graf Baudissin, *Archiv für Religionswissensch.* 18 (1915), pp. 173-239; E. Fascher, *Deus invisibilis* (*Marburger theol. Studien*, I), 1930; R. Bultmann, *Z.N.W.*, 29 (1930), pp. 169-92.

15 Cf. Plato, *Timaeus*, p. 28c: τὸν μὲν οὖν ποιητὴν καὶ πατέρα τοῦδε τοῦ πάντος εὑρεῖν τε ἔργον καὶ εὑρόντα εἰς πάντας ἀδύνατον λέγειν.

16 Hebrew is entirely lacking in verbal adjectives, e.g. ὁρατός, ἁπτός, etc., like the adjectives which in English are formed by adding the suffix '-ible' or '-able'. In Hebrew it is sometimes possible to use the passive participles (esp. the *niph'al* participle) in the sense of the Latin gerundive. Cf. Gesenius Kautzsch, *Hebrew Grammar*, para. 116, e.

17 It is characteristic that the Jewish philosopher of religion, Philo of Alexandria, under the influence of the Greek tradition, is at pains to reinterpret 'hearing' in the Old Testament as 'seeing', and accordingly he changes the voice of God on Sinai into an illumination. Cf. H. Leisegang, *Der Heilige Geist* I, pp. 215, 219ff.

18 Hans von Soden, *Was ist Wahrheit?* 1927; Rudolf Bultmann, *Z.N.W.*, 27 (1928), pp. 113-63.

19 Cf. esp. also Ps. 104.

20 Cf. Joh. Pedersen, *Revue d'Histoire et de Philosophie religieuses*, 1930, pp. 317-70.

21 M. Aurel., XII 8, 2: εἰς τὸ πᾶν ἀεὶ ὁρᾶν.

22 The Book *Qoholeth* (=Ecclesiastes) has been worked over in order to tone down the extreme scepticism.

23 The Book of Job has been worked over in the interests of the Jewish belief in divine chastening and retribution, above all by the insertion of the discourses of Elihu.

24 Isa. 26.19; Dan. 12.2, 13.

25 Cf. Baudissin (see above), III, pp. 379-98.

26 Cf. G. F. Moore (see n. 6), II, pp. 48f.

27 Cf. Baudissin, III, pp. 325-36; Jahweh is presented as Father, but the creation of the people as his son is regarded as having been achieved through his operation in history.

28 Cf. Baudissin, III, pp. 649f.

29   The principle dates are: 722 B.C., the fall of the northern kingdom of Israel. 597, the first deportation of the southern kingdom of Judah. 586, the second deportation. 538, the edict of Cyrus permitting the return of the exiles.

30   Psalms 47, 93, 96, 97, 99 are enthronement hymns.

31   See n. 24.

32   The ecstasy of the prophets is not that of mystical union: it is the medium for the reception of revelation.

33   Of course, there were secular songs in Israel—songs about work, victory, love and the like. Cf. Joh. Hempel, *Die althebräische Literatur* (Handbuch der Literaturwissensch.) 1930, pp. 24-9. Otto Eissfeldt, *Einleitung in das Alte Testament* (Neue theol. Grundrisse) 134, pp. 95-114. It is characteristic that the poetry collected together in the so-called Song of Songs (love or nuptial poetry) was only taken into the Canon as a result of its reinterpretation in terms of the relationship between God and Israel.

34   On these, see Walter Baumgartner, *Die Klagegedichte des Jeremia*, 1917.

35   Cf. Baudissin, III, pp. 438f.

36   This concept of wholeness is rendered by the Greek τέλειος at Matt. 5.48. Hence it does not mean 'perfect', in the Greek sense of the highest stage of a development. Cf. Frederick C. Grant, *The Earliest Gospel*, 1943, pp. 218-23. The ethical term 'straight' is derived from handicraft.

37   Cf. Baudissin, III, pp. 432-42.

38   See p. 27 and 33f.

JUDAISM

Bibliography

ENGLISH

The basic work on the history, religion and literature of Judaism: Emil Schürer, *History of the Jewish People in the Time of Jesus*. 1885-91, 5 vols, Edinburgh, Clark, various translators.

Cf., further, George Foot Moore, *Judaism in the First Centuries of the Christian Era. The Age of the Tannaim*, I-III, 1927, 1930. Robert H. Pfeiffer, *History of New Testament Times*, New York, Harper, 1949.★

A. C. Welch: *Post-Exilic Judaism*.★

OTHER LANGUAGES

Wilhelm Bousset, *Die Religion des Judentums im späthellenistischen Zeitalter*, 3rd Ed., edited by Hugo Gressmann (Handb. zum Neuen Testament, 21), 1926.

Cf. also the book by G. Hölscher mentioned under "The Old Testament Heritage."

Notes

1 On the significance of the synagogue and on its worship, see Schürer, op. cit., II, ii, pp. 52-89; G. F. Moore, op. cit., pp. 281-307; on its relation to the Temple, ibid., II, pp. 12-15.

2 The 'praise of the fathers', Ecclus. 44-50 is characteristic.

3 On the Jewish mission, see Moore, op. cit., I, pp. 323-53.

4 On the Sadducees and Pharisees, cf. esp. Schürer, op. cit., II, ii, pp. 10-43; Hölscher, op. cit., pp. 218-23, and Moore, op. cit., I, pp. 56-71. The account of Judaism given in this book takes no account of the Jewish sects mentioned briefly in Philo and Josephus. This is because they make little difference to the overall picture. In recent years the manuscripts discovered in the Dead Sea caves (the so-called Dead Sea scrolls) have shown that these Jewish sects were more important than it was hitherto possible to suppose. Since the texts discovered have not yet been published in their entirety, it is not yet possible to draw an accurate picture of the sects from which they originate. But it is fairly certain that the sects in question are Essenes, about which our information has hitherto been scanty. They are a product of syncretism. The authority of the Old Testament is accepted without question, but motifs from a dualistic cosmology are combined with the Old Testament tradition, and in connexion with this process there emerges a terminology akin to that of both the Johannine and Gnostic literature. It is possible that we have here a Jewish type of Gnosticism, or at least a Gnosticism in an embryonic stage, and that despite the absence of the Gnostic redeemer myth. The prominence of baptisms and lustrations may suggest that they had some connexion with the Gnostic or pre-Gnostic baptist sects of the Jordan district (for this cf. Joseph Thomas, *Le mouvement Baptiste en Palestine et Syrie*, 1935).

Whether the emergence of John the Baptist is to be connected with these Essene sects, and whether their views had any influence on the earliest Christian churches, or even on the preaching of Jesus, cannot at present be determined. Probably not. But it is probable that later Jewish Christianity was influenced by these sects. Indeed, Oscar Cullmann is on perfectly good ground with his thesis that the remnants of the Essene movement by the Dead Sea passed into Jewish Christianity (in *Neutestamentliche Studien für Rudolf Bultmann*, 1954, pp. 35-51).

Walter Baumgartner is publishing periodical reports on the progress of research into the texts of the Dead Sea scrolls in the *Theologischer Rundschau* (hitherto 1948-9, pp. 329-46, and 1951, pp. 97-154). A good introduction to the subject in English is available in H. H. Rowley, *The Zadokite Fragments and the Dead Sea Scrolls*, 1952, and in German in Hans Bardtke, *Die Handschriftenfund am Toten Meer*, 1952 (with a German translation of some important texts), Georg Molin, *Die Söhne des Lichts. Zeit und Stellung der Handschriften am Toten Meer*, 1952.

5 On the Rabbinic schools and the rise of the tradition, see Schürer, op. cit., II, i, pp. 323-79; Moore, op. cit., I, pp. 93-109, 251-62, 308-22. Cf. also W. Kümmel, *Z.N.W.*, 33 (1934), pp. 105-30.

6 On the terminology: 'Mishna'=repetition, 'Tosephta'=addition, supplement. The scribes of the Mishna are the 'Tannaim', their successors are the 'Amoraim', who commented on the Mishna and continued it. Their work is the 'Gemara' (completion), which, together with the Mishna forms the 'Talmud' (doctrine). On the rabbinic literature see Schürer, op. cit., I, i, pp. 117-66; Moore, op. cit., I, pp. 123-73.

7 On the sabbath see esp. Moore, op. cit., II, pp. 21-39.

8 On the *Shemah* and *Shemoneh 'Esre*, see Schürer, II, ii, pp. 77-87.

9 Cited after Bousset (see above), p. 124.

10 A special technique called 'Erubh', was developed, with the purpose of getting round the regulations of the law while literally fulfilling them; cf. Schürer, II, ii, pp. 7, 37, 120.

11 On Jewish ethics cf. esp. Bousset, op. cit., pp. 137-140; Moore, op. cit., pp. 79-197. Moore, pp. 263-66, very properly emphasizes that the negative ethic does not imply asceticism.

12 On the attempts to find a dominant, basic principle behind the laws, see Bousset, op. cit., p. 138; Moore, op. cit., II, pp. 82-8. On the *Testament of the Twelve Patriarchs*, a late-Jewish document (from the Maccabean age?), which has come down to us in Greek,

Armenian and Old Slavonic (and worked over by Christian hands) see Schürer, op. cit., II, iii, pp. 114-24; Bousset, op. cit., pp. 14f.; O. Eissfeldt, *Einleitung in das Alte Testament*, 1934, pp. 687-90.

13 One of the Mishna tractates, the 'Pirke Aboth' ('Sayings of the Fathers') is a collection of pronouncements of scribes in the age of the Mishna.

14 Cf. Moore, op. cit., II, pp. 5-8.

15 Cf. Bousset, op. cit., p. 130. Further information in H. Strack and P. Billerbeck, *Kommentar zum Neuen Testament aus Talmud und Midrasch*, III, 1926, pp. 397f.

16 Pirke Aboth (see n. 13), 1, 3. Trans. W. O. E. Oesterley.

17 Pirke Aboth, 2, 8.

18 On the motives of ethical behaviour, see esp. Moore, op. cit., II, pp. 89-111. Further, Reinhold Sander, *Furcht und Liebe im palästinischen Judentum*, 1935: Erik Sjöberg, *Gott und die-Sünde im palästinischen Judentum*, 1938 (in this book, on the motive of obedience, see p. 23, 2).

19 On the belief in retribution, cf. Moore, op. cit., II, pp. 89-93, 248-56; Sjöberg, op. cit. (see n. 18), pp. 21-5, 95-109.

20 Δι' ὧν τις ἁμαρτάνει, διὰ τούτων κολάζεται. Similarly Test. Gad, 5.10: δι' ὧν γὰρ ὁ ἄνθρωπος παρανομεῖ, δι' ἐκείνων κολάζεται.

21 Pirke Aboth (see n. 13).

22 Wolfgang Wichmann, *Die Leidenstheologie*, 1930.

23 Talmud b. Berakhoth 28*b*.

24 On the universality, power and origin of sin, cf. Moore, op. cit., I, pp. 460-96.

25 Cf. Sjöberg (see n. 18), pp. 125-53; Moore, op. cit., I, pp. 507-34.

26 Cf. esp. the great prayer for forgiveness, IV Esra 8.20-36. On confessions of sin and penitential prayers, see also Moore, op. cit., II, pp. 213f.

27 On cultic atonement and the substitute for it after the cessation of sacrificial worship, see Moore, op. cit., I, pp. 497-506. Sjöberg, op. cit., pp. 175-83; Hans Wenschkewitz, *Die Spiritualisierung der Kultusbegriffe*, 1932; Hans Joachim Schoeps, *Die Tempelzerstörung des Jahres 70 in der jüdischen Religionsgeschichte* (Conjectanea Neotestamentica VI), 1942, pp. 28-35.

28 Cf. Sjöberg, op. cit., pp. 154-69; Adolf Schlatter, *Der Glaube im Neuen Testament*, 4th Ed., 1924, pp. 29-32.

29   Cf. Albert Schweitzer, *The Quest of the Historical Jesus* 1910 and
     1931. The literature on the subject is vast; we need only mention
     Maurice Goguel, *La Vie de Jésus*, 1932 (Eng. Tr., 1933). On the
     proclamation of Jesus, see particularly Rudolf Bultmann, *Jesus*,
     2nd Ed., 1929 (Eng. Tr., *Jesus and the Word*, 1934); T. W. Manson,
     The Teaching of Jesus, 1935.

30   Cf. Günther Bornkamm, 'Der Lohngedanke im Neuen
     Testament,' *Evangelische Theologie*, 1946, pp. 143-66.

31   Matt. 23.23 adds: 'these ought ye to have done, and not to
     leave the other undone'. The clause appears to have been absent
     from the original Lucan text, and is probably an addition of the
     first Evangelist.

32   The sayings preserved in Matt. 5.17-19 ('Think not that I am
     come to destroy the law or the prophets . . .'), which assert the
     permanent validity of the law down to the smallest letter, are
     assuredly no genuine sayings of Jesus, but later products of the
     community.

33   A rabbinic saying runs: 'The sabbath is given over to you, and
     not you to the sabbath'; see Strack-Billerbeck (see n. 15), II, p. 5,
     on Mark 2.27.

34   Thus the invocation in the *Shemoneh 'Esre*; cf. also the pom-
     pous invocations in the penitential prayer in IV Ezra 8.20ff.

35   The 'Psalms of Solomon' are a collection of songs from the
     first century B.C. Broadly speaking, they breathe the atmosphere of
     Pharisaic piety. Cf. Schürer, II, iii, pp. 17-23; Eissfeldt (see n. 12),
     pp. 665-9. The translation of *Shemoneh 'Esre* is taken from the
     Authorized Daily Prayer Book, 4th Ed. (S. Singer.)

36   On the apocalyptic literature, i.e. the literature enshrined in
     those writings which, invariably under the pseudonym of one of
     the saints of old time, purport to give revelation about the end and
     the signs preceding it (and frequently in association with this,
     about God's purpose in history and about cosmic mysteries), see
     Schürer, II, iii, pp. 44-141; Eissfeldt, pp. 673-87.

37   From the synagogue prayer, 'Kaddish', Trans. Singer (see
     n. 35).

38   'Messiah' means 'anointed one', It is simply the designation of
     the king, especially the king of the age of redemption. The Greek
     rendering, 'Christos', eventually became a proper name in Hellen-
     istic Christianity.

39 Babylonian mythology influenced Hebrew eschatology and in particular its royal theology from quite an early date (cf., e.g., Hugo Gressmann, *Der Messias*, 1929; W. Staerk, *Die Erlösererwartung in den östlichen Religionen*, 1938; further, the work of Sigmund Mowinkel, and more recently the publications of the Uppsala school, for the Old Testament, in particular those of Ivan Engnell). Notwithstanding, we have in late Jewish apocalyptic a new influx of oriental mythology, esp. Iranian. On this topic cf. Bousset, op. cit. (see above), pp. 469-524.

40 In the Old Testament Satan has not yet become the Devil. The figure of the Devil entered Judaism from Iranian sources, and appears here under various names, of which 'Satan' is only one (meaning enemy or accuser). On the belief in demons and the devil in Judaism, cf. Bousset, op. cit., pp. 331-42.

41 From the 'Assumption of Moses', an apocalyptic document, which, however, emanates from the first (or second) century A.D. Eng. Trans. by R. H. Charles, in Charles, *Apocrypha and Pseudepigrapha of the Old Testament*, Vol. II, 1913, pp. 407-24.

42 On the resurrection of the dead, see p. 46.

43 Texts from IV Esra are quoted from translations by G. H. Box in Charles, op. cit., pp. 542-624, and of the Syrian Apocalypse of Baruch from the translation by R. H. Charles in Charles, op. cit., pp. 470-526.

44 Owing to the slavish translation of the Aramaic term for 'man' by the Greek ὁ υἱός τοῦ ἀνθρώπου, the designation 'Son of Man' has become traditional.

45 In the (almost certainly) genuine sayings of Jesus handed down in the tradition, there is hardly anything about the contrast between this age and the age to come. The passages which speak of the 'sons of this age' (Luke 16.8, 20.34f.) and of the reward of his followers in the age to come (Mark 10.30), are secondary. The use of συντέλεια τοῦ αἰῶνος in Matt. 13.49 may be original (though it is certainly secondary in the interpretation of the parable of the tares, Matt. 13.39f. and in Matt. 24.3). The use of καιρὸς οὗτος in Luke 12.56 in the sense of the present, which immediately precedes the eschatological end, is undoubtedly original though it is secondary in Mark 10.30, where it is contrasted with the ἐρχόμενος αἰών. On the criticism of the synoptic tradition, see my *Geschichte der synoptischen Tradition*, 2nd Ed., 1931, a concise

summary of which is available in *Die Erforschung der synoptischen Evangelien*, 2nd Ed., 1930.

46   Cf. Mark 8.38; Matt. 24.27, 37, 44; Luke 17.24, 26; 12.40; Luke 12.8f. (put into the first person by Matt. 10.32f.); Luke 17.30.

47   Cf. Mark 12.18-27; Luke 11.31f.; Matt. 12.41f.; Matt. 25.31-46, etc.

48   Mark 2.19*b* and 20 are a later product of the early Church. [Cf. J. Jeremias: *The Parables of Jesus*, 1954, pp. 42 and 82 (Translator).]

49   The ἐντὸς ὑμῶν of Luke 17.21 cannot be interpreted as 'within you' (which is quite incompatible with the concept of the Reign of God). Nor can I regard the frequently advocated translation 'in your midst', i.e. now, 'in my person' as correct.

50   In the context in which Mark and Matt. place the saying, the subject of ἐγγύς ἐστιν is undoubtedly 'he', the 'Man'. But the verse was originally an isolated logion, and perhaps Luke 21.31 is right when it amplifies by making the subject the βασιλεία τοῦ θεοῦ.

51   The prophecies alluded to in Matt. 11.5 are Isa. 35.5f., 29.18f., 61.1.

52   The Fourth Gospel has reshaped the preaching of Jesus so as to make him proclaim himself as the Son of God and demand faith in his person.

53   The Evangelists, of course, identify the Son of Man whose coming Jesus foretells with Jesus himself, and in this the tradition of the Church has followed suit.

54   The saying attributed to Jesus in Matt. 16.18 about Peter as the rock on which he will build his Church is a product of the early Church, although its authenticity has recently been defended by Protestant scholars. On the critical side, cf. Rudolf Bultmann: *Theol. Blätter* 20 (1941), pp. 265-79, and Werner G. Kümmel, *Kirchenbegriff und Geschichtsbewusstsein in der Urgemeinde und bei Jesus* (Symb. Bibl. Upsal., I), 1943. On the whole question of the 'Church' in the teaching of Jesus and in primitive Christianity, cf. Olaf Linton, *Das Problem der Urkirche in der neueren Forschung*, 1932; Niels A. Dahl, *Das Volk Gottes*, 1941.

55   Literature on Hellenistic Judaism: the second volume, div. iii, of Schürer (n. 1) deals with Hellenistic Judaism, and esp. with Philo and his teaching. Cf. further the work of Bousset (see above).

On Philo, the great works of Emile Bréhier, *Les idées philosophiques et religieuses de Philon d'Alexandrie*, 1907, and Harry Austryn Wolfson, *Philo, Foundations of Religious Philosophy in Judaism, Christianity and Islam*, 2 vols., 1947. Monographs: Hans Windisch, *Die Frömmigkeit Philos*, 1909; Isaac Heinemann, *Philons griechis.he und jüdische Bildung*, 1932; Joseph Pascher, *Η ΒΑΣΙΛΙΚΗ ΟΔΟΣ, Der Königsweg zu Wiedergeburt und Vergottung bei Philon von Alexandria*, 1931.

56 Philo, *de spec. leg.*, I, 260. Translations of Philo's works in Loeb Classical Library (Heinemann) by F. H. Colson and G. H. Whitaker (Vols. I-V), by F. H. Colson (Vols. VI-IX), and Ralph Marcus (sup. Vols. I and II).

57 Philo, *de migr. Abr.*, 1ff.

58 Philo, *de congr. erud. gr.*, 1-88, 121-57; *de Abr.*, 68-88; *de Cher.*, 3-10; *leg. alleg.*, III, 244.

59 Philo, *de somn.*, I, 167-72; *de Abr.*, 52-9; *de Jos.*, 1; *de sobr.*, 65; *de Praem. et Poen.*, 27.

60 The 'Wisdom of Solomon' is a document emanating from Alexandrian Judaism, the first part apparently deriving from a Hebrew original. It is earlier than Philo, and was probably written in the first century B.C.

61 Wisd. 7.21-8.1.

62 On Philo's attitude to the cultus, cf. the work of Wenschkewitz mentioned in n. 27, pp. 67-87.

63 On the criticism passed by Hellenistic Judaism on pagan religion and its worship, see esp. Wisd. 13-15.

64 The so-called Fourth Book of Maccabees depicts Jewish martyrdoms under the theme:

εἰ αὐτοδέσποτός ἐστιν τῶν παθῶν ὁ εὐσεβὴς λογισμός (1.1)

or: εἰ αὐτοκράτωρ ἐστιν τῶν παθῶν ὁ λογισμός (1.13)

65 Wisd. 9.15:

φθαρτὸν γὰρ σῶμα βαρύνει ψυχήν
καὶ βρίθει τὸ γεῶδες σκῆνος νοῦν πολυφρόντιδα.

66 Philo, *de migr. Abr.*, 120f.

67 Cf. the passages from Philo collected by Bousset, op. cit., pp. 441f.

68 Philo, *quaest et sol. in Exod.* II, 51.

69 Philo, *de opif. mundi*, 69-71. Further passages in Bousset, op. cit., pp. 450f.; Bultmann, *Z.N.W.*, 29 (1930), pp. 189-92.

70   On this cf. esp. Pascher's book mentioned in n. 55; see also
Wolfson, op. cit. (see n. 55), I, pp. 36-51.

THE GREEK HERITAGE

Bibliography

ENGLISH

Gilbert Murray, *Five Stages of Greek Religion*, Oxford, 1925.*
Werner Jaeger, *Paideia, The Ideals of Greek Culture*, trans. by Gilbert
Highet, Oxford, Blackwell, I, 1946 (from German 2nd Ed. of 1936),
II, 1944, and III, 1945 (from German manuscript).
Michael Rostovzeff, *The Social and Economic History of the Hellenistic
World*, Vol. I, Oxford, 1941.
William Chase Greene, *Moira. Fate, Good and Evil in Greek Thought*,
1948.
A. J. Festugière, *Personal Religion among the Greeks*, 1949.
M. P. Nilsson, *History of Greek Religion*, 1949.

OTHER LANGUAGES

Jacob Burckhardt, *Griechische Kulturgeschichte* (available in Kröner's
Pocket Editions, Vols. 58-60).
Fritz Taeger, *Das Altertum. Geschichte und Gestalt*, 4th Ed. 1950.
Histories of Greek religion, dealing mainly with the development of
the cultus and of the deities:
Ulrich von Wilamowitz-Moellendorff, *Der Glaube der Hellenen*, 2
vols., 1926, 1932.
Otto Kern, *Die Religion der Griechen*, 3 vols., 1926-38.
Cf. also Wilhelm Nestle, *Die griechische Religiosität in ihren Grund-
zügen und Hauptvertretern von Homer bis Proklos*, 3 vols. (Sammlung
Göschen, 1032, 1066, 1080), 1930, 1933, 1934. Wilhelm Nestle, *Vom
Mythos zum Logos*, 2nd Ed., 1941. Walter F. Otto: *Die Götter
Griechenlands*, 1929 translated 1955, under the title *The Homeric
Gods* (Thames and Hudson); brings out the intellectual content
behind the belief in the Olympian deities. Very important on this
subject: Bruno Snell, *Die Entdeckung des Geistes. Studien zur Entstehung
des europäischen Denkens bei den Griechen*. 3rd Ed., 1955. Cf. further:
Max Pohlenz, *Der hellenische Mensch*, 1947: *Griechische Freiheit*,
1955. Ernst Howald, *Die Kultur der Antike* (Erasmus-Bibliothek),

1948. Hermann Fränkel, *Dichtung und Philosophie des frühen Griechentums*, 1951. Werner Taeger, *Die Theologie der frühen griechischen Denker*, 1953.

Notes

1 Plat, *Prot.*, 322*a*-323*c*.

2 Soph., *Ant.*, 332ff. Trans. Jebb.

3 Ibid., 368ff.

4 Zeus already appears as judge over wicked rulers in Homer, *Il.*, 16, 384ff.

5 Cf. W. F. Otto (op. cit., see Bibliography), p. 104ff.; see also Snell, op. cit. (see above), pp. 43-64.

6 Solon, Fr., 3.30-9. Trans. I. M. Linforth (Fr. XII, 30-9 in Linforth).

7 Herod., VII, 102. Trans. Rawlinson.

8 Herod., VII, 104.

9 Aesch. *Pers.*, 192ff. Trans. Gilbert Murray.

10 Aesch. *Pers.*, 241ff.

11 Thucyd., II, 37, 1. Trans. Crawley.

12 Heracl., Fr. 114., in Diels *Fragmenta der Vorsokratiker I*. Trans. by J. Burnet, (Fr., 91*b*) in *Early Greek Philosophy* (1908).

13 Cf. Rudolf Hirzel, *ΑΓΡΑΦΟΣ ΝΟΜΟΣ* (Vol. XX of *Abhandl. der phil. Classe der Königl. Sächs. Gesellsch. d. Wissensch.*), 1900.

14 Soph., *Ant.*, 449ff. Trans. Jebb.

15 Aesch. *Eum.*, 516ff. Trans. Gilbert Murray. The first sentence, which is difficult to translate, runs in Greek as follows: ἔσθ' ὅπου τὸ δεινὸν εὖ; the conclusion: (τις) ἔτ' ἂν σέβοι δίκαν;

16 Aesch. *Eum.*, 690ff. (Gilbert Murray.) The beginning in Greek: ἐν δὲ τῷ σέβας ἀστῶν φόβος τε συγγενής. . . .

17 Cf. Bultmann, '*Polis und Hades in der Antigone des Sophokles*,' in: *Theologische Aufsätze für Karl Barth*, 1936, pp. 78-89.

18 Homer, *Il.*, 5. 440ff. Trans. Lang, Leaf and Myers.

19 Homer *Il.*, 6. 146ff.

20 Hymn. Hom. in Apoll., *Pyth.*, 11ff. Trans. H. G. Evelyn-White (Loeb).

21 Hes. *Works and Days*, 1ff. Trans. H. G. Evelyn-White (Loeb).

22 Pindar, *Isthm.*, 3-4, 4f.; 5, 52; *Pyth.*, 1, 41f.; *Ol.* 9, 28ff.; *Pyth.*, 5.23ff. Trans. Sir. J. E. Sandys (Loeb).

23 Aesch., *Suppl.*, 96ff. Trans. Gilbert Murray.

24 Homer, *Od.*, 4.499ff.

25 Aesch., *Pers.*, 820, 827f. Trans. Gilbert Murray.

26 Fragment from the *Niobe* of Sophocles.

27 Soph., *Ajax*, 764ff., 758f. Trans. Jebb.

28 Soph., *Ajax*, 124ff.

29 Heracl., *Fr.* 32. Trans. Burnet (see n. 12), (*Fr.* 65).

30 Aesch., *Ag.*, 160ff. Trans. Gilbert Murray.

31 Eur., *Tro.*, 884ff. Trans. A. S. Way (Loeb).

32 Eur., *Alc.*, 962ff. Trans. A. S. Way (Loeb).

33 Cf., e.g., Pindar, *Ol.*, 1, 25ff.; *Pyth.*, 3.13ff.

34 Protag., *Fr.* 1. Trans. Kathleen Freeman: *Companion to the Pre-Socratic Philosophers*, 1946, p. 348. On the translation and interpretation cf. W. Nestle: *Vom Mythos zum Logos*, pp. 269ff.

35 τὸν ἥττω λόγον κρείττω ποιεῖν.

36 Aristoph., *Clouds*, 901f., 1038ff. Trans. B. B. Rogers (Loeb).

37 Aristoph., *Clouds*, 1399f.

38 Aristoph., *Clouds*, 1420ff.

39 Thales (in Diels, *Die Fragmente der Vorsokratiker*, I), A 13.

40 Plato, *Rep.*, VI, p. 485*b*. Trans. Cornford.

41 So Empedocles and Democritus. Cf. Erich Frank: *Plato und die sogen. Pythagoreer*, 1923, p. 112.

42 Plato, *Phaedr.*, 229e-230a. Trans. H. N. Fowler (Loeb).

43 It is impossible to reproduce in translation the full meaning of the Greek λόγος; it includes 'word', 'thought', 'basic principle' and 'reason'. For the following: Plato, *Phaed*, 99e.

44 Plato, *Apol.*, 36c.

45 Plato, *Apol.*, 36d.

46 From the abundant literature on Plato, cf. esp. Paul Friedländer, *Platon I, Eidos, Paideia, Dialogos*, 1928. The second volume (1930) gives an analysis of the Platonic writings.

47 Cf. Hans-Georg Gadamer, *Plato und die Dichter*, 1934.

48 Plato, *Rep.*, II, pp. 369b-74e.

49 Plato, *Symp.*, 211b. Trans. W. R. M. Lamb (Loeb). Cf. *Phaed.*, 78d., etc.

50 Plato, *Rep.*, VI, p. 500c.

51 Plato, *Tim.*, 90c/d. Trans. Jowett. On this see Frank, op. cit. (See n. 41), p. 107.

52 Plato, *Laws*, XIII, p. 967e. Trans. R. G. Bury (Loeb). On this see Frank, op. cit., p. 29f.

53 On Plato's use of myth, see Frank, op. cit., pp. 88ff., and Gerhard Krüger, *Einsicht und Leidenschaft. Das Wesen des platonischen Denkens*, 1939.

54 Ἐπέκεινα τῆς οὐσίας (Plato, *Rep.*, VI, p. 509b). According to Plotinus, however, the ἀρχή, the ἕν, also lies ἐπέκεινα νοῦ and ἐπέκεινα γνώσεως (*Enn.*, V, 3, 11, 20, 29; 12, 48f.; 13.2f. Ed. Bréhier). ˙

55 Arist., *Met.*, A 2, pp. 982b, 11f.

56 Anax., in Diog. Laert., II, 10 (in Diels, Fr. A 1).

57 Anax. in Clem. Alex. *Strom.*, II, 130, 2 (in Diels, Fr. A 29).

58 Arist., *Eth. Nic.*, K 8, p. 1178b, 7f., 32.

59 Plato, *Gorg.*, 507e–508a. Trans. W. R. N. Lamb (Loeb).

60 Cf. Frank, op. cit., p. 1, also pp. 95f. and 352, n. 124.

61 See n. 3 on Chapter I, p. 200.

62 On the 'dialectic of the "bounded" and "boundless" as the *Leitmotif* of Greek philosophy', see Frank, op. cit., p. 63, and the whole section pp. 46–92, and on the discovery of the irrational, p. 224.

63 See p. 121.

64 Democr. Fr. B 102, 191, also A 167. On this, Frank, op. cit., pp. 95f.

65 Frank, op. cit., p. 2, and the whole passage, p. 2–19.

66 Cf., further, Plato, *Tim.*, 87c: πᾶν δὴ τὸ ἀγαθὸν καλόν, τὸ δὲ καλὸν οὐκ ἄμετρον, καὶ ζῷον οὖν τὸ τοιοῦτον ἐσόμενον ξύμμετρον θετέον.

67 Cf. Ivo Bruns, *Das literarische Porträt der Griechen im 5. und 4. Jahrh.*, 1896; F. Leo, *Die griech.-römische Biographie nach ihrer literar. Form*, 1901, Georg Misch, *Geschichte der Autobiographie*, I, 1907.

68 Thucydides is quite sure that his work will be welcomed by those who want to get a 'clear picture of the past, and hence human nature being what it is, an equally clear picture of the future'. Cf. Ernst Howald, *Vom Geist antiker Geschichtsschreibung*, 1944, pp. 82f.

69 Cf. H.-G. Gadamer, *Deutsche Literaturztg.*, 1932, pp. 1979–84, reviewing Günter Rohr, *Platons Stellung zur Geschichte*, 1932.

HELLENISM

Bibliography

ENGLISH

Franz Cumont, *The Oriental Religions in Roman Paganism*, Chicago, 1911.

Edwyn Bevan, *Stoics and Sceptics*, Oxford, 1913;* also his *Later Greek Religion*, London, Dent, 1927.*

A. D. Nock, *Conversion*, Oxford, 1933.*

W. K. C. Guthrie, *Orpheus and Greek Religion*, 1952.*

OTHER LANGUAGES

On the concept of Hellenism, cf. Richard Laqueur, *Hellenismus*, 1925.

Books dealing with the subject: Julius Kaerst, *Geschichte des Hellenismus*, I, 2nd Ed., 1917; II, 2nd Ed., 1926.

Paul Wendland, *Die hellenistisch-römische Kultur in ihren Beziehungen zum Judentum und Christentum*, 2nd Ed., 1912.

Martin Nilsson, *Geschichte der griechischen Religion*, II (Handb. d. Altertumswiss., V, 2, 2), 1950.

There is an abundance of material in Karl Prümm, S.J., *Religionsgeschichtliches Handbuch für den Raum der altchristlichen Umwelt*, 1943.

Since 1941 the *Reallexikon für Antike und Christentum* has been appearing in instalments, edited by Theodor Klauser in association with others. On the first section see esp. Max Pohlenz, *Die Stoa*, 1948, Supplementary Vol., 1949, and by the same author, *Stoa und Stoiker* (*Texte und Einführungen*) in the Bibliothek der alten Welt, 1950.

Notes

1 Cf. Wilhelm Dilthey, *Weltanschauung und Analyse seit Renaissance und Reformation* (Ges. Schriften, II), 1912.

2 Chrys. (H. v. Arnim, *Stoicorum veterum fragmenta*, I, p. 154, 7ff.): ἡνῶσθαι μὲν ὑποτίθεται (sc. ὁ Χρύσιππος) τὴν σύμπασαν οὐσίαν, πνεύματός τινος διὰ πάσης αὐτῆς διήκοντος, ὑφ' οὗ συνέχεταί τε καὶ συμμένει καὶ συμπαθές ἐστιν αὐτῷ τὸ πᾶν.

3 Cleanthes (H. v. Arnim, I, p. 118, 24ff.):
ἄγου δέ μ', ὦ Ζεῦ, καὶ σύ γ' ἡ πεπρωμένη,
ὅποι ποθ' ὑμῖν εἰμι διατεταγμένος,
ὡς ἕψομαι γ' ἄοκνος, ἢν δέ γε μὴ θέλω
κακὸς γενόμενος οὐδὲν ἧττον ἕψομαι.

4 Epict., *Diss.*, IV, 4, 33. Trans. W. A. Oldfather. (Loeb).

5 Epict., *Diss.*, I, 12, 17.

6 Epict., *Diss.*, I, 9, 6f.

7 Epict., *Diss.*, II, 16, 42.

8 Epict., *Diss.*, I, 16, 15-21.

9 Epict., *Diss.*, III, 5, 5-11.

10 Epict., *Diss.*, I, 11, 33.

11 Epict., *Diss.*, I, 25, 28.

12 Epict., *Diss.*, I, 18, 22.

13 Epict., *Diss.*, III, 20, 12-15.

14 Epict., *Diss.*, II, 26.

15 Cf. Hans Jonas, *Augustin und das paulinische Freiheitsproblem*, 1930, p. 13; and the whole section, p. 8-16.

16 Jonas, op. cit., p. 12.

17 Literature: the relevant sections in the works of Cumont and Wendland (see above). Franz Boll, *Sternglaube und Sterndeutung* (Aus Natur und Geisteswelt 638), 2nd Ed., 1926. Hugo Gressmann, *Die hellenistische Gestirnreligion* (Beih. zum Alten Orˉ ̲nt, 5), 1925. Wilhelm Gundel, *Sternglaube, Sternreligion und Sternorakel* (Wissensch. und Bildung, 288), 1933. Viktor Stegemann, 'Fatum und Freiheit im Hellenismus und in der Spätantike'. *Das Gymnasium* 50 (1939), pp. 165-91. Franz Boll, *Sternglaube und Sterndeutung*, 4th Ed. (no longer in 'Aus Natur und Geisteswelt'), by W. Gundel, 1931. Dom Jacques Dupont, O.S.B., *Gnosis. La connaissance religieuse dans les Epitres de Saint Paul* (1949), C. VII, § 1. Cf. Rudolf Bultmann, 'Zur Geschichte der Lichtsymbolik im Altertum' *Philologus*, 97 (1948), p. 1-36.

18 Cumont, op. cit. p. 134, cf. also pp. 207f.

19 Pliny, *nat. hist.*, II, 22. Trans. H. Rackham (Loeb).

20 Men., Fr. 291.

21 Athen. Mitteil. 35 (1910), p. 458.

22 Cf. Hans Jonas, *Gnosis und spätantiker Geist*, I, 1934, pp. 159-61.

23 On Epictetus, see pp. 139ff.

24 Sen., *de prov.*, 5, 7f. Trans. J. W. Basore (Loeb).

25 Cf. Cumont, op. cit. p. 178. Cf. also Philo's critical remarks on the 'Chaldeans': *de migr. Abr.*, 178-86; *de somn.*, 153f. Cf. Festugière, op. cit. 118-21, 134.

26 Vettius Valens, IX, 8, after Cumont, op. cit., p. 178. Cf. also Corp. Herm., 10.25.

27 Sen. *ad Helv.*, 8. 5. Trans. R. M. Gummere. Cf. Corp. Herm. 5, 3-5.

28 Sen. *ad Marc.*, 18.5f. (Is Poseidonius the basis of this? Cf. also Cicero *de nat. deor.*, II, 56; *Tusc.*, I, 19, 44.)

29 Sen., *Ep.*, 102, 21-9: the trans. are all from the Loeb edition. Cf. also the description of the beatific vision in Plut., *de genio Socr.*, 590bff., and see Bultmann, op. cit. (see n. 17), pp. 26-9.

30 Cf. Cumont, op. cit., pp. 164f.

31 Cf. Boll, op. cit. (see n. 17), p. 32.

32 Cf. Bultmann, op. cit., pp. 23ff.

33 On the Aeon, cf. e.g. Cumont, op. cit., p. 150.

34 Cf. Cumont, op. cit., pp. 126f., 145.

35 Apul., *Met.*, XI, 15. Trans. S. Gaselee (Loeb).

36 Lact., II, 16; cf. Jonas op. cit. (see n. 22), pp. 203f.

37 Corp. Herm., 12, 9.

38 Cf. R. Reitzenstein, *Die Hellenistischen Mysterienreligionen.* 3rd Ed., 1927, p. 301.

39 Clem Alex. *Exc. ex Theod*, 71f. Trans. R. P. Casey.

40 On demonology see Cumont, op. cit., pp. 152f.; Bousset, op. cit. (see Bibliography to Chapter II), pp. 331-42.

41 Cf. Cumont, op. cit., pp. 182-93, and the notes, pp. 300-6. The magic papyri provide a wealth of illustration; see *Papyri Graecae Magicae*, ed. Karl Preisendanz, I, II, 1928, 31.

42 On the Mystery Religions, see R. Reitzenstein, op. cit. (see n. 38); J. Leipoldt, *Die Religionen in der Umwelt des Urchristentums* (*Bilderatlas zur Religionsgeschichte*, 9-11); Hugo Gressmann, *Die orientalischen Religionen im hellenistisch-römischen Zeitalter*, 1930. Also F. Cumont, see above.

43 On Mithraism, cf. the works of Cumont, and, in addition to the work cited above, see esp. *Die Mysterien des Mithra*, German Ed. (3rd), 1923. Stig Wikander has promised an entirely new interpretation of Mithraism: see his preliminary essay, *Feuerpriester in Kleinasien und Iran*, 1946.

44 A treatment of the symbolism in the mystery cults is given in Albrecht Dieterich, *Eine Mithrasliturgie*, 2nd Ed., 1910, pp. 92-212.

45 Firm. Mat. *de errore prof. rel.*, 22.1:
θαρρεῖτε μύσται τοῦ θεοῦ σεσωσμένου,
ἔσται γὰρ ἡμῖν ἐκ πόνων σωτηρία.

46 Φάρμακον ἀθανασίας is found in Ign. *Eph.* 2. 20, and in a liturgical papyrus (H. Lietzmann, *Messe und Herrenmahl*, 1926, p. 257, trans. Dorothea Reeve, 1955, under the title, *Mass and Lord's Supper*, p. 210, n. 2); φάρμακον τῆς ζωῆς, Act. Thom., 135, p. 242, I, Bonnet; φάρμακον τῆς ἀφθαρσίας, Stob. Exc. from the κόρη κόσμου in W. Scott, *Hermetica*, I, p. 460,13. The expression is derived from the terminology of the mystery religions. See W. Bauer on Ign., *Eph.*, 2, 20 in the *Handb. zum Neuen Test.*, Supplementary Vol. II.

47 On Isis as the universal goddess, cf. Cumont, op. cit., p. 89. On Isis as Madonna, see F. Heiler, *Zeitschr. für Theol. u. Kirche*, New Series, I (1920), pp. 417-47.

48 Apul., *Met.*, XI, 25. Further texts are listed in Cumont, op. cit.; see esp. Werner Peek, *Der Isishymnos von Andros und verwandte Texte*, 1930.

49 Cf. Cumont, op. cit., pp. 29f., 94f.

50 Cf. Reitzenstein, op. cit. (see n. 38), pp. 46ff., 242ff.

51 A detailed account of the history of the study of Gnosticism is given in Hans Jonas, *Gnosis und Spätantiker Geist*, I; *Die mythologische Gnosis*, 1934. Gnostic texts in a German translation in Hans Leisegang, *Die Gnosis* (Kröner's Pocket Ed. No. 32).

52 This phrase comes from Harnack's *History of Dogma*.

53 See, e.g., Lietzmann, *The Beginnings of the Christian Church* (Eng. Trans., 1937), pp. 354-97.

54 Jonas, op. cit., p. 80.

55 See Leisegang, op. cit.; on the discussion of the problem of the relevance of the Mandaean Texts as sources for early Gnosticism, see the article by H. Schlier in *Theol. Rundschau*, New Series, 5 (1933), pp. 1-34, 69-92.

56 Cf. Joseph Thomas, *Le Mouvement Baptiste en Palestine et Syrie*, 1935.

57 The Mandaean Texts are the scriptures of the Mandaean communities, and their cultus and ritual can be reconstructed from them. The present state of these communities is described by E. S. Drower, *The Mandaeans of Iraq and Iran*, 1937.

58 Plot., *Enn.*, II, 9.

59 The basic elements of the myth are developed at great length in the systems of the particular Gnostics or Gnostic sects. These developed forms may be disregarded here.

60 Mandaean texts from the *Ginza*, trans. by M. Lidzbarski, 1925, pp. 570, 13ff.; 591, 7; 388, 8f.; 155, 3; 433, 9f.

61 Hippolyt. *El.*, V I. p. 103, 2ff., trans. by R. Reitzenstein, *Textbuch zur Religionsgesch.*,² 1922, pp. 215f.

62 See 'The Ideal of the Stoic Wise Man', p. 135.

63 Jonas, op. cit., p. 197.

64 I Cor. 2.14, 15.44, 46; Jas. 3.15; Jude 19.

65 The separation of the concepts of εἱμαρμένη and πρόνοια is characteristic: in Stoicism they are used synonymously to designate the law and order of the universe or the rule of φύσις. In Gnosticism εἱμαρμένη is the law and order of the universe, while πρόνοια is divine providence, which has no longer a cosmological but a soteriological import, leading the Gnostics to σωτηρία. Cf. Jonas, op. cit., pp. 172-8. Equally characteristic is the change in the meaning of πέρας and ἄπειρον; see Jonas, p. 163, 1.

66 God is characterized by attributes such as ἄγνωστος, ἀκατο-νόμαστος, ἀποκεκρυμμένος, ξένος, etc.; his nature is character-ized, not by λόγος, but by σιγή. Cf. W. Bousset, *Hauptprobleme der Gnosis*, 1907, p. 84; Jonas, op. cit., pp. 243-51.

67 Jonas, op. cit., p. 176.

68 *Corp. Herm.*, I, 27f.; 7, 1-3.

69 Cf. *Corp. Herm.*, 13, 3; Porphyr. *ad Marc.*, 8; *Act. John*, 26-9, etc.

70 See 'Star Worship, Fatalism and Astrology', p. 154.

71 Thus e.g., the process of 'rebirth' or deification is accomplished in the hearing (or reading) of the word which communicates the λόγος τῆς παλιγγενεσίας: *Corp. Herm.*, 13. On this, see R. Reitzenstein, *Die hellenist. Mysterienreligionen*, 3rd Ed., 1927, pp. 52, 64.

72 Odes of Solomon, 25. The song is also found in the Gnostic document '*Pistis Sophia*', Ch. 69. Eng. Trans. G. S. Meade, London, 1921, and G. Horner, S.P.C.K., 1924.

PRIMITIVE CHRISTIANITY

Bibliography

ENGLISH

F. J. Foakes Jackson and Kirsopp Lake, *The Beginnings of Christianity*, Part I, Vols. I-V, 1920-33 (not a complete treatment of the subject, but a critical edition and exposition of the Acts of the Apostles, with important excurses).

Maurice Goguel, *The Birth of Christianity*, Eng. Trans., 1953.

L. Duchesne, *Early History of the Christian Church*, Vol. I, 1950.

Hans Lietzmann, *The Beginnings of the Christian Church*, Eng. Trans., 1937.

Clarence T. Craig, *The Beginning of Christianity*, 1953.

Also relevant are the various Theologies of the New Testament, e.g. Ethelbert Stauffer, *New Testament Theology*, Eng. Trans., 1955 (S.C.M.).

Adolf von Harnack, *The Mission and Expansion of Christianity in the First Three Centuries*, 2 volumes, Eng. Trans., 1904-5.

Also significant: Ch. 1 of Ernst Troeltsch, *The Social Teaching of the Christian Churches*, Eng. Trans., 1931.

Rudolf Bultmann, *Theology of the New Testament*, 2 vols., Eng. Trans., 1952, 1955.

Fundamental, and still deserving of thorough study: Karl Weizsäcker, *The Apostolic Age*, Vols. I, II, 1894-5.

Old, but still instructive treatments of the subject: Otto Pfleiderer, *Primitive Christianity*, 4 Vols., 1900-11.

Paul Wernle, *The Beginnings of Christianity*, I, II, 1903-4.

OTHER LANGUAGES

Rudolf Knopf, *Das nachapostolische Zeitalter*, 1905.

Modern works: Johannes Weiss, *Das Urchristentum*, 1917.

Eduard Meyer, *Ursprung und Anfänge des Christentums*, I, II, 1921; III, 1923.

More extended treatment: Adolf Jülicher, 'Die Religion Jesu und die Anfänge des Christentums bis zum Nicaenum' (in *Die Kultur der Gegenwart*, ed. Paul Hinneberg, *Die christliche Religion*, I), 2nd Ed., 1922. Hans von Soden, *Die Entstehung der christlichen Kirche* (*Geschichte der christlichen Kirche*, I), ('Aus Natur und Geisteswelt', 690), 1919. Hans Achelis, *Das Christentum in den ersten drei Jahrhunderten*, 2nd Ed., 1925.

Theologies of the New Testament: e.g. H. J. Holtzmann (2nd Ed., 1911), H. Weinel (4th Ed., 1928), Adolf Schlatter (2nd Ed. under the titles: I, *Die Geschichte des Christus*; II, *Die Theologie der Apostel*, 1921). The following monographs are also of especial importance: Adolf Schlatter *Der Glaube im Neuen Testament* 4th Ed., 1927; Wilhelm Bousset, *Kyrios Christos*, 2nd Ed., 1921.

Notes

1   The characterization of Christianity as a syncretistic religion derives from Hermann Gunkel, *Zum religionsgeschichtlichen Verständnis des Neuen Testaments*, 2nd Ed., 1910.

2   Cf. Walter Bauer, *Rechtgläubigkeit und Ketzerei im ältesten Christentum*, 1934.

3   The people who denied the resurrection whom Paul is combating in I Cor. 15 are clearly Gnosticizing Christians. They did not, as Paul supposes, deny a continuation of the life of the baptized after death (he admits that they had themselves baptized for the dead in v. 29), but maintained the standpoint of the false teachers attacked in II Tim. 2.18, who said 'the resurrection is passed already'.

4   Cf. Ernst Käsemann, *Leib und Leib Christi*, 1933; further Heinr. Schlier, *Christus und die Kirche im Epheserbrief*, 1930; E. Käsemann, *Das wandernde Gottesvolk. Eine Untersuchung zum Hebräerbrief*, 1939.

5   See 'The Stoic Ideal of the Wise Man', p. 142f.

6   Cf. Epict., *Diss.*, IV, 12, 19: πρὸς τὸ μὴ ἁμαρτάνειν τετάσθαι διηνεκῶς.

7   That 'to be justified' (δικαιωθῆναι) does not mean 'to become righteous' in a moral sense is shown particularly clearly by Paul's quotation of Ps. 51.6 in Rom. 3.4, where δικαιωθῆναι is predicted of God.

8   Thus in Jewish apocalypses, IV Ezra and Syr. Baruch. Cf. Strack-Billerbeck (see n. 15 on Judaism), III, pp. 227f.

9   See 'Jewish Legalism', p. 69.

10   See 'The Stoic Ideal of the Wise Man', p. 138.

11   See ibid., p. 141.

12   See ibid., p. 144.

13   See 'The Divine Covenant', pp. 41f.

14   See 'The Proclamation of Jesus', p. 79.

15   See 'Gnosticism', p. 163.

16   See 'Gnosticism', p. 166.

17   See 'Man and his Relation to Time', p. 183.

18   See p. 189.

19   See 'Primitive Christianity as a Syncretistic Religion', p. 177.

20   See 'Gnosticism', p. 164.

21 That in Phil. 2.6-11 Paul is quoting a traditional Christological hymn has been demonstrated by Ernst Lohmeyer (*Kyrios Jesus*, Sitzungsber. der Heidelb. Ak. d. Wiss., Phil.-Hist. Kl., 1927-8, 4. Abh., 1928).

22 See 'The Hope of Israel', pp. 82f.

23 The radical elimination of apocalyptic eschatology in the Fourth Gospel has to some extent been redressed by the ecclesiastical redaction which the Gospel has undergone. This redaction sought to reintroduce the traditional view. Hence 5.28f., 6.51-8 and further minor additions.

24 See 'Gnosticism', p. 168.

25 Cf. Rom. 7.5: ὅτε γὰρ ἦμεν ἐν τῇ σαρκί.

26 For Paul the primary meaning of faith (πίστις) is obedience (ὑπακοή). E.g. what Rom. 1.8 and I Thess. 1.8 call the 'faith' of the churches, which has become known everywhere, is in Rom. 16.19 called their 'obedience'. It is the ministry of the apostle to produce the 'obedience of the Gentiles'. Unbelief is disobedience; cf. Rom. 10.3, 16, 11.30-2, etc. Thus Paul can coin the term, 'obedience of faith' (ὑπακοὴ πίστεως) (Rom. 1.5).

27 Cf. H. Gunkel, *Die Wirkungen des Heil. Geistes nach der populären Anschauung der apostolischen Zeit und der Lehre des Apostels Paulus*, 3rd Ed., 1909. Ernst Käsemann, 'Die Legitimatät des Apostels', *Z.N.W.*, 41 (1942), pp. 33-71. Rudolf Bultmann, *Exegetische Probleme des zweiten Korintherbriefes* (Symbolicae Biblicae Upsalienses, 9), 1947.

28 See 'Man and his Relation to Time', p. 184.

29 See ibid., p. 185.

30 See 'Gnosticism', p. 166.

31 See 'Man and his Relation to Time', pp. 185f.

INDEX OF NAMES AND SUBJECTS

INDEX OF SCRIPTURE REFERENCES

Old Testament

Rudolf Bultmann

Rudolf Karl Bultmann was a professor at Marburg from 1921 until 1951, when he became emeritus professor. Born in 1884 and educated in Germany, he qualified for the Theological Faculty in 1910, and was appointed lecturer in New Testament studies in 1912. In 1916 he was appointed university lecturer at Breslau, and in 1920, professor at Giessen. Among his translated works are *Jesus, The Theology of the New Testament,* and *Essays.*